ENVIRONMENTALLY SUSTAINABLE BUSINESS:

A LOCAL AND REGIONAL PERSPECTIVE

Peter Roberts

P·C·P

Paul Chapman
Publishing Ltd

Paul Chapman Publishing Ltd
144 Liverpool Road
London
N1 1LA

British Library Cataloguing in Publication Data

Roberts, Peter
Environmentally Sustainable Business:
Local and Regional Perspective
I. Title
338

ISBN 1–85396–240–6

Typeset by Anneset, Weston-super-Mare, Avon
Printed and bound by Athenaeum Press Ltd., Gateshead, Tyne & Wear

ABCDEFGH 98765

To Jo and Richard

Contents

Preface

Almost inevitably many of the books that have been written in recent years on the subject of business and the environment reflect the background and experience of authors who either work in business or are business school academics. Whilst many of these books offer a comprehensive and excellent treatment of the general nature of the relationship between economic activities and the environment, most of them adopt a perspective that either treats the environment as a relatively uniform condition within which all businesses operate irrespective of their location, or they focus upon a particular aspect of the environment that is of importance to an individual company or to a sector of industry. A further weakness apparent in some existing books is that they fail to acknowledge the significance of major spatial differences in the structure and performance of economic activities.

The intention of this book is to correct this apparent imbalance and, whilst covering much of the same territory as the existing literature, to present an analysis that places particular emphasis upon the importance of spatial factors in the business and environment relationship and the potential for the development of environmentally sustainable business. This emphasis is intentional and it reflects the experience and views of the author.

Location and local economic and environmental conditions are important matters, and they influence almost all aspects of the business and environment relationship. A company in Batley faces a very different combination of circumstances, challenges and opportunities compared to a business, of a similar size and in the same sector of activity, that is located in Bodmin, Bournemouth or Blaenau Ffestiniog. Geography matters, and it exerts a considerable influence upon the evolution of economic activities. It also represents an important platform upon which future business responses to the challenge of the environment can be constructed.

Individual towns, cities and rural areas display very different environmental and economic characteristics. These characteristics reflect both the influence of the natural environment and the present-day inheritance from previous eras of economic activity. The current state of the natural and built environment reflects the outcome of the many changes that have occurred in the nature of the relationship between ecological and economic processes. An important constraint upon future business activities will be the extent to which new forms of economic activity that respect the environment will prove to be viable within the context of particular local and regional economic and environmental circumstances.

Most business operations interact directly with the natural environment at a local or regional level, and it is at this spatial scale that any real change in the way in which we view and manage our environment is likely to occur. This standpoint also reflects an essential message of recent years – think globally, act locally.

This central philosophy has exerted a considerable influence upon the content and structure of this book. An important theme in the book is the origin and nature of the interactions that occur among business, environment and place, and the influence and implications of this triangular relationship for the future evolution of the interface between business and the environment. Less emphasis is placed in this book than in other texts upon the implications of the business and environment relationship for intracompany issues. Greater attention is paid to providing an assessment of how business functions within the context that is provided by local economic and environmental conditions.

Although the book does contain a discussion of the wider definition of sustainable development, including both the environmental and the socioeconomic elements, the main emphasis is upon the environment. A considerable gap exists in the present literature with regard to the wider implications for business of the sustainable development debate, but this text does not seek to fill this gap.

Case studies play an important role in the book. Some of these studies have been derived from the author's own work in Yorkshire and Humberside, and they inevitably reflect the particular environmental and economic conditions, problems and opportunities that are evident in that region. Further case studies are presented from other areas of the UK and world wide. What many of these case studies demonstrate is that imagination and enterprise are vital ingredients for the achievement of environmental sustainability and for the development and management of a successful business.

This book is of relevance to the wide range of subject areas that cluster around the business and environment relationship. It will also perform the function of providing a guide for managers, in both the private and public sectors, who are seeking to understand what they can do in order to enhance the environmental performance of their business and to improve the quality of life and economic attractiveness of a particular locality.

No book can hope to cover the entire span of environment and business issues and this text is no exception to this general rule. Readers who wish to explore particular topics in greater depth are referred to a variety of additional sources of information and understanding.

The structure and organisation of the book is relatively straightforward. It starts by examining the global level and works progressively towards the local; this progression is reflected in the structure of the book. The first part (Chapters 1 and 2) introduces the subject; the second part (Chapters 3, 4, 5 and 6) examines a number of important contextual and operational themes, whilst the third part considers a range of key issues that are of particular importance in the development and management of the business and environment relationship.

The progression that forms a major element in the structure conveys the reader from global environmental concerns to the local field of action. This progression is deliberate and is intended as a means of expressing the need to think globally but act locally. Chapter 1 presents a broad overview of the emergence of environmental problems and assesses the major characteristics, trends and key ideas that are associated with the relationship between business and the environment. Chapter 2 develops this introductory material further and explores the origins and impacts of a number of the more important environmental problems that confront business organisations. The second part of the book is organised in a number of thematic chapters. These chapters consider the economics of the environment (Chapter 3); the social, political and legal aspects of the interface between business and the environment (Chapter 4); questions of business organisation, operation and structure (Chapter 5); and the characteristics and applicability of the techniques, methods and procedures that are available to conduct environmental analysis and assessment (Chapter 6). The third part of the book is concerned with the generation and implementation of approaches to business development and management that place emphasis upon the environment. Chapter 7 examines the contribution and role of the environment in the generation of corporate strategies and the importance of adopting an approach to the management of environmental issues that will result in enhanced performance in the future. Chapter 8 looks at the business opportunities that are available in the growing market for environmental goods and services, whilst Chapter 9 takes this view further and considers the ways in which environmentally sustainable businesses can play an influential role in the development of local and regional economies. A final chapter presents conclusions about the nature of environmentally sustainable business development and discusses some of the most important questions that surround the future relationship among business, the environment and place.

The origins of this book reflect the experience of the author. As a child in rural Wales my father first taught me the rudiments of how to live within the capacity of the environment, and for the past thirty years I have sought the knowledge that is necessary to understand better the interaction between economic and environmental processes. Many friends and colleagues have helped me on this pathway of learning. Cecil Mann, Tim Shaw, Brian McLoughlin, John Holliday, Ken Carter and Bill Ogden were early

companions in this quest. In more recent years colleagues at Leeds
Metropolitan University and the Leeds Environmental Business Forum have
provided encouragement, case studies and insights. Thanks are also due to
Christine Leigh, Andy Gouldson, Richard Welford and my postgraduate
students for their advice and constructive criticism. Marianne Lagrange and
her staff at Paul Chapman Publishing have helped throughout, whilst
Michelle Huby has performed a miracle in translating my hieroglyphics into
the finished text. The diagrams are in tribute to the skill of Adrian Riley and
his colleagues. To all of these, and to many other friends and colleagues, I owe
a considerable debt of thanks.

Throughout, I have been helped and encouraged by my wife, Jo, and my
son, Richard; and it is to them that I dedicate this book.

Peter Roberts

Abbreviations used in the text

APC	–	air pollution control.
BATNEEC	–	best available techniques not entailing excessive cost.
BPM	–	best practicable means.
CBA	–	cost-benefit analysis.
CBI	–	Confederation of British Industry.
CEA	–	cost-effectiveness analysis.
CEST	–	Centre for the Exploitation of Science and Technology.
EA	–	environmental assessment.
EIA	–	environmental impact assessment.
ENDS	–	Environmental Data Services.
EPA	–	Environmental Protection Act 1990.
ES	–	environmental statement.
GIS	–	geographical information system.
HMIP	–	Her Majesty's Inspectorate of Pollution.
IPC	–	integrated pollution control.
IPCC	–	Intergovernmental Panel on Climate Change.
NIMBY	–	not in my back yard.
OECD	–	Organisation for Economic Co-operation and Development.
PPP	–	polluter pays principle.
SEA	–	strategic environmental assessment.
RPAA	–	Regional Planning Association of America.
UKCEED	–	UK Centre for Economic and Environmental Development.
UNEP	–	United Nations Environment Programme.
WCED	–	World Commission on Environment and Development.

1

Introduction:
Setting the scene and identifying some
major trends and issues

The environment has become an important issue for many businesses in recent years, and equally the attitude and behaviour of business is crucial to the future condition of the environment. The form and content of the relationship between business and the environment is the central concern of this book, and this relationship is both multilevel and highly complex. 'Relationship' is the term employed to express the many processes of interaction between the environment and the ways in which business uses resources at all stages in the production, distribution, marketing and final consumption of goods and services. By using the term relationship a dynamic, rather than a static, interaction is implied. The dynamic nature of this relationship results both from the characteristics that are inherent in any environmental system, and from the ever-changing nature of business as it seeks to adapt to new market demands and pressures.

At the outset it is important to recognise that the relationship between business and the environment changes through time and between places. Temporal and spatial influences upon the business and environment relationship can be observed and understood in many ways, and it is the intention of this book to illustrate the implications of both of these influences. The book also attempts to suggest ways in which the relationship can be managed to the mutual advantage of both business and the environment.

By approaching the interaction between business and the environment in such a manner, the central territory of the relationship can be defined. The concept of managing for and with the environment implies the adoption of an approach that addresses the full range of management issues. Indeed it is an approach that treats environment as a central concern in all aspects of business decision-making and operation. This suggests that it is no longer possible or satisfactory to regard environmental matters as irrelevant, or to treat them in a tokenistic manner. The environment should be regarded as one of the dominant factors in the development and implementation of business strategies and as an essential element in the cultivation of the relationship between a company and the locality in which it is situated.

Why has the environment emerged as a crucial concern in the 1990s and, more specifically, what events and actions have created the conditions whereby environmental concerns are now taken seriously by both hard-pressed and prosperous companies? Three broad explanations for the emergence of environmental concerns in business can be identified:

1. There has been a growing awareness and appreciation of the depth, breadth and seriousness of the environmental consequences that result from previous eras of economic growth, and from dominant attitudes in business which regard the environment as a provider of free goods rather than as a set of finite and precious resources.
2. This greater awareness and appreciation has been heightened by a series of major industrial accidents and crises. The consequences of environmental failure, evident in incidents such as those at Bhopal and Chernobyl, have become instantly visible to citizens throughout the world through the medium of television. Such messages provide a powerful and legitimate focus of concern for governments, businesses and citizens alike.
3. Governments, citizens and companies have realised that the varying degree of emphasis which is placed upon the environment in different countries, and which is reflected in legislation, both distorts the terms of trade and places uneven burdens upon the public and private sectors. In some countries companies are required to incorporate the costs of good environ-mental practice within their internal economic structures, whilst in other countries governments, or individual citizens, are left to count the cost of environmental irresponsibility.

These explanations are offered in an attempt to dispel the commonly held view that environmental concerns are solely the prerogative of a few cranks and eco-freaks. Many political and business leaders now recognise and accept the need to treat the environment as an equal partner alongside other economic, social and operational priorities. This realisation has taken many years to take root, but the evidence of environmental degradation can no longer be ignored and action to place environment at the centre of business decisions is now seen as both necessary and urgent.

Significantly the realisation of the importance of the environment is not confined to industrialised nations. Any doubts that environmental protection is now a global concern are surely dispelled by the commitments made by governments, business leaders and representatives of the voluntary sector alike at the United Nations Conference on Environment and Development held at Rio de Janerio in 1992. The environment is a global concern due to the fact that most resources are finite and because there will almost always be repercussions as a result of any decision taken unthinkingly to exploit the capacity of the environment. One person's additional purchase may represent another person's loss of a traditional way of life and, equally, a company's new source of raw materials may endanger the habitat of a rare species. This global dimension is vital, and there is a real need to move away from a position whereby an individual economic act is viewed in isolation and towards the adoption of a stance where the totality of environmental concern is recognised as a prerequisite for a more sustainable future.

Whilst it is essential that environmental problems should be recognised and treated in a holistic manner, and acknowledged as matters of international importance, it is also essential to recognise and emphasise the importance of place in fully understanding the interface between business and the environment. It is at a local or regional level that the majority of the outcomes of production and consumption can be seen. It is also at this level that many of the attempts to improve the environmental performance of business will occur and such efforts will be, in part, conditioned by the circumstances prevailing in the local or regional ecological and economic environments. The locality also provides the place where business decision-makers can best be influenced by local and sectoral peer groups and by the community who live adjacent to the individual factory, office complex or retail park. This theme is taken further in later chapters of this book.

How have we arrived at this position, and what symbols can be identified that mark this awakening of greater concern for the environmental dimension of business? It is not possible to identify a single act or acknowledgement of the problem; rather, greater concern for the environment in business can be seen to result from a cumulative series of individual actions. As indicated above, three major explanations can be isolated and these themes have pushed environment towards the top of the business agenda. These explanations can be used to guide the investigation of the growth of environmental concern in business that provides the substance of the rest of this chapter.

The environmental awakening of business

Thirty years ago this book would have been regarded by most business leaders, at best, as a contribution to science fiction or, at worst, as a futile demonstration of an unnecessary concern with irrelevant issues and arguments that would hinder economic efficiency. Today, many of the views that were advanced during the 1960s and 1970s regarding the possible finite nature of the capability of the environment to absorb the damage imposed by pollution, excessive resource consumption and the other consequences of industrialisation (see, for example, Goldsmith *et al.*, 1972; Meadows *et al.*, 1972) are now accepted as proven facts.

The scientific demonstration of the existence of very real limits to growth has been accompanied by a marked change in the attitudes of governments and businesses towards the environment. This change in attitude is typified by the changes that have occurred in the boardrooms of many major companies. In the most advanced companies environmental directors now share a boardroom table that was once the exclusive domain of production engineers, marketing directors, personnel managers and accountants. In these companies the environmental dimension is no longer viewed as an expensive luxury; rather, it is seen as a vital component in responsible corporate behaviour. This implies a transformation in attitudes, away from the old style approach of how little can we get away with in order to comply with minimalist environmental regulations, and towards a view that places environment at the centre of corporate planning and business activity.

This awakening of business to the needs and values of the environment has taken place in a number of stages. During the 1960s the doomwatchers challenged business with the prospect of environmental catastrophe, but they failed to achieve anything but a marginal shift in attitudes. The first significant moves towards the adoption by business of a more responsible attitude towards the environment occurred in the early 1970s. A first wave of environmental pioneers, chiefly major enterprises in the USA and West Germany, began increasingly to identify and adopt operational practices which placed greater value upon the environment. By the late 1970s some of the largest multinational companies were applying methods of environmental impact assessment and environmental audit (Royston, 1979), whilst small and medium enterprises in Germany were reporting their positive achievements with regard to a wide range of environmental concerns. It is difficult to judge whether state regulation (or the threat of it) or changing consumer attitudes and preferences have provided the major stimulus for this change in attitudes. Some business leaders claim that commonsense business economics and clear moral dictates mattered more. Whatever the precise reason, by the late 1970s the greening of business was well under way.

During the late 1970s and throughout the 1980s the response of businesses was, in part, co-ordinated and further stimulated by the actions of various business interest groups. The International Chamber of Commerce, working with the United Nations Environment Programme, organised the first World Industry Conference on Environmental Management in 1984. Such actions helped to ensure that the messages of early best practice elsewhere were transmitted to the UK and to other less environmentally aware nations. By the mid-1980s the Confederation of British Industry and other organisations had accepted the logic of moving towards accepting a greater sense of responsibility for the environment and were actively advocating the benefits of adopting enhanced environment attitudes to their membership. Other initiatives followed, including the establishment of Business in the Community and the gradual evolution of a network of local environmental business clubs and forums (Marshall and Roberts, 1992).

A second strand in the development of enhanced business attitudes towards the environment can be identified in the shift which occurred within the environmental movement during the late 1970s. For most of the preceding period the environmental movement had maintained a strong anti-business stance but, during the 1970s in the USA and elsewhere, environmental campaigners realised the power which they possessed. This realisation led to a series of campaigns to influence business behaviour and, in turn, to the forging of alliances among business, government and the environmental movement. The argument behind this move was that business could and would adapt to more environmentally acceptable forms if consumer and campaigner power was exerted in a targeted manner. Following the success of this movement in North America, green consumerism emerged in Europe during the 1980s, becoming a powerful force behind the changed images, if not products, developed and marketed by companies in order to gain a share of this sizeable and growing market. Although some of the initial enthusiasm and support for green processes and products diminished, especially under recession conditions, a number of companies changed their production methods and product profiles in response to changed consumer attitudes and the increased power and influence of the environmental movement.

From this analysis of the rise of enhanced environmental attitudes in business it is possible to identify a number of important trends. These trends reflect the change in priority and emphasis that is placed by some businesses upon a wide range of environmental matters. Attitudinal and other changes can be seen to have occurred in relation to a number of important issues:

- There has been a shift in the attitude of some companies away from a grudging minimum level of compliance with a prevailing regime of environmental regulation and towards a more proactive role in setting and maintaining new standards of behaviour.
- Some businesses have gone further and have moved beyond the requirements for environmental performance as specified in current legislation and towards a willing participation in both enhancing their own level of performance and stimulating a higher degree of environmental responsibility in other companies.
- The arena within which the above changes have occurred has widened with companies becoming more concerned about the overall performance of their business, rather than restricting environmental concerns to, for example, the minimisation of any pollution associated with production processes.
- The above changes have been linked to a shift in attitudes, from a concern solely with the environmental problems and potentials of an individual company, to a more general concern with the role of the company in the local environment within which it is located.
- There has also been a move from a position whereby the operation of a company, especially with regard to environmental matters, is cloaked with secrecy, to a greater degree of openness and willingness to disclose information.

Each of these changes is now explored in more detail.

Proactivity

Many companies have traditionally adopted a stance of complying, often at a minimum level, with current environmental legislation. Whilst this stance can be explained and understood by reference to the prevailing ethos of the time at which such a pattern of behaviour was initially formulated, it ignores the very real costs that are associated with such an approach. In the planning of additional fixed investment it is important to anticipate future environmental conditions and legislation. Such foresight can help a company to avoid potential problems, including the need for costly modifications to be made to plant or for changes to be made in its overall method of operation. In addition, the intelligent manager will wish to anticipate the future attitudes of consumers, bankers, insurance underwriters, government and other organisations who influence the performance of a company. All these actors are likely to require a higher level of environmental performance in the future. Proactivity on environmental matters is no longer a luxury but has become an important element in the forward planning of a responsible business.

Leadership

Whilst a change in attitude within an individual company may represent an important step forward, it is neither sufficient nor satisfactory to view that company in isolation. Few, if any, industrial processes exist in isolation, and most are linked, backwards and forwards, to a range of other activities. The responsible company takes its pivotal role seriously and can, for example, influence component producers by specifying that they should comply with a level of environmental performance that meets its environmental specifications. This leadership role can extend to other companies in the same sector or to other companies in a locality. The development of local and sectoral networks is an important means for the transmission of good practice, especially of cases that are easily accessible and are willing to share their experiences.

An integrated and holistic view

Environmental responsibility is often initially thrust upon a business organisation because it is required to comply with health and safety or pollution standards. Through the development of a positive approach to environmental management, which allows for the achievement of the required level of performance, some companies have discovered that other aspects of their business also benefit from the application of enhanced standards. For example, a company may have to undertake a review of its waste incineration policy in order to allow for the attainment of a higher standard of performance in relation to a specified level of atmospheric emission. Such a review may indicate that energy savings are possible if waste is burnt in a more efficient manner and if the heat that is generated by combustion is used for space heating purposes. An integrated and holistic approach to the environmental problems and potentials of a company may yield positive economic as well as environmental results.

The local role

Some companies still confine their concern for the environment to the conditions that exist within the factory walls. This attitude ignores both the wider potential for environmental damage to occur and the likelihood that environmental benefits may be identified if a wider view is taken. Benefits may accrue both to the individual company itself and to other companies in the locality. Such benefits will also advantage the host community. Major companies can and do offer technical and management expertise to smaller and medium enterprises in a locality, and they may also enhance their profile and public image by playing an active role in a local environmental business club or forum. This, at a local level, is clearly akin to the wider leadership role that a company may perform within its own sector of economic activity.

Openness

Many of the changes in stance and attitude which have been discussed so far are associated with the demonstration of a greater willingness on the part of an individual company to recognise and disclose the nature of the environmental impacts of its operations. The move from closed to more open attitudes is often a precondition for a company to play an active role in its own sector of industry or within a local area. In addition, a number of other benefits may be associated with the adoption of a more open attitude. Chief amongst these is a clearer view of what the company needs to do in order to put its own house in order. An important element in this process of self-realisation is the identification of what the company can do to help itself in improving its environmental performance. It is also important to identify other potential sources of assistance, including the expertise possessed by trade associations, other companies, local authorities, water authorities, energy utilities, academic institutions and a range of other public bodies. Mutual trust and respect are important elements in establishing the conditions for greater openness and mutual benefits can result from the more precise definition of the problems that face a company, and the identification of how such problems might be tackled in a manner which is to the mutual advantage of the company itself and the environment more generally.

Some major trends and issues

In charting the growth of environmental concerns in business a number of important features can be observed. These features mirror many broader environmental trends that have emerged during the past twenty to thirty years.

A helpful and relatively simple method for identifying the significance of environmental trends has been provided by the authors of *Beyond the Limits* (Meadows, Meadows and Randers, 1992). They use the term 'overshoot' to indicate the value and meaning of what are often seen as incomprehensible or contestable statistics. Overshoot means to go beyond a limit without meaning to do so. The limit may be a social convention, a legal requirement or the carrying capacity of a particular local environment. It does not really matter how the limit is defined, the important thing is that overshoot is recognised. This concept is very helpful in establishing a better understanding of how any one of a range of actions can overstep the mark, and in demonstrating the likely consequences of overshoot.

The concept of overshoot is introduced at this point in order to allay any fears that the reader might have regarding the complexity or quantity of the scientific evidence which is available in order to measure the relationship between business and the environment. Whilst it is important to question and evaluate specific elements of the evidence in detail, the real purpose of considering trends and indicators is to gain a better appreciation of the direction and speed of any change that has occurred, or is still occurring. In addition, the most important reason for considering the origins and outcomes of the more important environmental trends that have gained momentum during the past three decades is the need to understand how we have arrived at the present situation and what may occur in future if such trends continue without modification.

Ideas such as overshoot are also important because they encapsulate and express the way in which society may move, often without realising it, from a state of equilibrium to a position where resource consumption is dangerously excessive. Four key elements have been identified by Meadows, Meadows and Randers (*ibid.*) that chart the progression towards overshoot:

1. The occurrence of rapid motion, action or change.
2. The existence of barriers or limits beyond which the motion, action or change should not go.
3. Difficulty of control.
4. Overshoot.

Beyond overshoot a number of possible consequences may materialise. Catastrophe or disaster is one option, whilst another outcome is the introduction of a corrective mechanism of some kind. In the view of the authors of *Beyond the Limits* correction is possible, and this could provide the basis for a more sustainable future.

Having defined overshoot and explained the implications of the concept, it is possible to understand the importance of attempting to chart some of the major trends in the pattern of resource consumption and the emergence of a number of environmental problems that are associated with the process of economic growth. Some of the most important macrotrends of particular relevance to the relationship between business and the environment are summarised in Table 1.1. As can be seen from these statistics, at global level the rapid increase in the level of population, an increase of 47 per cent between 1970 and 1990, was accompanied by a rise of over 124 per cent in the number of registered automobiles, a 136 per cent rise in electricity generating capacity, a 126 per cent increase in the consumption of coal and a 125 per cent increase in the consumption of natural gas. These statistics illustrate the rapid shift that has occurred in both the volume and the nature of consumption towards a higher level of resource use. Such a pattern of resource use is clearly unsustainable over the longer term.

The importance of the evidence presented in Table 1.1 is that it demonstrates both the major trends in resource consumption that are associated with economic growth and the wider implications of such trends in terms of the changing pattern of human activity that reflect the consequences of such growth. Human behaviour and, by implication, the capacity of the environment to absorb the damage which is created by excessive consumption, can be seen to be related both to the availability of products – increasing car usage clearly relates to the availability of cars themselves – and to the ways in which products or services are provided; for example, there are many alternative means of generating electricity and some of these are more environmentally sustainable than others.

Table 1.1   Worldwide growth in selected human activitives and products, 1970–90

	1970	1990
Human population	3.6 billion	5.3 billion
Registered automobiles	250 million	560 million
Oil consumption per year	17 billion barrels	24 billion barrels
Natural gas consumption per year	31 trillion cubic feet	70 trillion cubic feet
Coal consumption per year	2.3 billion tonnes	5.2 billion tonnes
Electricity generating capacity	1.1 billion kilowatts	2.6 billion kilowatts
Kilometres driven per year (OECD) countries only:		
by passenger cars	2,584 billion	4,489 billion
by commercial vehicles	666 billion	1,536 billion
Municipal waste generated per year (OECD countries only)	302 million tonnes	420 million tonnes

Source: Adapted from Meadows, Meadows and Randers (1992).

One of the most direct illustrations of the long-term consequences of economic growth can be seen in the growth and incidence of atmospheric pollution. Global carbon dioxide emissions increased from just under 4.8 billion tonnes of carbon per annum in 1971 to over 6.2 billion tonnes of carbon per annum in 1988 (OECD, 1991a). Closer to home, carbon monoxide emissions in the UK increased in the period from 1970 to 1990. The total estimated emissions of carbon monoxide in 1990 were 6.7 million tonnes, of which some 90 per cent were caused by road transport (Department of the Environment, 1992a).

These broad indicators of the growth and implications of resource use and environmental problems have direct cost implications. A recent study prepared by ECOTEC (1989) for the UK Department of the Environment suggested that the cost of pollution control in the UK had risen from £2.4 billion in 1977–8 (£3.8 billion in 1984 prices) to £4.5 billion in 1985–6 (£4.1 billion in 1984 prices). Table 1.2 indicates the distribution of these costs in relation to the elements of the natural environment that are affected by pollution.

Table 1.2   Estimated total pollution costs 1977–8 and 1985–6 in the UK

Element of environment	Total costs (£m)
1977–8	
Air	590
Water	850
Land	790
Noise	180
Total	2,410
1985–6	
Air	1,160
Water	1,600
Land	1,550
Noise	130
Total	4,450

Source: Adapted from ECOTEC (1989).

There are noticeable differences in the incidence of pollution and other environmental damage between localities. In general terms the degree of pollution tends to increase with city size (Goudie, 1990) and this trend is evident in a number of ways, including the level of concentration of pollutants in the atmosphere. Non-urban localities are estimated to experience one-fifth of the level of atmospheric pollution which is experienced in cities with a population of one million or more. Nitrogen dioxide levels in British towns and cities vary considerably; for example, the mean NO_2 level recorded at High Holborn, at 115.9 micrograms per cubic metre, exceeds the level of 57.9 micrograms per cubic metre recorded in Cheltenham, whilst both levels exceed the guide value of 56 micrograms per cubic metre recommended by the European Community (Elkin, McLaren and Hillman, 1991). Other major differences in the incidence of pollution are obvious to the casual observer, such as the excessive consumption of energy associated with a high incidence of traffic congestion, the pollution of land and watercourses, the existence of degraded or derelict land, the dumping of toxic and hazardous waste materials and the absence of facilities for the recycling of domestic and industrial wastes. These variations in local environmental conditions provide a baseline against which corporate and individual actions to enhance the environment can be measured.

Industry exerts a considerable influence on many aspects of the environment and this pattern of influence can, in many circumstances, determine local environmental conditions. Although some of the environmental consequences of the operations of manufacturing industry are global in scale, such as the rise in the level of greenhouse gases, others have a more localised impact. In general terms pollution emissions or resource requirements in 1987 represented on average for OECD countries:

- 15 per cent of water consumption (excluding cooling water);
- 25 per cent of nitrogen oxide emissions;
- 35 per cent of final energy use;
- 40–50 per cent of sulphur oxide emissions;
- 50 per cent of contributions to the greenhouse effect;
- 60 per cent of biological oxygen demand and substances in suspension;
- 75 per cent of non-inert waste; and
- 90 per cent of toxic substances discharged into water.

Some illustrations of the particular environmental impacts associated with industrial activities are provided in Table 1.3.

These impacts should be set within a frame of reference that includes the contribution of manufacturing industry to wealth. In 1988-9, industrial output represented one-third, in value terms, of aggregate GNP in OECD countries (OECD, 1991a). However, as the OECD observes, the influence of industrial activities extends far beyond manufacturing itself to include agriculture, transport, services and residential location. Manufacturing industry plays, and will continue to play, a leading role in determining the occurrence and severity of environmental problems, but equally it also provides a capacity to bring about a significant change in the level of priority accorded to the improvement of environmental conditions.

By isolating the major environmental responsibilities and potentials that are associated with manufacturing, it is easy to forget or underestimate the role played by a range of other business activities and their role in ensuring the implementation of policies that respect the environment. In reality, as consumers of manufactured products and as major direct and indirect users of a number of environmental resources, the service sector shares equal responsibility with manufacturing for ensuring that environmental resources are used in a sustainable manner.

Many other sectors of business, as well as other activities in the economy more generally, interact both directly and indirectly with the environment. Obvious examples include mining, forestry, the generation of electricity, transport, and construction. Less obvious examples are agriculture, tourism and leisure activities. In addition, a sectoral approach to the analysis of the relationship between business and the environment runs the risk of disguising the fact that all members of society are consumers. This implies that, above and beyond the sectoral dimension of the business and environment relationship, it is important to recognise that consumers and employees also interact with

Table 1.3 Environmental effects of selected industrial sectors

Sector	Raw material use	Air	Water	Solids/wastes
Textiles	Wood, synthetic fibres, chemicals for treating	Particles, odours SO_2, HC	BOD, suspended solids, salts, sulphates, toxic metals	Sludges from effluent treatment
Iron and steel	Iron ore, limestone, recycled scrap	Major polluter: SO_2, particulates, NO, HC, CO, hydrogen sulphide, acid mists	BOD, suspended solids, oil, metals, acids, phenol. sulphides, sulphates, ammonia, cyanides, effluents from wet gas scrubbers	Slag, wastes from finishing operations, sludges from effluent treatment
Petro-chemical refineries	Inorganic chemicals	Major polluter: SO_2. HC, NO, CO, particulates, odours	BOD, COD, oil, phenols, chromium, effluent from gas scrubbers	Sludges from effluent, spent catalysts, tar
Non-ferrous metals (e.g. aluminium)	Bauxite	Major local polluter: fluoride, CO, SO_2, particulates	Gas-scrubber effluents containing fluorine, solids and hydrocarbons	Sludges from effluent, spent coatings from electrolysis cells
Micro-electronics	Chemicals (e.g. solvents), acids	Toxic gases	Contamination of soils and groundwater by toxic chemicals	

Source: Adapted from OECD (1991a).

the environment through their household, shopping and leisure activities, and that the intensity and impact of these activities will vary between places. The full complexity of sectoral and other relationships is explored later in this book.

Key ideas and concepts

Three sets of ideas are central to any consideration of the relationship between business and the environment. The first set is concerned with questions of resource use and management and the notion of sustainable development. A second set of ideas is related to the emergence of corporate governance and the acknowledgement of the wider responsibilities of business organisations, both to the environment in general and to the locality in which a company is situated. The third set of ideas reflects the ways in which companies can operationalise and implement their commitment to the environment. Although each of these sets of ideas will be explored at greater length elsewhere in this book, it is appropriate to introduce them at this point in order to provide a foundation for their further development and discussion.

Resources and sustainable development

Although it is fashionable to regard concern for the environment as a discovery of the 1980s, in reality environmental matters have been considered to be important for many centuries. During the twentieth century one of the earliest attempts to conduct a comprehensive and detailed analysis and assessment of the relationship between economic growth and the environment was undertaken by members of what later became known as the Regional Planning Association of America. Charged with the task of developing new utility sources and stimulating the improvement of agriculture and the growth of manufacturing industry in backward rural areas of the USA, this group of environmentalists viewed the environment as a key element in the process of economic development. They advocated the use of procedures for development and industrialisation that placed particular emphasis upon

1. the conservation of natural resources;
2. the control of commodity flow; and
3. the development of the environment.

This view of the growth of economic activities in balanced regions (MacKaye, 1928) is very similar both in spirit and substance to the present-day notion of sustainable development. The ideas of MacKaye and his colleagues are discussed at greater length in Chapter 9.

The environment as a provider of a wide range of resources, and as the ecological context for socioeconomic activity, is at the heart of the concept of sustainability. Many of the conventional views of what constitutes a resource fail to make the important distinction between a resource as an intrinsic asset and a resource, as defined by the *Oxford Dictionary*, as a 'means of supplying a want'. This distinction is of great importance. In making decisions on the exploitation of resources it is essential to set such decisions in the context of a long-term perspective and to ensure that steps are taken to minimise any adverse consequences which may arise from current levels and methods of resource utilisation. In addition, even though certain resources are not used at present, they may be required in the future and should not be damaged or sterilised. Resources should be considered as dynamic assets that change their value over time. Neolithic flints, which were once highly valued, now have little but archaeological value, whilst many previously unwanted and unvalued materials, such as oil and bauxite, are now highly valued.

Resources can be categorised in many ways. The most helpful distinction is that which can be made between 'stock', or non-renewable, and 'flow', or renewable, resources (Rees, 1985). Stock resources are materials which have taken millions of years to form and they cannot easily be replenished except over geological time or, to a limited extent, through recycling. Flow resources can be defined as those which are naturally renewed within a short timespan. Some authors make a further distinction between 'flow' and 'continuous' resources. Flow resources include those items which can be depleted, sustained or increased by human actions, as compared with continuous resources that are available independent of human action but which are capable of modification (Blunden, 1985). Figure 1.1 illustrates the distinction between the various categories of resource and provides some examples.

The value placed upon a resource also reflects the changing nature of social values and perceptions. Environmental quality, when viewed as a resource, can be seen to be of lesser or greater value depending upon the perceptions and dominant value system of an individual observer or of a group in society. One person's unique and cherished landscape may be another person's potential site for a super-quarry, toxic waste tip or leisure complex. Although the value placed on resources by individuals and society as a whole has varied through time, with increasing affluence the level of environmental quality that is sought by citizens has generally tended to rise.

It was stated earlier that sustainable development, although a new term, does not represent a totally new idea. The importance of the idea of sustainable development is that it links the well established principle of responsible use of the environment to ideas such as social equity. The term sustainable development has been used by the World Commission on Environment and Development (WCED), also known as the Brundtland Commission, to express the view that development should be set within the limits of the environment. Put simply, economic growth should respect the carrying capacity of the planet and should not exceed it.

This idea is important for, whilst it accepts the inevitability of further growth, it also acknowledges the need for a degree of redistribution of resources and goods. Central to the idea of sustainable development are two key concepts:

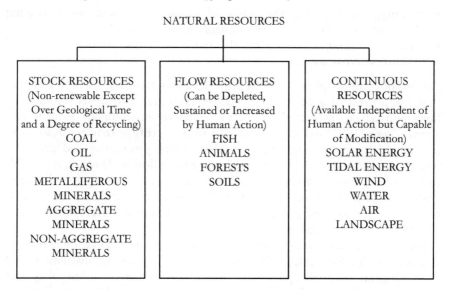

NATURAL RESOURCES

STOCK RESOURCES (Non-renewable Except Over Geological Time and a Degree of Recycling)	FLOW RESOURCES (Can be Depleted, Sustained or Increased by Human Action)	CONTINUOUS RESOURCES (Available Independent of Human Action but Capable of Modification)
COAL	FISH	SOLAR ENERGY
OIL	ANIMALS	TIDAL ENERGY
GAS	FORESTS	WIND
METALLIFEROUS MINERALS	SOILS	WATER
AGGREGATE MINERALS		AIR
NON-AGGREGATE MINERALS		LANDSCAPE

Adapted from: Rees (1985) and Blunden (1985)

Figure 1.1 Catergories of resource

1. The concept of needs, in particular the essential needs of the world's poor, to which over-riding priority should be given.
2. The idea of limitations imposed by the state of technology and social organisation on the ability of the environment to meet present and future needs.

In other words sustainable development is, in the view of the WCED, 'development that meets the needs of the present without compromising the ability of future generations to meet their own needs' (WCED, 1987, p. 8).

According to Pearce, Markandya and Barbier (1989), sustainable development encapsulates three key elements: environment, futurity and equity. These three elements can be seen to be integrated in sustainable development through the idea that 'future generations should be compensated for reductions in the endowments of resources brought about by the actions of the present generations' (*ibid.*, p. 3). This implies that only those environmental resources that can be replenished, recycled or replaced should be used and that resources should be developed in such a way that there is no permanent damage caused through the pattern and process of consumption. Extending this analysis it can be seen that the three key elements of environment, futurity and equity are concerned with

- *environment* – placing emphasis on the full costs of using natural, built and cultural environments in order to ensure that quality of life is maintained;

- *futurity* – considering the needs of future generations when making decisions about the use of environmental resources; and
- *equity* – placing emphasis on the more even distribution and use of resources across societies.

For business this implies a shift in attitudes away from a growth at any cost stance and towards a perception of the environment that treats resources as finite and which respects the three principles of environment, futurity and equity. Davis (1991) has argued that this shift in attitude requires business to re-examine its fundamental beliefs and to adopt procedures and processes which have greater regard for the environment. Following Davis, it is possible to identify six basic concepts that can be used to guide the required change in attitude and behaviour, and which have the ability to create the preconditions necessary for the emergence of sustainable business development; these concepts are summarised in Box 1.1.

Even though this book concentrates upon the environmental dimension of sustainable development, it is clear from the preceding discussion that environmental improvements are unlikely to emerge unless they are accompanied by the other elements of sustainable development. Environmental enhancement is, for example, unlikely to gain support in conditions where poverty and social divisions exist, and where it is apparent that positive environmental action is likely to exacerbate rather than reduce the gap between rich and poor.

Box 1.1 *Basic concepts for sustainable business development*

- *Discriminating development* – business should be discriminating in the use of resources in order to minimise waste and to prevent environmental and ecological damage.
- *Conserving resources* – preference should be given to the use of renewable resources and local resources should be used where possible.
- *Maximise the 4 Rs* – repair, reconditioning, reuse and recycling should be given priority in order to reduce the consumption of resources.
- *Creative work* – work should be organised in such a way as to make the fullest possible use of human abilities and to involve people in ensuring that activities are conducted in a sustainable manner.
- *Maximisation of non-material growth* – although growth which consumes resources has to be limited, this does not apply to activities, such as the arts, education and leisure, which do not consume excessive amounts of resources.
- *Self-directed personal investment* – opportunities should be created to allow investment to take place in activities which will support sustainability and which will serve the needs of individuals and communities.

Source: Davis (1991).

It is also possible to identify a number of basic principles that can be used to guide environmentally sustainable business development. These include

- the polluter should pay for any environmental damage caused;
- prevention of environmental damage is better than cure;
- do not use non-renewable resources faster than renewable substitutes can be found and do not use renewable resources faster than they can be replenished;
- minimise resource use and recycle and reuse materials; and
- co-ordinated and negotiated solutions, across sectors, are normally best.

Corporate governance and the environment

Corporate governance, otherwise known as corporate responsibility or socially responsible business behaviour, is concerned with the wider responsibilities of a company and the implications of such responsibilities for the internal operation of a business. This is no new concern and, as has already been seen in relation to environmental sustainability, fundamental arguments in support of including environmental matters on the business agenda were established in the early 1970s. The report of the Company Affairs Committee of the CBI on *The Responsibility of the British Public Company* (CBI, 1973), identified four major aspects and areas of interaction between a company and society as a whole; two of the four major aspects were pollution and conservation. This early acknowledgement of the central role of the environment in corporate governance parallels the general intensification of concern for the environment that gained momentum during the early 1970s.

Although there have been many variations in the intensity of the commitment of business to the environment, the environmental dimension of corporate governance is now well established (McIntosh *et al.*, 1993) and many companies place considerable emphasis upon the production and implementation of a corporate environmental policy, strategy or mission statement. The basic environmental principles that are incorporated within sustainable development form the foundation for the environmental dimension of most expressions of corporate commitment. This implies that companies should not only seek to improve their own in-house environmental performance but should also endeavour to protect the interests of all stakeholders including shareholders, employees, members of the local community, suppliers and customers.

The range and strength of concern for the environment that is experiential will vary according to the activities that are undertaken by an individual company. It is also likely that the range of concern will reflect local or regional environmental conditions. However, a typical environmental mission statement is likely to include matters related to the use of resources, the nature of production processes, transport operations, recycling and reuse, waste management and disposal, energy use, environmental awareness training and relationships with the local community. A typical environmental mission statement, from the Royal Bank of Scotland (1993), is illustrated in Box 1.2.

Box 1.2 Royal Bank of Scotland Corporate Environmental Policy Statement

- To ensure environmental implications are considered when assessing credit proposals.
- To conserve the usage of energy and raw materials.
- To endeavour to reduce wastage as far as possible.
- To endeavour to recycle materials as far as possible.
- To endeavour to avoid pollution of air, land or water.
- To improve the working environment.
- To observe and, if possible, exceed environmental regulatory standards.
- To play a part in community environmental initiatives.
- To train employees in good environmental practices.
- To use the products and services of suppliers whose environmental policies are compatible with our own.

The commitment of individual companies to the environment may extend beyond the adoption of a corporate environmental mission statement. Some organisations have established research foundations, whilst others participate at local, national and international levels in environmental business clubs or forums. A major reason for the establishment of an environmental business forum is to pool available expertise, knowledge and experience in order that small and medium enterprises in a locality may benefit from the resources possessed by larger companies. The precise form and organisation of an environmental business forum will vary according to the characteristics and environmental challenges that are encountered in a locality, but generally such an organisation will seek to involve both the business community and the public policy community in a partnership for the environment. The structure and operation of a forum is also likely to reflect prevailing conditions in the local economy, including the potential for the development of new environmental enterprises. The aims of the Leeds Environmental Business Forum are outlined in Box 1.3.

Corporate governance is the clearest illustration of the way in which business has embraced environmental challenges. By embedding environmental issues at the centre of business strategies it is likely that concern for the environment will continue to figure as an important element on the business agenda.

Operationalising and implementing environmental policies

Placing environmental concerns on the agenda is only the starting point in the sustainable development of business. In parallel with the adoption of a corporate environmental policy it is important that companies should identify and develop methods and procedures that allow for the achievement of their

---

Box 1.3   *The Leeds Environmental Business Forum*

The Mission of the Forum is to promote, encourage and support business practices which are aimed at the improvement of the Leeds and wider environment, and to publicise and disseminate the environmental achievements of the Leeds business community.

In order to achieve this Mission the Leeds Environmental Business Forum has the following broad objectives:

- To raise the awareness of the business community with regard to environmental issues.
- To act as a focal point for the collection, dissemination and exchange of information and actions relating to best practice in the environment, and to act as an interface with organisations and agencies responsible for environmental regulation.
- To share and distribute expertise and resources and to channel advice which will enable positive environmental action to occur.
- To develop a full programme of environmental projects based on partnerships between business, government and other appropriate organisations.
- To publicise the achievements of the Leeds business community in the environmental field, both within and outside the city.

---

aspirations. Although Chapter 6 of this book deals in detail with the subject of environmental assessment techniques and procedures, it is important here to outline the need for business to prepare at an early stage for the adoption of a more environmentally responsible stance.

Techniques such as environmental impact assessment and environmental auditing are beginning to emerge as standard items in the business toolkit. More recent developments have included the introduction of environmental management systems and the use of life-cycle analysis. The importance of these methods of analysis and assessment is that they provide a technical capability to measure the impact of a business upon the environment and to monitor the progress of a company in the achievement of the targets specified in a corporate environmental mission statement.

Views vary as to the desirability of regarding environmental matters as a separate issue in the operation of a business. Welford (1992a) has suggested that total quality management and environmental management should be seen as part of a single system of management and he argues that 'total quality and as such zero defects also means zero negative impact on the environment' (p. 25). This view is gaining ground and can be seen as a model of best practice to which companies should aspire.

Conclusions

This chapter has provided an introduction to the complex nature of the relationship between business and the environment. It has demonstrated that positive action by business is an essential prerequisite for an improvement in environmental conditions, and it has also indicated the importance of adopting enhanced environmental standards for the future success of business. The relationship between business and the environment can be seen to be symbiotic; both parties can gain advantages through positive action, whilst both parties will suffer if environmental matters fail to become a central plank of business concern.

The scale of the environmental problems confronting business is potentially immense, but there are signs of an improvement. More importantly, an increasing number of companies have now adopted corporate mission statements which place priority on the enhancement of their environmental performance.

2

Environmental problems and opportunities

In the preceding chapter it was stated that the business world faces a wide range of environmental challenges. These challenges exist in the form of both problems and opportunities. Some of the problems that face business have the potential, through the use of imagination and a willingness to learn from earlier mistakes, to be translated into new business ventures or new products. Some companies have, for example, discovered that by taking action to enhance energy conservation they are then able to develop new areas of expertise and technology that can provide products or the foundations of an entirely new business activity.

It is also important to distinguish between the perception of what constitutes a relevant range of environmental issues from inside a company, and the view from outside. Although an individual company may consider that it has done all that is required by law to ensure that its activities do not damage the environment, this may not be sufficient when its responsibilities are judged from the viewpoint of an individual investor or from a community perspective. A minimalist response by a company is more likely to antagonise than to placate the concerns of environmentalists, whilst the presentation of a green tinge, which is lacking in substance, can seriously damage the reputation of any business organisation. Any company that fails to convince its bankers, insurers or investors of its environmental credentials risks endangering or limiting its own future success. This issue has been recognised for some years and banking institutions, from the World Bank to smaller specialist industrial finance houses, now screen applicants for their environmental soundness (Schmidheiny, 1992).

Environmental problems exist and are recognised at a variety of scale levels, from the global to the local. What is less often acknowledged is that a cumulative process of environmental degradation is at work in many situations. For example, one company may locate adjacent to a river and discharge a controlled amount of effluent into the watercourse without causing any real harm to the aquatic environment. At a later date a second plant may be located further upstream, again discharging a relatively harmless and limited amount of effluent. It is only when the two discharges meet that a problem is caused. The result of the mixing of these two individual discharges, which are in themselves harmless, can create a cumulative problem (Berry and Steiker, 1974). This example illustrates the nature and process of cumulative environmental damage, and it also points to the need in many cases for a collective rather than an individual approach to be adopted in order to work towards a solution to environmental problems.

These introductory observations provide a framework for the analysis of environmental problems and the business opportunities which may emerge when solutions are sought and implemented. The remarks also introduce the spatial dimension of the business and environment relationship; a dimension that is absent in many of the existing attempts to analyse and assess the link between business and the environment. However, whilst it is important to acknowledge the importance of the interaction between environment and economic activity at a local level, it is also important to recognise that interactions occur between local and global levels. The nearest that many writers on businesses and the environment get to considering the spatial dimension is through the idea of the value or supply chain. Smith (1992) illustrates the use of the value chain in assessing the processes which occur within an organisation from an environmental as well as an auditing perspective. Although Smith's analysis is centred upon an individual business, the concept can be extended to investigate the full range of economic activities present in a locality and the implications of the business and environment relationship for an individual company and its suppliers and customers. Figure 2.1 illustrates these relationships by considering an individual company and its links to suppliers and customers.

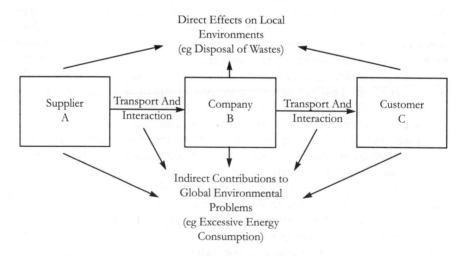

Figure 2.1   Environmental linkages

In this simplified model, whilst Supplier A may conform to the standards of environmental behaviour adopted by Company B, other suppliers may currently fail to adopt a positive attitude towards the environment. Likewise, although Company B may have implemented an environmental policy that conforms to the requirements of Customer C, it may fail to achieve the environmental standards demanded by other potential customers. More importantly, even in this simplified model, it can be seen that all three businesses contribute to both global and local environmental problems and that, in addition, the transfer of products between the organisations generates additional environmental costs. This model can also be seen in a positive sense, because it represents the potential that exists for mutual interaction between the three businesses as they work towards common environmental goals. It also demonstrates the potential for an increase in trading between companies in situations where all trading partners adopt higher environmental standards. This use of the value or supply chain illustrates the extent to which an individual company relies upon its suppliers in order to ensure that it operates to an acceptable environmental standard. As Peattie (1992) argues, it is likely that the environmental performance of any company will, in part, be predetermined by companies further back down the supply chain.

A further feature of the business and environment relationship, which is illustrated in Figure 2.1, is the likelihood, in many situations, that the activities of an individual company will have both a direct impact upon the local environment through its everyday operations – such as the disposal of solid waste materials to landfill – and an indirect impact on regional, national or global environments through its consumption of resources such as energy and raw materials. This distinction is somewhat artificial because, in reality, the intensity of the interaction that exists in the link between business and the environment should be considered as a continuum; some business operations have direct and indirect impacts upon the environment from the local to the global level, whilst other companies have a minimal and indirect impact solely at the level of the immediate locality.

An additional point worthy of consideration is the dynamic nature of the environment and business relationship that is encapsulated in the value or supply chain. Three factors combine that generate changes in the intensity and spatial impacts of the interaction between business and the environment. First, there is the issue of the rate of consumption of resources of various types, and the implications of consumption patterns for the balance between the use of stock and flow resources. In considering this issue it is important to acknowledge the contribution made by the recycling of materials and replacement of stocks. The consequence of an overexploitation of scarce resources would be to cause a previously balanced supply chain to fail to meet the conditions for continued sustainable development. A second issue is the availability of technology that can be used to help to reduce or eliminate any adverse environmental impacts associated with the production, exchange or movement of goods. Technological improvements may also allow for a higher proportion of materials to be reused or recycled. Third, it is important to acknowledge the existence of variations in the ability of the environment to absorb the negative impacts of economic activities. This issue has its origins in the concept of the environment as a dynamic rather than a static system, and it is based upon an ecological view of the world which is concerned with 'the study of the interconnectedness of nature, including human beings and their activities' (Button, 1988, p. 143). These three issues combine to ensure that the environmental implications of the operation of a value or supply chain are in a constant state of flux. They also point to the need for continuous monitoring in order to ensure that the relationships between businesses are ordered in such a way as to minimise any cumulative impact upon the environment, at all levels from the local to the global.

The origins and occurrence of environmental problems

It would be incorrect to suggest that environmental difficulties are solely a product of the continuous process of industrialisation that has occurred since the early days of the industrial revolution. There are a number of contemporary accounts of the occurrence of environmental damage, in both urban and rural areas, prior to the late eighteenth century, including the damage done to ancient woodlands due to overexploitation by charcoal producers, the excessive grazing of the downlands of southern England and the pollution of rivers resulting from the discharge of untreated domestic effluent. However, such early environmental impacts were inconsequential when compared with the effects of the mass industrialisation that occurred from the late eighteenth century onwards, coupled with the transformation of agriculture and the rapid growth of urbanisation.

The cradle of the industrial revolution is often said to have been Coalbrookdale in Shropshire where the Darby family enlarged their ironworks during the 1760s to become the largest works of any kind in Britain (Hoskins, 1955). In 1779 this ironworks supplied the cast-iron arches for the bridge which still spans the River Seven at Coalbrookdale; this impressive achievement, together with the mechanisation of the textile industry, the growth of coal mining and the industrialisation of the pottery sector, heralded the dawn of the industrial revolution.

Two centuries on, the negative environmental impacts that are associated with the rapid growth of an increasingly industrial society, chiefly living in large towns and cities, can be seen to be the dominant element in any assessment of the condition of the current global environment. At local, regional and global levels the processes of industrial growth have left their mark. The impacts of mining and manufacturing have been described in many contemporary accounts. Émile Zola, in *Germinal*, describes the environment of the Nord-Pas-de-Calais coalfield in the nineteenth century as

An uncultivated moor, of volcanic sterility, in which for ages a coal mine had been burning. The calcined rocks, of a sombre red, were covered by an efflorescence of alum as by a leprosy. Sulphur grew like a yellow flower at the edge of the rivers. At night, those who were brave enough to venture to look at these holes declared that there were flames there, sinful souls shrivelling in the furnace within.

(Zola, 1970, p. 231)

In Britain the effects of two centuries of continuous industrialisation has left a legacy of environmental problems that now challenge business. The consequences of the industrial revolution are not only experienced in mining and manufacturing areas, but they are also visible in the structure and distribution of the population, in the disposition of infrastructure and in the institutional framework of modern society. To change course both requires business to accept its immediate responsibilities towards the environment and also implies that business leaders should play a leading role in helping to change attitudes and patterns of behaviour in society at large. As Davis argues (1991, p. 17), 'business will be the main agent for bringing about change in the direction of development and this implies that a very heavy burden of responsibility falls on all business managers'.

However, even though the responsibilities placed upon business are considerable, many other sectors of society also have a major role to play in ensuring that sustainable development is translated from concept to reality. Government, at all levels, the voluntary sector and local communities also have a role to play in developing and implementing sustainable solutions to the cumulative and collective environmental problem. Cairncross (1991, p. 16) has noted that 'environmental policy is inevitably interventionist', and by proposing this she is suggesting that governments, and society as a whole, cannot ignore the choices that a greater concern for the environment imposes. Business policies that seek to transfer the costs of producing goods in a more sustainable manner will inevitably result in a higher price to the consumer, whilst the alternative approach, of paying higher taxes or service charges to the state or to service organisations, will impact in other ways upon the cost structure of business. There are certainly no free rides for business, for consumers or for society as a whole.

Environmental problems

What are the major environmental problems that confront business and how do these problems manifest themselves? There are a number of important distinctions which should be made clear at the start of any consideration of the occurrence and severity of environmental problems:

- First, there are matters related to the spatial scale and extent of environmental problems – are the problems local, regional, national or global?

- Second, there are issues of duration – are the problems of short duration or are they permanent?
- Third, there is the question of attribution – is a problem the sole responsibility of a single source?
- Fourth, there is the matter of perception as against reality – is a problem as severe as it seems?
- Fifth, there is the question of the costs involved in resolving environmental problems – what are the costs and who should meet them?

Each of these problems is an important matter, and they point to the need for environmental problems to be viewed in the round. The case for adopting an approach to the environment which is holistic has been stated by many authors. Stead and Stead (1992) put the argument for such an approach in simple terms: they claim that 'if people think holistically, they cannot help but recognise and consider the impact of their decisions on other parts of the ecosystem' (p. 131). This approach allows business managers to understand where their own organisation is positioned in relation to the ecosystem, and to appreciate that most actions of an individual organisation are likely to have some form of negative or positive impact on other activities. By adopting this approach, Stead and Stead claim that managers can develop an ecological perspective on which to base their decisions.

Developing holistic attitudes is an important task, because it is vital to recognise at the outset that environmental problems have no respect for boundaries. Pollution and other forms of environmental damage recognise neither the limits of a factory curtilage nor a national boundary. Emissions from British power stations cause considerable damage to the forests of Scandinavia, water pollution from industrial and domestic sources washes into the seas, whilst the toxic elements from solid wastes seep into aquifers. The 'tragedy of the commons' is a term that has been adopted to symbolise the environmental degradation of the global commons – the atmosphere, land and oceans. Garret Hardin (1968) used the well-known analogy of over-grazing of common land in order to demonstrate how it is in the collective interests of society to regulate and control the causes of deterioration of the environment. This matter is of immense significance and formed a major plank in the stance taken by the World Commission on Environment and Development (1987). Although the work of the World Commission concentrated upon the international dimension of the global commons, the deterioration in environmental conditions which affects the commons originates in the use of resources and the generation of emissions from individual homes, businesses and modes of transport. The holistic view is one which acknowledges this multiplicity of origins and accepts the reality that tackling the global problem starts in an individual backyard or in an individual factory.

We now return to the five key problems or questions that were listed earlier in this chapter. Whilst it is important to acknowledge the range and cumulative impact on the environment of the various sources and forms of damage, it is vital not to be overwhelmed. For this reason, if no other, each of the problems or questions is now considered separately.

Spatial scale and extent

As has already been demonstrated in the preceding paragraphs, some environmental problems are global in scale and impact, or have the potential to affect all human beings equally. Some of these global problems relate chiefly to the atmosphere (these problems include ozone depletion, global warming and acid rain), others relate to the oceans (such as toxic pollution) whilst other global problems affect the land. It is important to recognise that some of the problems that are encountered are specific to a particular element of the environment, whilst others have an impact on two or more elements. Three examples of these major environmental problems are presented below.

Ozone depletion is a problem that has received increasing attention during the past two decades. The ozone layer is found between 15 and 50 km above the surface of the earth; it absorbs some solar radiation and also, more importantly, it protects the earth from harmful ultraviolet radiation emitted by the sun (see Figure 2.2). Any significant reduction in the ozone layer 'may have serious consequences for life on earth' (Department of the Environment, 1992a, p. 28). It should be noted that, although the ozone layer has a beneficial effect, ground-level ozone in concentration is considered to be harmful.

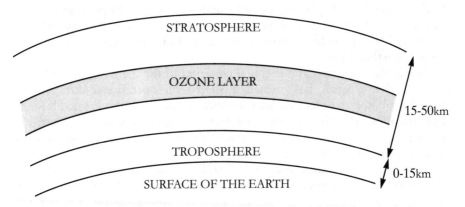

STRATOSPHERE

OZONE LAYER

15-50km

TROPOSPHERE

0-15km

SURFACE OF THE EARTH

Figure 2.2   Structure of the atmosphere

Depletion of the ozone layer leaves the surface of the earth exposed to the full effects of ultraviolet radiation. Excessive ultraviolet radiation can cause skin cancer and can have harmful effects on a range of materials including crops. In addition, the ozone layer, by absorbing radiation, generates heat in the upper atmosphere. This warm region of the atmosphere has similar temperatures to the surface of the earth and acts as an important control over the temperature, structure and circulation of the middle atmosphere (Farman, 1990). The depletion of ozone is at its most severe over Antarctica where an ozone hole now exists during very cold periods. The size of the ozone hole has been estimated by a number of observers; one such measurement estimated that 97 per cent of the ozone between 14.5 and 18.5 km altitude had been destroyed in the atmosphere above the British Antarctic Survey's monitoring station at Halley Bay (*ibid.*). There is also 'evidence of ozone depletions in winter at mid- and high-latitudes in the northern hemisphere' (OECD, 1991a, p. 19).

The main cause of ozone depletion is associated with the growth of inorganic chlorine in the stratosphere. Although chlorine is the major depleter, bromine also causes ozone reductions. The increase in chlorine and bromine in the atmosphere is mainly attributed to the emission of chlorofluorocarbons (CFCs), halons, carbon tetrachloride and other substances. The CFC industry began in the 1930s, but the major increase in the concentration of CFCs and other ozone depleting gases has been since the 1950s.

International acknowledgement and action on ozone depletion quickly followed the accumulation and presentation of scientific evidence on the existence and consequences of ozone depletion. The United Nations Environment Programme (UNEP) hosted and encouraged a series of international meetings to discuss what should be done to limit the consequences of depletion and to prevent further damage. The resulting agreement, signed by 36 nations in Montreal in 1987 (the Montreal Protocol), stipulated that production of five of the most commonly used CFCs should be frozen at 1986 levels, reduced by 20 per cent by 1993 and by a further 30 per cent by 1998 (Meadows, Meadows and Randers, 1992). The protocol was amended in 1990, and in this revised version it was agreed that the production of CFCs would be halted by the year 2000.

Clearly the reduction and eventual cessation of the use of CFCs and other ozone-depleting gases has created a short-term operational difficulty for businesses but, as we shall see later in this chapter, it has also created business opportunities. The effects vary from sector to sector but with support and encouragement from scientific organisations and governments business has discovered solutions (see Box 2.1).

Greenhouse gases, such as carbon dioxide and methane, occur naturally in the atmosphere. These gases trap the heat of the sun and have the effect of making the earth habitable. Since the industrial revolution the concentration of these gases has increased, resulting in an additional warming of the earth's surface (Figure 2.3).

Although the concentration of greenhouse gases in the atmosphere increased in the preindustrial era, prior to the industrial revolution 'abundances of the greenhouse gases were relatively constant' (Houghton, Jenkins and Ephraums, 1990, p. xv). With industrialisation, urbanisation and the development of agriculture, emissions of the greenhouses gases – carbon dioxide, methane, nitrous oxide and others – have increased rapidly. Initially

Box 2.1 *CFC reduction strategies*

Case 1: UTA Clifford
UTA Clifford manufacture motor vehicle steering wheels. CFC II has been used as a foam-blowing agent and has had the additional advantage of acting as a coolant, causing a skin to be formed on the outer surface of the wheel. A short-term solution was to use HCFC 22 as a blowing agent. A new biochemical process was introduced on a trial basis in mid-1992 with a view to moving towards the commercial production of ozone-friendly steering wheels.

Case 2: Royal Ordnance
Royal Ordnance have used CFCs in the cleaning of materials related to the manufacture of artillery fuses. Action has now been taken to minimise CFC usage, control emissions more tightly and to recycle solvents through the use of a distillation plant. This has reduced CFC consumption and has also resulted in considerable cost savings.

Source: Adapted from DTI (1992a; 1992b).

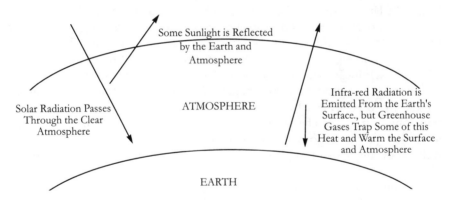

Figure 2.3 The greenhouse effect

it was thought that the effects of the additional greenhouse gases were absorbed by the atmosphere, but the limits of natural absorption have now been exceeded.

The Intergovernmental Panel on Climate Change, whilst accepting the difficulty of predicting future climate change, has estimated in their business-as-usual scenario that on current trends a rise in global mean temperature of 0.3°C will occur each decade, resulting in a likely increase of global mean temperature of about 1°C by 2025 and 3°C by the end of the twenty-first century (*ibid*).

Carbon dioxide is one of the major gases contributing to the greenhouse effect. In 1990 carbon dioxide emissions, by source, in the UK totalled 160 million tonnes of carbon. The chief contributor to emissions was the generation of power, representing some 30 per cent of the total. When emissions are attributed by the final energy end user – electricity, for example, is supplied to many sectors of the economy including business – the major users of energy and the largest producers of carbon dioxide are industry and agriculture (Table 2.1).

Table 2.1 UK carbon dioxide emissions by end user, 1990

Sector	Million tonnes of carbon	% of total
Households	41	26
Industry and agriculture	56	35
Commercial and public sector	24	15
Road transport	33	21
Other transport	5	3
Total	160	100

Source: Adapted from Department of the Environment (1992a).

Under the United Nations Framework Convention on Climate Change, signed by 150 nations by 1993, governments have agreed to draw up programmes of measures that are aimed to return emissions of carbon dioxide and other greenhouse gases to their 1990 levels by the end of the present century. Given the significant level of emissions that can be attributed to the operation of business, it is clear that the obligations contained in this convention are only likely to be achieved if business takes action to reduce energy consumption. This is a global challenge, which is most likely to be achieved at local level though the actions of companies, often working together to share technology, methods of implementation and more efficient energy generation plant.

The third and final example of a global environmental problem is concerned with the marine environment. Oceans and seas cover three-quarters of the earth's surface and they maintain a wide and varied range of forms of life. Given the extent of the marine environment, it is not perhaps surprising that it is used for waste disposal on a massive scale. In addition the seas and oceans are important for the transport of goods. Some of the many pressures on the marine environment are illustrated in Table 2.2.

Many of these pressures on the marine environment result either directly or indirectly from human activities, including industry and transportation. Two examples of pollution that are of particular concern at a global level are the discharge of synthetic organic compounds and of metals. Synthetic organic compounds are extremely stable, persistent and toxic; such compounds accumulate in the fatty tissues of aquatic organisms (OECD, 1991a).

Table 2.2   Pressures on the marine environment

Pressure	Substance or activity	Some sources
1. Waste inputs	Nutrients	Sewage, agriculture, industry
	Pathogens	Sewage, agriculture
	Oil	Industry, sewage, shipping
	Synthetic organic compounds	Industry, sewage, agriculture
	Radioactive wastes	Nuclear weapons, nuclear waste
	Trace metals	Industry, sewage, dumping
	Plastics and debris	Litter, shipping wastes
	Solid waste	Sewage, dumping, industry
2. Environmental restructuring	Coastal development	Dredging, industrial and other development
3. Resource exploitation	Fishing and shell fishing	Harvesting activities
	Petroleum development	Drilling, accidents
	Mineral development	Dredging, tailings disposal, extraction
4. Atmospheric climate change CO_2, CFCs		Energy, transportation, agriculture, industry

Source: Adapted from OECD (1991a).

Compounds of particular prevalence and concern include DDT, the PCBs, lindane and organotin compounds, especially tributyltin (or TBT). Such materials concentrate in the food chain and have the effects of retarding growth and reducing natural resistance to disease. Action to reduce the emission and concentration of synthetic organic compounds has been taken and, for example, legislation has been introduced to reduce the use of TBT in the manufacture of anti-fouling marine paints (see Box 2.2).

Metals are discharged into the oceans and seas in many different ways. Although many metals occur naturally in the marine environment, their level of concentration is such that they pose no real threat to the environment. However, discharges of concentrated metals can affect a range of marine forms of life through toxicity. A well-known case is that of mercury concentration in Minamata Buy, Japan, in the 1950s. This incident resulted from severe pollution of coastal waters due to discharges of mercury from chemical and fertiliser plants. Fish and other marine organisms were affected, as were the local population who consumed fish caught in the bay. Minamata disease spread amongst the local population, causing severe disability and death (Huddle, Reich and Stiskin, 1975).

Responses to pollution of the marine environment have been many and

---

Box 2.2   *Controlling the use of TBT*

TBT compounds have been used for some years in the manufacture of anti-fouling marine paints for use on the hulls of boats and ships. Increasing evidence of environmental damage to marine life, especially in two types of shellfish – oysters and dogwhelks – led to the introduction of measures to control the use of TBT. In France the use of TBT-based paints on small boats was banned in 1982. Monitoring of oysters showed a rapid recovery within a few years of the introduction of the ban. In the UK similar measures were introduced in 1986 and 1987 and recent research shows that by 1990 concentrations of TBT in seawater deriving from anti-fouling paints were a quarter of the 1986 figures. It now remains to extend the restriction of TBT use to other uses such as large ships and drydock facilities.

Sources: Department of the Environment (1992a) and OECD (1991a).

varied. Of particular relevance to UK business are the North Sea Conferences, which have agreed measures for the protection of the marine environment of the North Sea. At a global level the International Council for the Exploration of the Sea is concerned with the development of marine science and the provision of information to other international bodies such as the Oslo Convention (on the prevention of dumping from ships and aircraft) and the Paris Convention (concerned with the prevention of discharges into the sea from land-based sources). The International Maritime Organisation is concerned with safety at sea and protecting the marine environment by the prevention of pollution from shipping. Other specific European Community and national legislation on the marine environment reinforces these international agreements.

All these three examples are important because they demonstrate the occurrence of environmental damage and its significance at a global scale. However, whilst they are acknowledged as global environmental problems, the causes or points of origin of such problems are local, and it is also possible to point to similar, albeit smaller scale, effects at a local level. This is certainly the case in many instances of water and atmosphere pollution and is the general case with regard to the pollution of land.

Problems of duration
A number of issues related to the severity and duration of environmental damage at all spatial levels, from global to local, have been discussed in the preceding section. Some issues, such as global warming, need to be viewed over the long term and an appropriate context is provided by the geological timescale. Change in the global climate is a gradual process, but clearly any further deterioration in environmental conditions that is brought about by the

actions of the present generation will have an adverse impact on the quality of life of future generations. For reasons which are clearly associated with the concept of sustainable development, it is important to view the environmental consequences of social and economic actions, at least, in terms of the inter-generational inheritance.

Some of the actions which are taken by human beings have a permanent effect, whilst others are of a more transitory nature. Spatial scale and time sometimes combine to produce particular environmental effects at specific places. These effects can have direct implications for quality of life in an individual locality or region and can give rise to special efforts to safeguard a rare habitat or species. Such situations highlight many of the more important characteristics of the relationship between business and the environment and can result in the implementation of corrective actions which are to the mutual benefit of an individual company and society as a whole. Some companies have chosen to forgo the opportunity to expand their premises in order to safeguard a rare habitat, other businesses have rehabilitated despoiled areas of land in order to create nature reserves, whilst in a number of instances companies have decided to protect an area of adjacent land which is of particular ecological value by the designation of a no-go area within their own boundary. The benefit to the environment is obvious, whilst, for business, the benefits include an enhanced public relations image, the op-portunity to badge products and services to indicate a company's association with an environmental cause, campaign or approval scheme and, in some cases, a solution that benefits the environment can result in cost savings as well.

In examining the question of duration, it is therefore important to categor-ise the environmental consequences that are associated with the occurrence of economic activities on the basis of the degree to which such consequences are temporary or permanent, and the extent to which the particular consequence is related to a unique habitat or other feature of the environment. Figure 2.4 demonstrates the interaction between these temporal and spatial considera-tions and it provides some general examples. Clearly it is considered to be folly to pursue any action that will have a permanent negative effect upon the environment, especially if that action, or series of actions, will either endanger the future functioning of the global environment or eliminate a species forever.

This analysis and its implied categorisation illustrates the importance of the principles of sustainable development which were discussed in Chapter 1. In particular, it is important to note those issues that reflect the duration and scale of any environmental damage that results from economic activity, and to ensure that such consequences are reflected in the widespread adoption of the precautionary principle. Jacobs (1991, p. 98) argues that given that our 'understanding of the environment is in general highly underdeveloped', it is important to adopt 'safe minimum standards'. Jacobs also advocates the adoption of an approach to decision-making where 'prudent pessimism

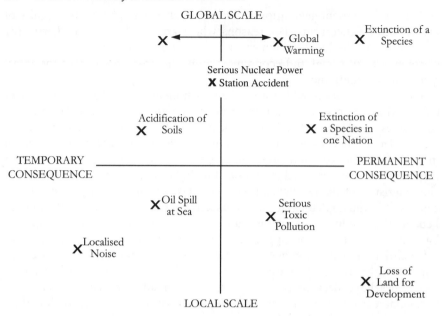

Figure 2.4   Duration and spatial scale of the environmental damage caused by economic activities

should be favoured over hazardous optimism' (*ibid*. p. 100). The precautionary principle urges that action should be taken 'where there are good grounds for judging either that action taken promptly at comparatively low cost may avoid more costly damage later, or that irreversible effects may follow if action is delayed' (Department of the Environment, 1990, p. 11). Given the limitations of scientific knowledge, it is suggested that precautionary action should be taken if it is suspected that environmental damage is likely to occur. The stance in favour of the 'global public interest' (Millichap, 1994, p. 21) is one which is now reflected in many national legislative programmes and in the actions that are proposed by the European Union in its Fifth Environmental Action Programme (Commission of the European Communities, 1992a).

Origin and attribution

Many of the major sources of pollution and other environmental damage have been described and analysed earlier in this chapter. However, it is helpful to consider whether the environmental consequences of business activities should be attributed to a particular company, to a sector of activity or to the wishes of society as a whole. As was demonstrated by the information presented in Table 1.3 and Figure 2.2, it is possible to attribute the origins of specific forms of environmental damage to particular industries, or to relate the origins of specific forms of environmental damage to particular industries or sectors of activity. Whilst this direct attribution of environmental consequences is helpful in particular cases, it is also important to understand the nature of environmental resource life-cycles and the methodologies which are used by scientists to identify and quantify environmental 'sources' and 'sinks' (see Box 2.3).

Box 2.3   *Sources and sinks*

Source: A point of origin of material or energy flows used by a system. Coal deposits are sources of coal in the short term; in the very long term forests are sources of coal. Forests are sources of wood in the short term; in the intermediate term soil nutrients, water and solar energy are sources of forests.

Sinks: The ultimate destination of material or energy flows used by a system. The atmosphere is the sink for carbon dioxide generated by burning coal. A landfill site is often the sink for paper made from a forest.

Source: Meadows, Meadows and Randers (1992).

These two areas of analysis and assessment are connected by their adoption of a common approach which seeks to track resources from their origin, or source, to their final end point, or sink. A major global assessment of the sources and sinks of greenhouses gases has been conducted as part of the IPCC programme of research. Whilst some sources and sinks are stable, others are unstable (Bennett and Chorley, 1980).

The IPCC analysis has considered a number of the greenhouse gases, including carbon dioxide, methane, nitrous oxide, CFCs and carbon tetrachloride, and has assessed the rate of change in the concentration of such gases. Some growth rates have been increasing over the past decade, whilst that of methane and some of the halocarbons has been decreasing. A specific investigation of each of these gases demonstrates that the sources vary from those which are natural to those which are anthropogenic in origin, that is, origins that are connected with human activities. One example is the origins of methane; here a combined annual emission of 500 teragrams originates from a variety of sources (see Table 2.3) and these emissions find their way into a number of sinks (Watson *et al.*, 1992).

Life-cycle analysis adopts a similar, albeit much smaller-scale approach to the tracking of individual resource flows. It attempts to consider materials or products from the cradle to the grave and to consider the interaction between the transformations through which the material passes with other methods and processes of resource use. The topic of life-cycle assessment is considered in more detail in Chapter 6; the main point to note at this stage is that,

Table 2.3   Estimated sources and sinks of methane in teragrams per year

Sources	*Natural*	Wetlands	115
		Termites	20
		Ocean	10
		Freshwater	5
		Methane hydrate	5
	Anthropogenic	Coal mining, natural gas and petroleum industry	100
		Rice paddies	60
		Enteric fermentation	80
		Animal wastes	25
		Domestic sewage treatment	25
		Landfills	30
		Biomass burning	40
Sinks		Atmospheric removal	470
		Removal by soils	30
		Atmospheric increase	32

Source: Watson *et al.* (1992).

although the procedures used to track resource flows by the life-cycle method are similar from place to place, the actual conditions that are encountered in individual localities differ considerably, thereby influencing the detailed nature of the assessment. For example, two companies, located in different places, may use the same source of materials, utilise identical methods of production and serve the same customers, but their approaches to the disposal of waste materials may differ because of the availability in one location of recycling facilities that are absent in the other locality.

Perception and attitude

People's perceptions vary as to what constitutes environmental damage or a hazard, and this variation occurs through time and between places. What was once seen as an acceptable or normal practice is now often considered to be undesirable or hazardous. Likewise, what is seen as a normal pattern of business operation in a less developed nation may be banned or severely restricted in the UK. These differences in perception matter, because they indicate the level of appreciation that a society has for the effects of business upon the environment.

Such differences in perception can be seen to exist at various levels. At global level it is clear that the awakening of society at large to the existence of many forms of environmental damage, such as global warming, has taken place at a point in time when the situation has become critical; at the point of overshoot, to use the term coined by Meadows, Meadows and Randers (1992).

One of the chief tasks assigned to the World Commission on Environment and Development was 'to help define shared perceptions of long-term environmental issues' (WCED, 1987, p. ix) and it is the accurate definition of what constitutes an environmental problem which has proved to be so important in generating support for sustainable development and in translating this concept into action. Cutter (1993) compares expert and public views on the scientific evidence for global warming and demonstrates the significant differences that occur in the acceptance of the evidence. She also notes that the public's perception of the actions which are required to reduce environmental damage may be flawed, or may lag behind reality. For example, whilst the public in the USA consider the major causes of the greenhouse effect to be the use of aerosol spray cans, the ozone hole, cutting down trees and air pollution, they fail to recognise the chief cause, which is the release of sequestered carbon through the burning of fossil fuels or deforestation (Kempton, 1991). Similar false perceptions cause a lag effect to occur; for example, in the same survey the public considered that the banning of aerosol sprays is an important policy option, despite the fact that sprays containing CFCs have been banned in the USA for over twenty years (Cutter, 1993).

The most important trend, despite many false perceptions and time lags in recognition, is the growing acceptance by governments, public and business alike that there are serious environmental problems. Pearce, Markandya and Barbier (1989) observe that 'the world has become greener and our understanding of the environment–economy interaction advances day by day'. They cite as evidence the results of a number of surveys of public opinion, including a survey conducted for the European Commission in 1986 (Commission of the European Communities, 1986), which demonstrated that 50 per cent of Europeans saw environmental protection as essential, whilst only 9 per cent put development as a priority (Table 2.4).

In line with the change in the public's perception of the importance of the

Table 2.4 Public perceptions in Europe of growth versus the environment (%)

	Priority on development	Priority on environment	Choice between the two
European Community	9	50	32
Belgium	8	35	49
Denmark	3	55	30
France	11	56	29
Germany	3	50	41
Greece	12	47	23
Ireland	23	40	26
Italy	6	55	32
Luxembourg	6	65	28
Netherlands	9	45	40
Portugal	11	38	33
Spain	12	47	17
UK	11	48	32

Source: Adapted from Commission of the European Communities (1986).

environment, the business community has also increasingly acknowledged the significance of environmental issues. Roome (1992) suggests that it is possible to identify two major sources of environmental concern that have caused business attitudes to change: scientific evidence and public perception. He argues that it is possible to categorise the positions that are adopted by business using these twin sources of change, thus resulting in four theoretical positions (Figure 2.5). In the case where both the scientific evidence and public concern about environmental impacts are high, Roome suggests that a company is 'forced into a reactive position' (*ibid.* p. 17), whilst in a position where the twin sources of concern are at a lower level the response of a company is discretionary and is often driven by management. This model is helpful in positioning the attitude and response of business, especially if it is also appreciated that other sources for change exist, such as those exerted by the value chain or by local peer group-pressure.

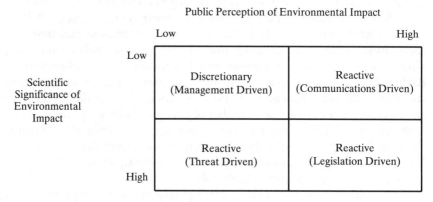

Public Perception of Environmental Impact

	Low	High
Low	Discretionary (Management Driven)	Reactive (Communications Driven)
High	Reactive (Threat Driven)	Reactive (Legislation Driven)

Scientific Significance of Environmental Impact

Figure 2.5 Assessing corporate vulnerability to changing environmental values

Source: Based upon Roome (1992)

At a sectoral level the responses of business can be seen to differ both within and between sectors, and between nations. A recent survey of managers in the automotive, oil and chemical, steel, metal processing and electricity sectors in Europe has identified some important differences in the way in which the environment is perceived and the relative importance of environmental problems and solutions to such problems (Vaughan and Mickle, 1993). Of the companies interviewed in this survey, chemical companies had gone furthest in integrating environment into management practice. The most interesting aspect of this survey is that it distinguishes between the various sources of pressure on a sector and identifies the relative importance of these sources on a country-by-country basis (Table 2.5). In general terms, European business perceives the environment in three ways: as a legislative constraint, as a business opportunity and as an integral part of business (*ibid.*). This reflects the results obtained from other surveys of business attitude and reinforces the four Ps advocated by Cannon that offer a strategic response to the challenges which confront business as a consequence of the growing significance of the environmental agenda. The 'four Ps' are pre-emption, participation, product development and positioning (Cannon, 1992).

The costs involved

The final issue to be addressed is how to determine the costs which are associated with the impact of economic activities upon the environment. Having determined the total costs it is also important to decide upon the distribution of such costs. Although this issue is considered in more detail in the next chapter, a brief discussion of this theme will be provided at this point for the sake of completeness.

It is difficult to provide a single detailed, accurate or comprehensive estimate of the costs that are associated with the impact of business upon the environment. Some studies have endeavoured to provide a comprehensive assessment of the relative costs on a continental or national basis. Whilst such assessments are helpful in terms of indicating the relative scale and severity of environmental problems, they offer little by way of guidance, or detail, that is of help in the development of future business policy. Nevertheless, these broad assessments are of considerable significance in that, compared with the situation obtaining even ten years ago, they do represent an acknowledgement of the importance of environmental issues in economic development. In its most recent assessment of the long-term prospects for the world economy, the OECD indicates the significance of environmental problems in determining the future rate of growth and notes that

> Especially for global environmental problems, the diversity of interests in the world community plus the high degree of uncertainty about the exact consequences imply that 'prisoners' dilemmas' lie in wait around every corner. This is why any solution will confront the world community with co-ordination problems of unprecedented complexity. In view of the sizeable contribution made by the developed countries towards the greenhouse effect and the income gap between these countries and the LDCs, any global bargain for these problems will undoubtedly require substantial offers of aid from the developed countries.
>
> (OECD, 1992, p. 40)

The costs that are associated with cleaning up or preventing environmental damage are considerable and they are likely to vary under different legislative regimes. Cannon (1992) distinguishes four tiers of environmental standard in Europe, ranging from highly developed, such as in The Netherlands, Germany and Switzerland, through moderately developed, including the UK and France, and relatively undeveloped, for example Portugal and Greece, to undeveloped, such as Poland, Romania and Bulgaria. This difference in

Table 2.5   Chemicals and petrochemicals sector: sources of pressure by country

	Non-governmental organisations	Public	Media	Employees	Trade unions	Trade bodies	Customers	Competitors
France	C	D	C	D	D	B	C	C
Germany	E	—	C	B	—	—	C	D
UK	C	C	C	B	E	D	B	C
Italy	A	A	D	E	E	B	C	B
Benelux	D	D	C	C	E	C	D	D

Note: Significance: A = Most
E = Least

Source: Adapted from Vaughan and Mickle (1993).

standards also suggest that the costs which are associated with the prevention and rectification of environmental damage will vary considerably, and indeed that is what can be observed in terms of the rate of increase in the percentage of gross domestic production (GDP) that is devoted to the environment. Those countries in the highly developed category tend to spend an increasing amount of GDP on the environment, for example expenditure in The Netherlands increased from 1.1 per cent of GDP in 1980 to 1.3 per cent of GDP in 1985 (Cairncross, 1991).

Actual spending on the environment in the UK in 1990–1 has been estimated at some £14 billion; of this the largest element was the £8.7 billion spent by enterprises, with the second largest element being the £4.8 billion spent by government (Department of the Environment, 1992). Environmental expenditure by companies varies considerably. Some of the largest organisations now spend a considerable proportion of both capital and revenue on implementing their environmental policies. Gray, Bebbington and Walters (1993) cite the example of Ciba-Geigy who now perceive the environment as one of the three pillars of their overall entrepreneurial responsibility, and this company spent a total of 1,330 million Swiss Francs on safety and environmental protection in 1989. A further example, which builds upon the example of Minamata disease referred to earlier in this chapter, indicates that the 15-year programme of dredging and reclaiming those areas of Minamata Bay that were contaminated by mercury cost the Chisso Company over 30,000 million yen. The company also paid over 90,000 million yen as compensation to persons affected by the disease (World Health Organisation, 1992).

It is easy to become dazzled by the large amounts of money which can be required in order to support an environmental initiative in a major multinational company. For most businesses the costs are more modest and may not represent any increase in the current level of capital expenditure. More importantly, there are a number of very good reasons why a company should take its environmental responsibilities seriously and develop corporate policies and an expenditure profile which match those responsibilities. To do otherwise could be seen as potentially or actually damaging to the future prospects of a company.

Environmental opportunities

Many of the environmental problems which have been discussed earlier in this chapter also represent actual or potential business opportunities. It is worth reminding readers of Max Frisch's dictum that 'crisis is a productive state provided you do not associate it with catastrophe' (quoted by Stohr, 1990, p. 1). Many crises provide a useful learning experience and, having invested in a new technology or developed a modified process, companies can find themselves in a position of market leadership. Opportunities are the reverse side of the environmental coin, and they reflect both the origins of the initial problem and a positive view of the future. Although a discussion of green business opportunities forms the substance of Chapter 9, and is also discussed elsewhere in this book, the broader issue of the opportunities for business development, which are associated with the growth of concern for the environment, are discussed in the remainder of this chapter.

Schmidheiny (1992) outlines the major reasons why business should view environmental issues as opportunities. In his view, six trends provide the foundations for a move towards greener business: customer pressure for greener products, insurance companies favour clean companies, banks are more willing to lend to environmentally sound businesses, employees prefer to work for environmentally responsible companies, environmental legislation is becoming more severe, and new economic instruments reward clean business operations. These trends have resulted in a number of companies adopting higher environmental standards for their own operations and, from the basis of their experience, such firms exert sectoral influence though the supply chain, and can influence local behaviour by means of peer-group pressure.

Enhanced environmental attitudes and behaviour are now seen as an essential prerequisite for long-term business success. The European Commission, in its study *Towards Sustainability*, identifies the business sector as having 'particularly significant impacts' on the environment and argues that 'it is essential to view environmental quality and economic growth as mutually dependent' (Commission of the European Communities, 1992a, p. 28).

In a recent report from the House of Lords Select Committee on the European Communities (1993), the case is taken further. This report notes the considerable size and the rapid rate of growth of the market for environmentally friendly products. The House of Lords report makes reference to an environmental protection industry world wide worth some £130 billion and a market for environmental protection equipment and services which will grow from $200 billion in 1990 to $300 billion by the end of the decade. Of this worldwide market, the European Union market is seen to be worth some $50 billion; Germany alone accounts for one-third of this market. In the world-wide market, Japan and Germany are seen to have gained a competitive advantage due to the early adoption in those nations of rigorous legislation, and they therefore have first mover advantages which, although powerful, are not inevitable. This assessment, from an impeccable source, illustrates the opportunity and the challenge to business.

There are three broad approaches to the development of environmental products and services. First, companies can develop, produce and market new products which allow entry into the market for replacement products, such as CFC replacement gases for use in foam blowing. Second, it is frequently possible to adapt existing products to meet the demands of the market for more environmentally friendly goods; examples would include the redesign of power station plant in order to ensure that it is less polluting or the adaptation of sewage treatment systems. Third, companies, from their own experience or by developing new skills, can offer design, research and consultancy services to other companies. These broad strategies for the reorientation of a company should be accompanied by increased attention to the environmental dimension of all aspects of a company's operations.

What particular environmental problems give rise to new business opportunities? In the view of the Centre for the Exploitation of Science and Technology (CEST), there are 13 key problems that require immediate attention and their solution provides an opportunity to develop new business ventures (CEST, 1990). These problems and the possible business opportunities (estimated to be worth £140 billion in the UK between 1991 and 2000) associated with them are outlined in Table 2.6.

These examples of the national and international business opportunities, which are associated with the market for environmental goods and services, are also reflected in more modest actions that can be taken by small and medium enterprises at a local level. New specialist niche markets have emerged that offer the opportunity for a company either to seek to satisfy market demand itself or to collaborate with other local companies in the establishment of new business ventures. Environmental cottage industries are now beginning to emerge in localities where existing companies have chosen to support a range of business activities associated with recycling and waste reduction, such as the secure recycling of confidential papers or the safe disposal of computer systems. Small-scale ventures such as these, many of which may be collaborative or partnership based, are the local equivalent of the larger-scale opportunities explored by the House of Lords and CEST. These new and innovative enterprises may also offer potential for the development of new economic complexes and linked activities.

The Advisory Committee on Business and the Environment (ACBE) has put the case for adopting a positive attitude towards the challenge of the environment: 'Improving your environmental performance is not an option – it is vital to every aspect of your business. It is a key factor for success' (ACBE, 1993a, p. 4).

Conclusions

Although widespread and severe, many of the environmental problems that result from business activities, and from human activities more generally, should not only be viewed as representing insurmountable obstacles. The solution to such problems requires a realistic view to be taken of the causes and consequences of environmental damage. This recognition is essential to the achievement of environmentally sustainable development. Many environmental problems, at global, national and local levels, have their origins in an approach to the process of industrialisation and economic growth which has regarded the environment as a free good. Such an approach has dominated economic life for almost two centuries, and it has paid little respect to the carrying capacity of the planet.

New approaches and strategies, which are aimed at allowing development

Table 2.6   Environmental problems and associated business opportunities

Problem	Cleaner products	Cleaner processes	Conservation
Greenhouse effect	Efficient boilers	Low carbon fuels	Insulation
Stratospheric ozone depletion	CFC replacements	Water based cleaning	Refrigerator maintenance
Acid rain	Low sulphur fuels	Coal washing	Energy saving
Water quality	Low phosphate	Low solvent use	Water management
Heavy metals	Low HM batteries	Cleaner metal finishes	—
VOCs and smells	Low solvent paints	Better storage	Traffic management
Persistent organics	Flame retardants	Non-Cl bleaching	—
Air quality	Cleaner cars	Pyrolysis	Traffic management
Noise	Control of acoustics	Better design	Traffic management
Waste management	Recyclable products	Low waste	—
Contaminated land	—	—	Better practices
Major spills and accidents	—	Risk assessment	Energy efficiency
Releases from biotechnology	Sterile releases	Containment	—

Source: Adapted from CEST (1990).

to occur in such a way as to allow for the simultaneous achievement of the environmental and economic goals of society, provide a number of important business opportunities. These opportunities offer businesses the potential to develop and market new products and to introduce new methods of production. In addition, it is possible to identify new modes of service delivery and of ways of organising and discharging work that minimise the call upon environmental resources. These new opportunities can also be extended to the development of new enterprises and can play an important role in the regeneration of old industrial areas.

3

The economics of the environment

As has been indicated in the first two chapters of this book, the resolution of many of the environmental problems that result from the operation of business activities almost inevitably involves a consideration of the economics of the environment. Two questions that are frequently asked about many of the environmental initiatives that have been proposed and implemented during recent years are, who should meet the costs involved in improving the quality of the environment, and what will be the impact of increased costs upon the performance of an individual company? These are complex questions, but they are fundamental to any meaningful analysis and assessment of the relationship between business and the environment. Put simply, to spend is to choose, and the choices are narrowing as the condition of the environment deteriorates.

The central economic concern for business has been expressed by Coopers and Lybrand (1990a, p. 1) in the following statement: 'It is evident that the real limits to economic growth are the capacity of the environment to deal with waste and the threats to the atmosphere from pollution and deforestation. Our scarcest resources are unpolluted air, water and soil.' This statement encapsulates many of the important economic issues that form the substance of this chapter: the theory and functioning of economic systems; the questioning of conventional attitudes to growth; the measurement and assignment of environmental costs and benefits; the role of tax and other measures in encouraging sustainable development; and, finally, the implications for business of the emergence of a new economic paradigm. Each of these issues will be considered within the context provided by the central organising framework of this book: a framework which seeks to relate the condition of the environment to the operation of economic activities across space. Because the economic implications of this relationship are of relevance at all spatial levels, from the global to the local, examples and illustrations will be provided of some of the key issues and approaches that confront political, business and community leaders, irrespective of their particular constituency or company roles and responsibilities.

Some initial concepts

In defining the key economic issues of relevance to the relationship between business and the environment, it is important to appreciate that many economists have paid little attention to environmental matters and do not regard the environment as a distinct entity or, if they acknowledge the existence of the environment, it has often been viewed as a free good. A criticism of this view of the economics of the environment is related to the vagueness with which the word environment is used, especially when the term environment is used mainly to refer to the range of issues that surround the discharge of pollution (Kneese, 1977). Traditionally business economists have had relatively little regard for environmental matters. The neoclassical economic doctrine assumes that the economy is an open system that is not constrained by any limits imposed by the environment, and that resources somehow enter the economic system in a response to the consumption of goods and services. O'Riordan and Turner (1983, p. 211) see the neoclassical economic system as one where 'resources apparently disappeared with the act of consumption and the economic system as a whole was geared to the fulfilment of one ultimate goal, the maximisation of welfare or utility, which could only be derived from the consumption act'.

The traditional concepts that have dominated much of economics are expressed in a particular set of terms that are fundamental to understanding the features and limitations of the market model. Some of these terms have already been defined earlier in this book, but these earlier definitions need to be extended or modified in order to ensure that they are clearly understood in relation to the economics of the environment.

Definitions

Resources are often defined by economists through the use of the term factors of production. The three main categories of resource identified by economists are as follows:

- *Natural resources* – including land and the other resources which exist on it and underneath the earth's surface, the seas and oceans and the atmosphere.
- *Labour resources* – including human labour and the skills, expertise and innovativeness associated with human abilities.
- *Capital resources* – this is the store of physical assets, including the resources and infrastructure which allow goods and services to be produced.

This definition of resources indicates that natural resources, which reflect the full range of characteristics and features of the environment discussed in

Chapter 1, are only one element in the broader view and definition of resources used by economists.

Resources are used or allocated in order to satisfy human wants. There are gradations in the definition of wants; fundamental wants are often referred to as needs and this particular want is taken to include the need for basic requirements such as food, clothing and shelter. More sophisticated wants can be satisfied once these basic needs have been met and such additional wants can be defined as including luxury goods and advanced services.

Demand is generated when a person or group in society wants a product or service and is able to pay for it. This process whereby demand is satisfied by the provision of a good or service generates a transaction that is known as supply. By supplying a good or service, the owner or producer of a resource is responding to the market stimulus generated by a consumer.

This simple transaction is the basic act in creating a market situation and in this situation the extent to which the supply of goods or services satisfies human wants and needs is defined as utility. Utility varies according to the circumstances in which a consumer is operating, but the important feature to recognise in this context is that the basic notion of utility is that a resource can satisfy a need and therefore it is said to have utility. Some economists have attempted to measure the degree to which the supply of certain commodities satisfies wants, but this is more of a theoretical challenge rather than a matter of concern for the environmental manager in business. The example of the traditional means of supplying water to domestic consumers can be used to illustrate the importance of the idea of utility for environmental economists. As Norton (1984) explains, under traditional tariff arrangements for water supply in the UK, water authorities supply domestic consumers an unlimited quantity of water upon the payment of a standard charge. He further observes that if only 'ten litres of water per week is supplied to a household, we might expect all of this water to be used for drinking, the satisfaction or marginal utility obtained from this initial ten litres being high', and because the consumption of water is not charged by the unit, additional consumption will occur and the 'extra satisfaction or marginal utility associated with the consumption of successive litres of water will diminish', eventually to zero (*ibid.* p. 46). The concept of utility is important because it indicates the value that is placed on environmental resources.

A final basic concept that is of importance in identifying the way in which economics treats the environment is the notion of the market. Markets are, in one sense, simply a means of expressing the supply of goods or services in order to satisfy demands whilst, in another sense, the concept of a market implies the processes that occur in order to satisfy demand as well as the actual physical act of supply.

Classical economics

Having defined these terms it is now possible to examine the various ways in which economists have considered the environment. Classical economists were concerned with analysing the power of the market to stimulate growth. Adam Smith argued that through the 'invisible hand', individuals acting in their own self-interest as consumers or producers could satisfy individual wants, but would also produce a beneficial outcome for society as a whole. Pearce and Turner (1990, p. 6) point to the fact that 'what was vital to economic and social progress was that economic transactions should be allowed to operate on the basis of freely competitive markets'. The important point to note is that the classical economists placed considerable emphasis upon the production of goods and therefore concentrated their attention on the ways in which the factors of production interact. For the classical economists, working in a preindustrial era, the environment was an important concern. Many of their ideas were based on the use of land and the concept of environmental limits was a key factor. Economic growth was limited by the shortage of good agricultural land and other natural resources; the fixed amount of agricultural land available placed a limit on production and diminishing returns occurred as increasing amounts of labour were applied, each additional increment of labour yielding a lower amount of production.

Marxist economics

The classical economists placed emphasis upon the use of labour and Marx took this labour theory of value further. In Marx's view natural resources were considered as raw materials – both initial source materials and the product of one industry when used by another – and these materials were transformed by the dominant factor of production, that is, labour. Through developing the labour theory of value, Marx argued that the 'value of a commodity was determined only by the amount of past and present labour which went into producing it' (Papp, 1977, p. 135). In summary, Marx adopted the view that natural resources were the gifts of nature, but these resources only had value when human labour was applied to them. Marx, in Papp's view, was 'not concerned with depletion of resources, nor particularly with the methods by which industries obtained their resources' (*ibid*. p. 136). This absence of concern for the environmental costs of resource use are evident in the pollution and other crises that currently beset the former Soviet economies.

Neoclassical economics

The dominant economic model, which has influenced much of the thinking of business and government, originates in the neoclassical school. In the neoclassical model particular emphasis is placed upon the scarcity of a commodity. The price of a commodity was seen to be a function of scarcity rather than a measure of labour costs. Although they gave less value to labour, all the factors of production were still recognised, but the introduction of scarcity value implies that even if a commodity requires little labour in its production, it still has value. Scarcity in the neoclassical model is determined by the interaction between supply and demand; this interaction determines the equilibrium market price for a commodity. Within this form of analysis there is an important environmental concept; this is that the pursuit of individual self-interest is also likely to improve social welfare. Individual preferences are also seen to reflect social desirability and this is represented in the idea of maximising social welfare. A Pareto optimum situation is one in which an individual can only act without making someone else worse off. This Pareto optimum situation does not imply social equity or a direct concern for the environment, but it does reflect the efficiency of a choice in fulfilling consumer wants in a free market.

Although the concept of Pareto optimality is important, it does not allow for the full incorporation of environmental concerns. This is because it is based upon a series of restrictive assumptions and does not, for example, consider the imperfections of much price information. Neither does it fully incorporate all of the externalities, or residual side effects, of production. Nevertheless, it does provide an argument in favour of intervention in circumstances where it is clear that the market situation is not maximising social welfare. This allows a simplified market system to be illustrated, incorporating the element of externalities or residuals that are ignored by the basic market model (Figure 3.1).

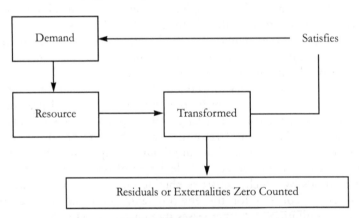

Figure 3.1 A simplified market model

Source: based on Roome (1992)

Modifications to the neoclassical view, which chiefly viewed economics as having a concern with the analysis of the pattern of economic activity and prices, a microeconomic view, were developed during the 1930s. Keynes argued that there were certain economic problems which required a view to be taken of broad economic aggregates, a macroeconomic view, and he advocated government intervention in cases where the market proved to be inadequate to the task of tackling such problems. Although Keynes concentrated on problems such as the management of growth in the economy so as to avoid mass unemployment, the notion of intervention did prove to be influential in both the study of economic growth and in assessments of the consequences of such growth for the broader welfare of society. Keynes's theory, whilst directed chiefly towards unemployment, does offer a number of parallels with important concerns in environmental economics. In particular there are affinities between the consideration of external diseconomies, such as pollution of the global commons, and the treatment given to issues of social welfare.

Ecological economics

Many other adaptations of the neoclassical model have been developed. Some of these attempt to incorporate environmental factors directly within the production process, such as the polluter pays principle, whilst others view the costs of dealing with environmental damage as part of the portfolio of activities known as intervention. What is known as the mixed approach attempts to relate environmental questions to the neoclassical paradigm that was developed initially to deal with relationships in a private market situation. As was stated at the beginning of this section, most economic theories regard the economic system as an open system, but in reality an economic system is a closed system. This closed system draws resource inputs from the environment and, as can be seen in Figure 3.1, it discharges its residuals into the environment.

One of the first economists to draw attention to this situation was Kenneth Boulding (1966). In his view human beings have operated a 'cowboy economy', in which resources are exploited without any real concern for the present or the future. This attitude is seen to originate in the emphasis placed by conventional economics upon the scale and rate of production. Boulding advocated a move towards a 'spaceship' view of the economy; a stance that requires the true valuation of finite resources and which places emphasis upon the minimisation of the use of resources. The aim of the 'spaceship economy' is to 'maintain, use and use again' (Cottrell, 1978, p. 7). In this way the aim of an economic system should be to maintain the capital stock upon which the system depends.

This view was taken a step further by Kneese, Ayres and D'Arge (1970) who argue for the use of a mass or materials balance approach. In their view the extraction of resources from the environment for the purposes of production does not alter their mass. Equally, the deposition of residuals, in total, does not affect the mass. In other words, whatever resources flow into the economic system must emerge from the system as waste. However, what does occur is that wastes or residuals are deposited into common property resources and thus 'market forces, whilst marvellously efficient in allocating owned resources, work to damage or destroy common property resources' (Kneese, 1977, p. 28). This view of the interaction between the economy and the environment is important, because it directs attention towards the spatial inequity often associated with the use of resources in the process of production, and especially in the generation of externalities. For example, a resource drawn from a remote source may be processed at a specific location in order to satisfy a demand of society, but the residual from that process may be deposited on the land surface as toxic waste, or it may be discharged into the water or the atmosphere. The locality in which production takes place therefore accommodates the disbenefits of resource use in order that society as a whole may benefit.

Although the introduction of the materials balance approach represents a considerable advance upon previous ways of considering the environment, a number of weaknesses have been identified in the original model that was put forward by Kneese, Ayres and D'Arge. Pearce (1976) has argued that the basic materials balance model only really deals with materials and energy flows up to the point of their entry into the environmental media (land, air and water) and that this fails to appreciate the importance of the capacity of the environment to receive and assimilate residuals. As he suggests, there is a considerable difference between a situation in which the environment can absorb the waste that is discharged and one where the quality and types of residuals being discharged are sufficient to overload the assimilative capacity. This modification, which is similar in many ways to the concept of the ecological carrying capacity of an environment, is especially important in dealing with pollution, and Pearce demonstrates the possibility of a basic incompatibility between the social optimum, determined through cost-benefit analysis, and an ecologically stable situation (Pearce, 1977).

These and other modifications to the materials balance approach provide public policy-makers, business managers and environmentalists alike with a helpful and practical model that allows for the identification of the main points of interaction between the economy and the environment. The materials balance approach, together with the modifications suggested by Pearce, also provides a useful contribution to the spatial management of the costs that are associated with the use of resources, especially in those regions and localities that are particularly subject to pollution and the deposition of wastes.

Linking the economic sphere to the environment in this way suggests a need to modify the neoclassical model in order to allow conventional analysis to be extended so that it can handle environmental problems. This is best achieved through an appreciation of the implications of the materials balance approach. In this modified or mixed approach, resources are not simply defined as stock resources but also include amenity resources, such as landscape and open space; likewise the sinks into which residuals may be discharged are considered to be resources and should be treated as such.

This wider view of the interaction between the economy and the environment enables the position of the individual business in relation to the environment to be defined. As an operating unit within the wider economy, a company faces the full range of choices regarding resource usage that confront society as a whole. The interactions that occur between what Pearce and Turner (1990) refer to as the economic matrix and the environment matrix, are similar in overall form and content to the relationship between the competitive environment and the ecologic environment that has been discussed by Smith (1992). These interactions, or relationships, are central to any consideration of the ways in which business can respond to environmental problems and challenges. As can be seen in Figure 3.2, such a relationship is best described as an interface between the internal economic operating environment of a company and the ecological environment. Flows between the two elements, working within the framework of the materials balance approach, should be fully costed and, wherever possible, any adverse effects of the process of production should be regarded by an enterprise as an operating cost.

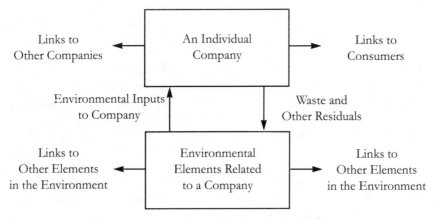

Figure 3.2   Link between economic and environmental factors

Many other aspects of the relationship between the economy and the environment, and between the operation of an individual company and the environment, are considered in the remainder of this chapter. However, these issues all depend upon the acceptance of the fundamental principles outlined in this section. Before discussing other aspects of environmental economics, it is important to note that none of the relationships that have been described are fixed or constant. Economics does not give a priority to one issue or group over another. It is therefore vital to consider each specific case on its merits and to determine trade-offs, and the assignment of responsibilities, within a dynamic rather than fixed framework of analysis and action.

The question of growth

As has already been discussed, growth is an important consideration in many of the attempts that have been made to explain how an economic system functions. Indeed, it is true to say that analysing the ways of achieving and maintaining growth has been a fundamental preoccupation of many economists.

Early classical economists were concerned with the limits to growth, indeed for Malthus the environmental limits that were imposed by the supply of agricultural land dominated his analysis. But for most of the period from the start of the industrial revolution to the 1960s, insufficient attention was paid to such limits. However, with the growing awareness of environmental problems that occurred during the 1960s, the growth orientation of conventional economic systems was questioned. The debate during the 1970s centred upon a discussion of the extent to which further economic growth was desirable or possible without inflicting lasting damage upon the environment. Various views were put forward, varying from what O'Riordan and Turner (1983) describe as the technocentric position – here growth is seen as desirable in itself with technology providing the capability to ensure the provision of substitutes for scarce resources – to an ecocentric view which favours the environment and rejects growth as an objective in itself. Some observers have taken the ecocentric position further, arguing in favour of a zero growth or negative growth stance in order to prevent an ecological catastrophe.

This intermeshing of ecologists and economists caused the emergence of concerns not only with the interaction between the economy and the environment but also with the spatial distribution of the benefits and disbenefits of growth, especially with regard to the relationship between developed and less developed nations. In this debate, which culminated in the work of the World Commission on Environment and Development, fundamental questions were raised with regard to the nature and operation of economic systems. Chief amongst such questions are the search for a way of maintaining growth without causing further damage to the environment, and ensuring that the benefits of future growth are better distributed between countries.

It is important here to distinguish between growth and development. Growth in a conventional sense is taken to imply economic growth and is measured in terms of an increase in income. Development is a wider concept and implies a simultaneous uplifting of social, economic and environmental conditions. This distinction lies at the centre of the debate over the choice of sustainable development as the preferred term for the concept espoused by the World Commission on Environment and Development. It is, however, more than an exercise in semantics, for sustainable development also encapsulates the ideas of inter and intragenerational equity and a commitment to the non-monetary components of welfare (Jacobs, 1991).

How does this definition of sustainable development affect the way in which we measure growth or development? Conventional measures of growth, such as Gross National Product (GNP) or Gross Domestic Product (GDP), pay little direct attention to the impact of economic growth upon the environment. As Rookwood (1993, p. 198) has noted these measures are flawed and misleading because they count 'bads as well as goods', and, as a result, environmentally necessary changes have been resisted because they could impede the growth of GNP or GDP. What is required are measures of growth or development that incorporate environmental factors and measure changes in the quality of life. A similar problem in relation to business accounting has been identified by Gray, Bebbington and Walters (1993, p. 13), who argue that 'conventional short-term profit measurement, performance reporting budgetary constraints and investment appraisal are highly likely to be in conflict with more environmentally benign initiatives'.

Alternative measures of growth and development seek to incorporate a wider set of considerations and use as their framework of reference the interactions implied in the materials balance approach. A review of some of the major methods for obtaining more complete and meaningful national and international accounts has been conducted by Pearce, Markandya and Barbier (1989). In their view it is important to provide a system of environmental accounting that

- provides a balance sheet which indicates a profile of what stocks of resource are available at a given point in time;
- shows the use made of the stocks, what sources they originate from and how they are added to or transformed over time; and
- ensures that the stock accounts and the flow accounts are consistent over time in order to allow the balance sheet in any one year to be derived from the balance sheet of the previous year plus the flow accounts of that year.

Their review of the various attempts to establish environmental accounts considers both physical and monetary approaches. Physical accounts represent the use and flow of resources in terms of the units of consumption appropriate to the particular resource in question, for example, the area of land taken for urban development, barrels of oil used or gallons of water consumed. Monetary accounts attempt to link the use of environmental resources to national income accounts and provide a valuation of the resources which are used in order to provide goods or services.

Each of these approaches has much to offer in terms of the value that is placed upon the environment. As will be discussed in more detail later when reference is made to methods of environmental assessment, the valuation of resources by using a physical unit of account provides a real calculation of resource consumption and, by using empirical evidence, the amount of a resource that is consumed can be related to its economic effects, such as the cost of treating waste materials. In the case of the monetary approach, a difficulty is encountered in assigning a monetary value to each transformation of a resource. In practice a mixed approach, which inter-relates the physical stock or flow of resources with a monetary value, may prove to be more satisfactory. The problem of implementing these improved accounting structures has been the subject of considerable research during the past twenty years; an early attempt to assign economic values to environmental issues resulted in the calculation of a measure of economic welfare by Nordhaus and Tobin (1972). Other suggestions include methods for the calculation of environmentally adjusted net national product, whereby an amount for the depreciation of human-made capital and for environmental depreciation is deducted from GNP (Jacobs, 1991) and for the provision of an index of sustainable economic welfare (Daly and Cobb, 1989).

In diagrammatic form the calculation of an account which seeks to incorporate environmental values can be seen to involve two stages. First there is a need to deduct an estimate of the resources used and, second, an estimate of the monetary value of environmental degradation (Steer and Lutz, 1993). Figure 3.3 illustrates this process and uses the baseline of net domestic product (NDP), that is GDP minus an allowance for the depreciation of human-made capital, for the calculation of what Steer and Lutz term an environmentally adjusted net domestic product (EDP). This is a difficult calculation to undertake for the reasons stated above, but it has the twin merits of allowing environmental values to be incorporated in the national accounts and of including an estimate of depreciation.

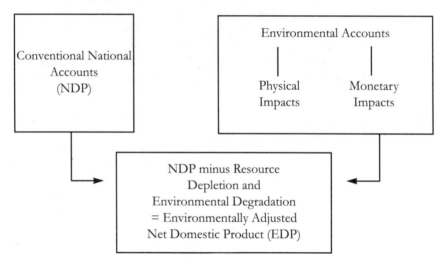

Figure 3.3   A green national account

Measuring environmental progress in terms of business performance faces many of the difficulties described above. Conventional accounting makes provision for the direct costs of business operations, including an allowance for depreciation, but makes no real attempt to incorporate the wider environmental costs associated with the operation of a specific process or a company as a whole. Some countries have now introduced a requirement that companies should disclose details of their impact on the environment. Since 1989 Norwegian corporations have been required to provide details in their annual report of emission levels, contamination and the measures adopted to prevent environmental damage (Roberts, 1992). One example of a company that has responded to this new requirement is Norsk Hydro, who in 1989 produced a special report on its domestic activities with regard to the environment and followed this initial action, in 1990, with a fuller report on the worldwide activities. This pathbreaking report produced positive results for the company in terms both of its own operations and its public image.

Many aspects of business accounting already have to incorporate environmental concerns. The direct costs of complying with legislation, the provision of allowances for the costs associated with the clearance of contaminated land and the costs of environmental control within a plant provide some examples. The real challenge is to extend this limited assessment in order to allow the full costs of the interaction between business and the environment to be recognised and incorporated; a form of materials balance approach within business accounting is required. This need for a change in stance has been recognised by the European Commission who argue in their plan *Towards Sustainability* (Commission of the European Communities, 1992a, p. 29) for the 'improved management and control of production processes including a system of licensing linked to integrated pollution prevention and control, environmental auditing, effective environmental valuation and accounting'.

An important role for accounting in business is to develop information systems that are capable of capturing the costs of adopting more environmentally responsible business practices (Owen, 1992). This challenge is similar in nature, and in its complexity, to the task of calculating the national environmentally adjusted net domestic product that was illustrated by Figure 3.3. The longer-term challenge has been defined by Bebbington and Gray (1993) as the need to develop a sustainable cost approach to accounting. This approach aims to provide a business organisation with the information it requires in order that it may determine if it 'leaves the biosphere at the end of the accounting period no worse off than it was at the beginning of the accounting period' (*ibid.* p. 8). This is a major task, but it is a fundamental reform if business is to account for the impact of its activities upon the environment.

Measuring environmental costs and benefits

Many of the approaches that have been discussed earlier in this chapter provide clues as to the ways in which the environmental costs and benefits that are associated with economic activities can be assessed. However, in practice, few policy analysts or business managers have either the training or time that is required to construct a complex macroeconomic model. A number of standard techniques and procedures have been developed during recent years that are intended to assist decision-makers in making choices about economic investments. These techniques and procedures vary from soft procedures for screening investment decisions to complex econometric models. A number of these approaches are reviewed in the following section; in conducting this review the major features and capabilities of these approaches are contrasted with their weaknesses and limitations. A fuller review of methods for environmental impact assessment and environmental auditing is presented in Chapter 6.

Cost-benefit analysis (CBA) has been used for the past thirty years to assist decision-making. The fundamental premise is a simple one, that is, that an investment should only be undertaken if the benefits outweigh the costs. In cost-benefit analysis an attempt is made to assign monetary values to costs and benefits and, in order to allow these costs and benefits to be considered over time, a discount rate is used to convert these future values to their present value. Although the concept is a simple one, many complexities and difficulties are encountered in attempting to assign costs and benefits.

The fundamental rationale for CBA is to be found in the study of welfare economics. This branch of economics is concerned with social welfare maximisation and it attempts to indicate to decision-makers whether or not a policy or project is likely to assist in the enhancement of social welfare.

Examples of the use of CBA abound. Both public and private sector investments have been subject to assessment using CBA and in many cases the results have proved to be of great assistance in informing a decision, including those cases where the outcome has been the realisation that the initial specification of the proposed action is inherently flawed and needs to be re-defined. Some examples of the use of CBA include the assessment of major public and private transport projects. The Third London Airport Study was a classic case of the use of CBA and it yielded many interesting lessons. Other examples include the use of CBA to assess new energy generation and transmission facilities; large-scale commercial and leisure developments, such as new science and warehousing parks, shopping centres and sports complexes; potentially hazardous industrial installations; water control and management schemes; new towns; and large projects in environmentally sensitive areas. As Schofield (1987, p. 5) notes: 'the method applies at a variety of levels of analysis and in a wide selection of fields.'

Despite the widespread use of CBA, there are a number of difficulties that limit its usefulness and, in some cases, its validity. In summary, these doubts relate to the choice of discount values, the ability to place a value on certain environmental features, and especially those features that cannot be replaced, the estimation of secondary effects, the definition of risk and the question of intergenerational equity. Whilst it is impossible in an introductory text to rehearse all the arguments that are related to these issues, two of them are central to decision-making in business (discount values and replacement) and they are dealt with in more detail below.

The choice of discount rate is often crucial to the success of a project, and a clear result from the application of a test rate can form the basis for a decision on whether or not to proceed. In CBA the choice of a discount rate can have considerable influence over the weight that is given to environmental considerations through the calculation of a net present value (Box 3.1). Many public and private projects are intended to operate for many years and the costs and benefits associated with them occur throughout their life. The costs associated with major schemes often peak at the start of a project, for example, the construction of a dam or a new industrial site, whilst the benefits tend to be distributed throughout the project. Tietenberg (1992) cites the example of a tidal power scheme on the border between Canada and the USA. The US government applied a discount rate of 2.5 per cent, whilst Canada used a rate of 4.125 per cent. The higher Canadian rate led to the conclusion that the project was likely to yield a negative net benefit, whilst by using the US rate the project produced a positive net benefit. Pearce, Markandya and Barbier (1989) take the argument further and point to the case of forestry. The benefit in this case is a tree that takes 50 years to grow; and the benefit is 'reduced to comparative insignificance in terms of present values' (*ibid.* p. 137). In such a case the result is that the tree will not be grown unless special treatment is applied to afforestation and future generations will have 'forgone a benefit which they cannot reproduce' (*ibid.*), because they will have to wait 50 years for a tree to grow.

Box 3.1 *Discount rates: calculation and influence on projects*

In order to calculate a net present value (NPV) it is necessary to discount future costs and benefits to a common base. This can be obtained from the formula

$$\text{NPV of expected } \pounds x \text{ in year } t = \frac{x}{(1 + i)\ E}$$

where i = annual interest rate. Discounted at a rate of 10 per cent, the present value of £100 in one year's time is

$$\frac{100}{(1 + 0.1)} = \pounds 90.90$$

and in two years' time is

$$\frac{100}{(1 + 0.1)^2} = \pounds 82.60$$

By altering the rate to 5 per cent, the present value of £100 in two years' time is

$$\frac{100}{(1 + 0.05)^2} = \pounds 90.70$$

The higher the rate of interest and the longer the period of years, the smaller the NPV. Projects that produce benefits in the distant future will therefore appear to be less attractive.

The second issue of importance for business is the question of the value that is placed on the possibility of replacing or restoring an environmental resource. Ignoring the fact that an unrealistically low value may be placed upon certain features of the environment, the problems that are associated with finding a replacement for a lost environmental asset are extremely difficult to address. These difficulties arise because the environmental values in question are intangible, or because the values placed on environmental assets vary from generation to generation. Whilst it is difficult to assign a value to matters such as water quality, it is almost impossible to decide upon the value to be assigned to a particular landscape. Although pioneering work in recent years has helped to reduce such difficulties (O'Riordan, Wood and Shadrake, 1992), two important problems remain: first, what is an irreversible effect; and, second, can an adequate replacement be found?

With regard to the first problem, O'Riordan and Turner (1983, p. 100) express the view that 'Irreversible damage effects may serve to reduce an individual's options to experience the environmental good in question' and that an option value may be defined as 'a benefit accruing to an individual as a result of his retaining an option to consume the good at some time in the future'. The option value can be seen as a premium for risk avoidance, but it is a complex and controversial calculation. On the question of providing a replacement, the views of analysts vary. The Department of the Environment (1991) notes that any attempt to value an environmental resource may fail to measure public preferences and that the value placed on a resource by the community may be greater or less than this. Pearce and Turner (1990) offer a more optimistic outlook and suggest that a shadow project elsewhere, funded by an amount added to the cost of a project, may substitute rather than replace the lost environmental asset. It may, in their view, be possible to restore a partly degraded wetland elsewhere in the same region in order to substitute for the loss of a particularly valuable wetland due to the development of a project.

Even with all these doubts and difficulties, CBA still offers a helpful and useful approach to the measurement and determination of the environmental costs and benefits that are associated with projects. However, the most important factor that determines the value and validity of CBA is the extent to which a realistic value is assigned to the features of the environment. It is the weakness in the practice rather than in the theory of CBA that has caused most concern. As Jacobs (1991, p. 197) observes, in the case of the assessment of new trunk roads in Britain 'government decision-makers are much more impressed by a project with high net present value despite major environmental costs than by one with significant environmental benefits but a smaller financial return'.

By applying the criteria that are central to the concept of sustainable development to CBA, it is possible to arrive at a modified form of analysis that meets some of the current criticisms. In some cases this implies the adoption of the true long-term benefits that are associated with projects and costs, rather that the acceptance of apparent short-term values. Pearce (1991) points to the example of the subsidisation of fertilisers, pesticides and irrigation water in the third world. These costly approaches are associated with the excessive use of resources and the occurrence of environmental degradation through the salinisation of soils and other consequences of their use. By removing the subsidies an overall gain results, both for the environment and for national government budgets. This example of a win-win policy reflects potential benefits that are 'extensive in scope and suggest a small and perhaps even negative national cost to improving environmental quality' (*ibid.* p. 8).

A more elementary method, which can be used to calculate any potential gain or loss that may be associated with a proposed action, is known as cost-effectiveness analysis (CEA). This method can be used when it is difficult or impossible to arrive at a good measure of the benefits associated with an action. In essence it involves specifying the desired outcome of an action, testing the extent to which alternative options meet the objective and identifying the option that achieves the objective at least cost. The objective, or target, used in CEA is usually specified by the political or corporate process and may, for example, represent the desired outcome in terms of the development of new plant capacity or the installation of new process equipment. The main limitations to the use of CEA relate to the definition and specification of the details of the objective. If it proves difficult or impossible to measure the characteristics of one or more of the options, then CEA in Wimpenny's (1991, p. 43) opinion 'becomes ambiguous'.

Many other techniques and procedures have been suggested for the assessment of projects, but most of them either suggest alternative ways of calculating the costs and benefits to be included in CBA or they provide partial solutions. For a fuller review of the available techniques the reader is referred to Schofield (1987), Pearce and Turner (1990), Wimpenny (1991), Tietenberg (1992) and Pearce (1993).

Within a business, the most helpful approach to the assessment and measurement of environmental impacts has been suggested by Gray, Bebbington and Walters (1993, p. 148) who argue that 'unless environmental considerations are embedded into the core functions of the accounting and financial systems, those functions will not only be unsupportive of organisational change towards a greener orientation, they will actually prevent it'. From this starting point a company can build its approach to the measurement of the environmental costs and benefits that are associated with all aspects of its operations. In developing this approach it is important to ensure that it is transparent and capable of external verification and review.

One of the major difficulties that confronts a business is that experience on how to inject an environmental dimension into company financial systems is very limited. Gray, Bebbington and Walters (*ibid.*) have revealed that fewer than 40 per cent of UK companies have any environmental factors integrated into their financial investment appraisal process and less than 20 per cent have incorporated environmental issues into their budgeting systems. This neglect of environmental concerns means that it is often difficult for managers to compare a potential environmental solution with the conventional approach to an investment decision.

There are a number of specific problems that require attention if a business is to introduce environmental values into its accounting and financial procedures. The first of these relates to the use of discount rates and the methodology of discounted cash flow analysis. As was identified in the case of CBA, the choice of a discount rate, the period of time over which an investment is assessed and the identification of the environmental implications of all the stages in a project are crucial elements in determining the viability of an environmental solution. Too high a discount rate may undervalue the potential contribution of an alternative approach that places greater emphasis on the environment, whilst the full costs of the future disposal of hazardous plant or materials may not be taken fully into account in defining the true costs associated with a project. As Owen (1992, p. 9) has observed, 'using lower discount rates for particular environmental benefits would ensure that a significant present value would attach to them'. The selection of an appropriate time horizon for assessing a project is frequently even more important. Anticipating future environmental standards and assessing a project over its expected lifespan may, for example, reveal that making an investment decision now that incorporates environmental criteria may save having to retro-fit pollution control equipment in the future. By adopting methods of investment appraisal that place value on the environment, companies may be able to avoid technically difficult to solve and costly problems in the future. Anticipating the future condition of the ecological environment is now as important to the development of a corporate strategy as forecasting future economic circumstances.

For most companies the most important step forward would be to introduce environmental criteria and considerations into the budgetary process. This may imply, for example, that corporate policy is adjusted in order to determine the rate of charge that should be made on any transfers between divisions that incorporate or entail an environmental problem or residual. In such cases a system of rewards and penalties could be introduced that is designed to reinforce and encourage positive behaviour (*ibid.*). Quite clearly this approach would also encourage the minimisation of waste and a reduction in the consumption of raw materials and other resources.

The full range of company activities should be brought within the process of environmental accounting and financial management. This issue is taken further in Chapters 5 and 6. Adjusting the role played by accountants is also important. Davis (1991) suggests that if accountants are to continue to play a leadership role it is unlikely that this will be because of their knowledge of finance, rather it will be because they have accepted the new challenges of the environment and have realised the importance of introducing environmental concerns into all aspects of a company's activities. This holistic approach is reflected in the CBI's approach to environmental auditing and management (CBI, 1990) and in the advice offered by Business in the Environment (BiE, 1992). Box 3.2 summarises some of the main areas of business activity that could be subject to an environmentally sensitive accounting and financial system. The old maxim holds true for the environment as with all other aspects of business activity – if you cannot measure it, you cannot manage it.

Box 3.2 *Some key items of concern in an environmental accounting system*

- Raw material inputs
- Energy inputs
- Water and other resource inputs
- All manufacturing and associated processes
- Plant and building maintenance
- Planning, environmental and operating permits
- Local environmental conditions
- Research and development activities
- Product design
- Design of plant, equipment and processes
- Design of buildings and infrastructure
- Layout of facilities
- Aesthetic considerations
- Emission and effluent control
- Accident and emergency procedures
- Notification procedures
- Transportation
- Waste management, recycling and waste disposal
- Storage, containment and intraplant transfer
- Training and staff awareness
- Decommissioning, abandonment, restoration and reclamation
- Corporate strategy and its overall impact

Tax and related instruments for environmental control

Having isolated and discussed the ways in which the environmental dimension can be reflected in economic and business decisions, it is important to review ways in which the objectives of sustainable development can be reflected in the price that is charged for goods and services. As has already been discussed, although market mechanisms can and do reflect the value of some environmental resources, there are certain imperfections in the operation of markets that prevent the full valuation of all resources. An important step forward has been the adoption of the polluter pays principle (PPP). In its *Guiding Principles Concerning International Economic Aspects of Environmental Policies*, agreed in 1972, the Organisation for Economic Co-operation and Development discussed the desirability of ensuring that the polluter should bear the expense of carrying out the measures decided by public authorities to ensure that the environment is in an acceptable state (OECD, 1972). This mechanism is designed to ensure that the true cost of producing goods and services is reflected in the price charged and, as such, a part or all of any increase in the cost of production will be passed on to consumers.

In addition to this general principle, it is also important to recognise the need for the adoption of additional financial inducements, both taxes and subsidies, which seek to encourage higher environmental standards.

The OECD (1991b) has suggested three major economic instruments that can be used to achieve higher standards:

- Environmental charges or taxes.
- Marketable permits.
- Deposit-refund systems.

Environmental taxes are of two kinds: user charges and effluent charges. Such taxes or charges are set on a product, or the resource inputs used to make a product, and raise the cost of production. These taxes allow a polluter to choose how to adjust to the required environmental standard, either by paying the tax or, if the costs of eliminating the cause of pollution are low, by modifying the production process and thus eliminating pollution. One example is the concept of a carbon tax; the European Commission has proposed such a tax which should be levied half on the carbon content of different fuels and half upon the energy content (Pearce, 1993).

An alternative method is the introduction of marketable or tradable permits. Such permits are based upon the idea of setting limits to pollution and allowing polluters to pollute up to the defined level. These permits are then sold to companies who are allowed to trade their right to pollute. As Gabel (1992) observes, if two companies hold permits then company A, which finds it expensive to operate within its quota allocation, may purchase additional quota rights from company B. Company B can sell its quota because its cost of complying with environmental limits is relatively low.

The third instrument suggested by the OECD is the deposit-refund system. In such systems a deposit is paid, in advance, on potentially polluting processes or products. If pollution is avoided then a refund is made. A simple example is the use of a deposit paid on bottles, but the principle could be extended to many other products.

The alternative to charges or taxes is the use of a subsidy to reward positive environmental behaviour, such as reclaiming derelict land or installing pollution abatement equipment. A problem with the use of subsidies is that the costs of reducing or eliminating pollution do not always fall upon the original polluter.

For business, the introduction of financial instruments to control environmental damage will generate the need to include the costs of compliance within the costs of production. By having to pay a tax on their operations, or by having to purchase a permit to pollute, companies will be required to investigate the alternatives. In some cases, such as the proposed carbon tax, the option of reducing energy consumption may prove to be more attractive than paying the tax. Some companies have already adopted such an approach and have achieved substantial cost savings (an example of energy saving by Sainsbury's is provided in Box 3.3).

Box 3.3   *Energy saving by Sainsbury's*

- Sainsbury's has systematically reviewed store design over the last 15 years to arrive at the concept of a 'low energy store'.
- The modern supermarket uses only 60 per cent of the energy used by a similar store built 10 years ago.
- Key savings have been achieved by improvements in lighting technology, increasing the efficiency of refrigerators, using the heat from the refrigeration system to heat domestic water and ventilation air, recycling heat from instore bakery ovens, introducing computerised building energy management systems and monitoring energy use.

Conclusions

In tracing the evolution of the changing attitudes of economists to the problems and potentials of the environment, this chapter has sought to demonstrate that the recognition that the environment is not a free good, and that it needs to be managed with the same expertise that is essential to business success, is a precondition for future economic progress. The World Commission on Environment and Development (1987, p. 9) has expressed the challenge in the following way:

> Yet in the end, sustainable development is not a fixed state of harmony, but rather a process of change in which the exploitation of resources, the direction of investments, the orientation of technological development, and institutional change are made consistent with future as well as present needs. We do not pretend that the process is easy or straightforward. Painful choices have to be made.

The process of change in economic and business thinking that is implied by the concept of sustainable development is one that shifts the burden of responsibility. It is no longer acceptable for a business to ignore the environmental consequences of its operations and it is vital that environmental concerns become embedded in corporate strategy. This suggests the need for a true value to be assigned to environmental resources; such a value may be significantly above the spot price that is currently paid for raw materials. In addition, a company may have to consider its entire production and marketing strategy in order to ensure that it can operate within the new parameters that are set by the economics of sustainable development. A change of this magnitude will not occur overnight. During the changeover period some companies may have to rely upon end-of-pipe techniques to mitigate the worst effects of environmental damage, whilst others will continue to pay pollution taxes until they can achieve the raised environmental standards.

In accepting the reality of the new economics, business is accepting a radical agenda. But this agenda is essential both to the achievement of sustainable development and for future business success. Implementing the agenda implies changing attitudes within companies and in the broader business community. Proactivity is essential; act now, or lose market share in the future, is the choice that faces many companies. A corporate commitment to the economics of the environment and a shift in the culture of business are vital elements in the process of change.

At a local level the response of business will vary with prevailing economic and environmental circumstances. In some localities and regions it has proved possible to move relatively rapidly towards achieving the conditions necessary for the attainment of sustainable development. This may result from an inheritance of a less environmentally damaging economic structure, it may be because the local environment has a greater capacity to absorb the consequences of business operations or it may be due to the influence of environmentally minded business leaders. Local networks of businesses acting in collaboration can assist individual companies by setting an example, sharing technologies and other solutions, and by demonstrating the benefits that emerge as business moves towards accepting its new responsibilities.

Alain Lipietz (1992, p. 48) has summarised the argument for considering economics and environment as two sides of the same coin, and to relate them to the conditions obtaining in a particular place:

> economics is the science of the human activities of production and distribution. Ecology as a science extends this viewpoint: above and beyond the activity itself, it considers the environment where the activity takes place, the interaction between them, and changes in the environment as a result of the activity.

4

The sociopolitical and legal context

The 1980s saw the coming together of many diverse political doctrines and the emergence of a consensus on the importance of giving higher priority to the better management of the environment. This was no accidental or casual change in stance. In one sense it represented a common concern amongst previously opposed ideologies for the future of the environment as the fundamental resource of the planet. A revolution in thinking on this scale cannot be ignored, especially when it reflects the changing social values and attitudes of voters. By the early 1990s concern for the environment had resulted in the emergence of a commitment by governments to the sustainable management of the planet.

Business is at the centre of this process. As a supplier of goods and services, it depends for its future prosperity on meeting the demands of citizen-consumers in a manner which reflects their changing aspirations and values and, as an essential component of modern society, it influences, and is influenced by, political attitudes. Like it or not, business has to respect the social and political conventions of the broader community within which it operates and, at a more immediate level, it has to function within a framework of law and regulation that is determined by society. In addition, at local and national levels, peer group pressure exerts considerable influence on business behaviour.

This chapter examines three aspects of the sociopolitical framework within which the business and environment relationship has evolved and will continue to evolve into the future. The first part of the chapter considers some of the major aspects of the changing political and organisational context and the emergence of a new consensus amongst governments of all political complexions concerning the environment. This is followed by an assessment of changes in social values and priorities, including an analysis of some of the more important social trends and attitudes that have helped to shape the demands placed upon business by consumers. The final part of this chapter provides a brief review of some of the most important areas of UK and

European policy and legislation that regulate and influence both the internal and external functions and operations of businesses, at all scale levels and in all member states of the European Union.

Political and organisational issues

Traditionally, political ideologies have been influenced by, and are reflected in, various views of the way in which the economy functions. As was explained in Chapter 3, these views vary from those of the classical economists, through the approach advocated by Marx to the modern-day modified market stance. This relationship between economic theory and political ideology is reflected in the ways in which various approaches have encompassed the question of the environment, particularly with regard to the origins and consequences of environmental problems. Through an appreciation of the major factors that have stimulated changes in political attitudes, and accompanying adjustments in economic theory and practice, it is possible to demonstrate and explain the origins of the current move towards an international political consensus on the environment and the importance of the role played by business in the improvement of environmental conditions.

The report of the World Commission on Environment and Development (WCED, 1987) provides an insight into how and why political attitudes towards the environment have changed. In part there was already a considerable degree of international agreement with regard to the importance of the environment as a key global concern. Both the 1972 UN Conference on the Human Environment and the work of the Independent Commission on International Development Issues (or the Brandt Commission) identified the complex nature of the relationship between the environment and economic growth, including the occurrence of social inequities between north and south and growing threats to global security. In the view of the Brandt Commission, these inter-related issues had generated a number of risks and significant instabilities in the international community, and the resolution of such problems required agreement on a number of areas of mutual interest and action. Brandt saw that this 'mutuality of interests can be spelled out clearly in the areas of energy, commodities and trade, food and agriculture, monetary solutions and inflation control, financing of projects and programmes, technological innovations, ground and space communications', together with the 'depletion of renewable and non-renewable resources, throughout the planet, the ecological and environmental problems, the exploitation of the oceans, not to forget the unbridled arms race, which both drains resources and threatens mankind' (Independent Commission on International Development Issues, 1980, p. 20). This diagnosis set the scene both for the Brandt Commission's own recommendations (Box 4.1) and for the later work undertaken by the World Commission on Environment and Development.

Building upon the work of the Brandt Commission, and that undertaken by a wide variety of other international groups, the World Commission on

---

Box 4.1 *The Brandt Commission: major recommendations*

The work of the Brandt Commission concentrated upon problems of poverty and global inequity. The final report of the commission included among its recommendations:

- an action programme must be launched to provide emergency and long-term aid to the poorest countries;
- there must be an end to mass hunger and malnutrition;
- a programme of *détente* and disarmament is required;
- the need for development policies to include national population programmes; and
- the need to check the strain on the global environment.

This final recommendation was seen as fundamental because the strain on the global environment threatens the survival and development opportunities of future generations.

Environment and Development (1987, p. ix) placed particular emphasis upon four key tasks:

- to propose long-term environmental strategies for achieving sustainable development;
- to recommend ways concern for the environment may be translated into greater co-operation among developing countries;
- to consider ways and means by which the international community can deal more effectively with environmental concerns; and
- to help define shared perceptions of long-term environmental issues and the appropriate efforts needed to deal successfully with the problems of protecting and enhancing the environment.

As has already been discussed in Chapter 1, the work of the WCED led to a detailed definition of what constitutes sustainable development, and the creation of a broadly based consensus on how it may be achieved. The political importance of this consensus should not be underestimated because, prior to 1987, it was far from clear that world leaders were willing to consider the probability of achieving a compromise between economic growth and the environment. As Cairncross (1991, p. 15) has observed, the virtue of the work of the commission in defining and generating agreement on the concept of sustainable development was that 'it allows people to think of compromises: of ways to temper the impact of growth, without sacrificing it entirely'. By achieving agreement on the basic principles of sustainable development, the WCED provided the impetus for a number of specific processes of elaboration and implementation to be defined and to proceed. One important step forward in the work of the commission was the recognition that, although many institutions and agencies are involved in the management of the environment and the economy, most of these institutions 'tend to be independent, fragmented, working to relatively narrow mandates with closed decision processes' (WCED, 1987, p. 9). The commission's call for co-operation, partnership and multilateral working at global level, also implies the need for the development of co-operation both within the major sectors of the economy and at national and local levels.

Industry, especially with respect to those companies that operate at multinational scale, was seen by the WCED as the most important sector as it was 'perhaps the main instrument of change that affects the environmental resource bases of development, both positively and negatively', and it was argued that industry and government would 'stand to benefit from working together more closely' (*ibid*. p. 329). As was discussed in Chapter 1, this call had already been acknowledged through the establishment of the World Industry Conference on Environmental Management in 1984. However, following the call by the commission, and acknowledging the need for closer co-operation at all levels from the global to the local, a nested hierarchy of partnership has developed with business leaders participating in a range of activities that are aimed at the translation of the concept of sustainable development into reality. Faulkner (1992, p. ii) has identified in this new partnership the need to 'recognise that the convergence of people, processes, politics and the environment on this planet has placed on the table global management issues'.

In placing particular emphasis upon the need for co-operation between governments and business, and by stressing the need for the creation of a partnership approach to the solution of environmental problems in a manner that takes into account the wider aspirations of society, business and environment organisations, such as the Leeds Environmental Business Forum (see Box 1.3), represent the base of a pyramid of action and implementation. This approach, which is built from the grassroots, is an essential element in the achievement of the objectives of sustainable development.

Given the definition of partnership that has emerged in recent years, and which is now accepted as providing a model for action, the aims and aspirations of business in relation to the environment are only likely to be realised if the global to local 'pyramid of partnership' includes a number of active participants drawn from government, the private sector and the wider community (Figure 4.1). A new three Ps emerges from this discussion of the politics of the environment: partnership, persuasion and prioritisation. The first element, partnership, has already been described. The second element, persuasion, will involve the creation of a model of partnership wherein mutual trust and joint working replace antagonism and suspicion. The third element, prioritisation, is essential because, whilst the challenges of the environment are many, the financial, technical and human resources required in order to develop and implement proactive strategies are limited in their supply and availability.

Figure 4.1 Partnerships for business and the environment

This pyramid of partnership for business and the environment demonstrates the opportunities that have emerged in many localities in recent years to make progress on a number of significant environmental issues. The establishment of the environment as a subject area where political agreement has become more important than conflict has helped to provide a basis for joint working between the business community and a range of other actors on subjects which, whilst they are strictly speaking outside the normal remit of business, provide the basis for improving the relationship between a host community and an individual business. An example is the important role that has been, and still is, played by business leaders in both the initial development and the later extension of the activities of the Environment City movement. This provides an ideal example of how a national partnership can work with local groups in the pursuit of a common agenda of issues that are of equal relevance to business, the community and local government actors. All of the Environment Cities, of which there are four in the UK (Leicester, Middlesbrough, Leeds and Peterborough), work to a common model of structure and organisation that allows for a considerable degree of latitude at local level and for the establishment of an appropriate local partnership. The Environment City movement is a partnership among the Royal Society for Nature Conservation, the Wildlife Trusts Partnership and British Telecommunications plc, with support from local and central government; the operational model is illustrated in Box 4.2.

Partnerships, such as that promoted by the Environment City movement, provide business with an important opportunity to make a contribution, at all levels from the local to the global, to the achievement of sustainable development. By working with appropriate governmental and voluntary bodies, business organisations are able to demonstrate their commitment to environmental enhancement and, in doing so, can ensure that they are working

---

Box 4.2   *The Environment City movement*

Formed in 1990 with two central themes: partnership and a holistic approach. Initial funding was provided by the Department of the Environment. Since 1992 sponsorship has been provided by BT. Emphasis is placed on the networking of good practice and mutual learning.

Each Environment City has a structure based on eight Specialist Working Groups (SWG), each responsible for a key sector of activity:

- Energy.
- Transport.
- Waste and pollution.
- Food and agriculture.
- Economy and work.
- Built environment.
- Natural environment.
- Social environment.

Each SWG has representatives from the public, private and voluntary sectors, plus specialist advisers. In each Environment City a central management group is responsible for the development and review of strategy and for the overall control of the programme of activities.

---

within a framework of activity that has gained a degree of public and legal endorsement.

Such a situation is far preferable to the traditional position of many companies and entire sections of the business community *vis-à-vis* local communities and the environmental lobby. In some local situations there is little attempt by business to explain its behaviour or to make a contribution to the overall social and environmental welfare of the local community. Antagonism and a mutual distrust of the motives of others has resulted in the absence of any agreement on the basic questions to be asked about the business and environment relationship. In such situations it is impossible to achieve even the most elementary level of agreement, and there is no real foundation for any form of local partnership or progress. It is only by breaking with the antagonisms of the past, and by accepting that mutual benefits can flow from co-operation, that it is possible to move from the traditional stance of distrust and separateness to a situation where co-operation becomes the norm.

The political challenge represented by the environment has led to the development of a number of new approaches that attempt to bring together the various actors who have a stake in ensuring the achievement of a more sustainable world. The change in attitude that has brought about this adjustment can be seen to represent a move from an approach that is essentially adversarial in nature to one which is based on the principle of mediation (Chapman, 1991). Mediation is a way of resolving political and other disputes through the intervention of an impartial or neutral third party. The mediator has no decision-making power and, as a consequence, has to rely upon skills of negotiation and an ability to present a situation in such a way as to assist the various parties in understanding and resolving their separate positions. Mediation is well known in business as a means of resolving commercial disputes and it can equally be used to resolve environmental disagreements. The business community in the UK has supported the use of a mediation approach and the CBI has assisted in the establishment of the Centre for Dispute Resolution. Many of the largest companies in the UK are members of this centre.

Despite the emergence of local to global co-operation and the creation of partnerships for the environment, and notwithstanding the emergence of new approaches to the resolution of conflicts between individual businesses' requirements and the condition of the environment, many situations still exist where there is an inherent potential for conflict. In such situations there is little alternative but recourse to the law (this is dealt with in the final section of this chapter), or to procedures aimed at providing some form of direct payment or compensation for an economic act that causes, or may cause, environmental damage.

Political attitudes towards the creation of compensation funds vary. Some political commentators and governments see such payments as a component part of the trade-off between environment and growth. A classic case in the UK is the Zetland County Council Act 1974. This Act provided the Shetland local authority with the power to acquire land that was required for oil associated development, and to establish a fund from oil revenues in order to ensure that the local community might obtain a direct long-term benefit from oil developments. This concept of prior compensation is, however, the exception rather than the rule. The normal situation is one where any environmental damage that may occur as a result of an industrial operation is subject to regulatory control and the payment of compensation following the event.

There is one final question to be asked in relation to this consideration of the politics of the environment: how permanent a feature of the political landscape is the priority currently given to the environment? In previous waves of environmental awareness and concern the presence of environmental lobbyists and pressure groups has been seen as a passing fancy – the muesli and sandals brigade on the march again. The strength of the present political commitment to the environment is unlikely to dissipate so quickly; as McGrew (1993, p. 13) has noted, 'the British Conservative Party has been repackaged as the original party of conservation and the Labour Party as a shade of Red-Green'. This new commitment can be seen in a variety of statements made by politicians across the party divide. Ann Taylor (1992, p. 19), the then Shadow Minister for Environment Protection, has stated that 'we must make an explicit, and an explicitly ethical, commitment to sustainability, in the sense of ensuring equality of opportunity between ourselves and future generations', whilst John Gummer, the Secretary of State for the Environment, has indicated that 'The United Kingdom is determined to make sustainable development the touchstone of its policies' (Department of the Environment, 1994, p. 5).

These political commitments are all the more important because, at national level, they represent a point of coincidence between top-down global political agreements, such as that reached at the Earth Summit held in Rio de Janeiro in 1992 and reinforced by Agenda 21 (the work programme on the environment for the next century), and bottom-up political pressures that emanate from the environmental concerns of voters and subnational political, business and community interests. A further cause for optimism regarding the long-term future of the environmental movement is provided by the improved organisation of the various environmental pressure groups, and by their proven ability to co-operate with each other on matters of common interest. Such groups have also developed substantial technical expertise and have negotiated a number of alliances with business interests.

In the final analysis political and organisational structures reflect the changing aspirations and attitudes of society, and this theme is explored in the following section.

Social attitudes and aspirations

Political attitudes and stances are often seen as a mirror of the views and aspirations of society at large. The increased prominence given to environmental matters by consumers and citizens has been translated into political preferences and this, more than any other factor, can be seen to provide the basic reason for the greening of political attitudes. The surge in the vote for the Green Party in the 1989 elections for the European Parliament reflected this upsurge in popular concern for the environment and it helped to galvanise the traditional political parties into action.

Popular concern for the environment has its origins in a broader-based social concern, which in turn has its origins in the growing fear that the costs associated with the established 'growth at any price' philosophy of the postwar world are too high a price to pay for improved prosperity, and a realisation that the price that has to be paid for this increased prosperity is a deterioration in the quality of life. The clearest manifestation of this change in consumer attitudes and preferences can be seen in the growth in the number of public protests against major infrastructure proposals. The long-running dispute on the line of the route for the fast rail link from the Channel Tunnel to London is a case in point, but other protests have occurred in relation to proposals for motorway building, chemical plants, incinerators, airports, coalmines, new housing estates, industrial and retail parks and many other forms of physical development. The NIMBY (not in my back yard) syndrome is well known, but little understood.

The complexities inherent in many decisions related to the environment mean that, whilst the NIMBY syndrome is a convenient catchphase, it is a poor description of the underlying tensions. In many cases where public protest is raised against a proposed development there are at least two groups involved: those who oppose a project on grounds that it damages their environment or the environment that they seek to protect, and those who either without reservation, or with some notion of a trade-off in mind, support the proposal. This is not a new problem; in the past most planning applications for major projects have attracted both supporters and opponents. This could be seen as a peacetime equivalent of the guns-or-butter debate. Even within an individual community there may be different views as to the merits, or otherwise, of a development that has a significant effect upon the environment. This argument was encapsulated in colourful fashion by one of the witnesses at the public inquiry into the proposal for exploratory drilling at Capel Hermon; the witness was of the view that

> There are far too many people who regard the County of Merioneth as some form of Indian Reservation inhabited by the Welsh equivalent of the Blackfoot, Sioux and Apache Indians. We believe that if the Government wishes to conserve certain areas to the detriment of the development of those areas then there should be compensation to the area to be conserved.
>
> (Searle, 1975, p. 93)

It is apparent that there is no single or simple way to define or describe the views of the public, and it is even more difficult to classify those who support or oppose a project into convenient categories.

However, despite the many underlying tensions, a general trend of growing social awareness about, and concern for, the environment can be detected. This has developed from protests that are related to development schemes into a variety of forms of direct consumer action. Increasingly sophisticated and knowledgeable consumers register their protests in the supermarket, the garage forecourt and in their choice of investment trust or personal equity plan. One of the best-known examples relates to the purchase of aerosols that use CFCs as a propellent. In Britain, Friends of the Earth mounted a campaign to demonstrate the harm done by CFCs and published a pamphlet indicating aerosol brands that were CFC free. As Elkington and Burke (1989, p. 137) observe, 'just days before Friends of the Earth followed up with a list of the brands that did contain CFCs, the eight largest aerosol manufacturers announced that they would phase out CFCs by the end of 1989. Those companies alone accounted for 65 per cent of the UK toiletries market'. The power wielded by the consumer had made its mark.

These and other manifestations of changed attitudes indicate the importance for business of understanding and responding to the evolving views of society. At one level this can be accomplished by conducting regular surveys of consumer attitudes (some of the evidence in this field will be reviewed later), but at another level such surveys can miss important underlying trends. It is often difficult to distinguish cause from effect, or to provide a realistic assessment of the strength of feeling expressed by an individual consumer. This problem is at its most severe when you confront an individual with a simple yes-no choice, or when you attempt to measure the strength of environmental opinion among a group of residents who also depend for their livelihood upon the manufacture of an environmentally damaging product. The apparent dichotomy that exists between the role that is played by a citizen as a guardian of the local environment and as an employee of a local company can be resolved if the needs of the community are satisfied through the adoption of an approach to the resolution of environmental problems that also meets the needs of business.

Social attitudes vary between places and what is considered to be an acceptable practice in one locality, region or nation may be unacceptable in another place. This spatial variation in the acceptability of the existence of an environmental hazard or a pollution threat may result from the economic circumstances prevailing in a particular place. The social acceptability, or otherwise, of environmental problems also reflects the long-established images and perceptions of industry that are held by the residents. Some years ago a proposal to remove a large colliery spoil heap in the Stoke on Trent area was opposed by local residents; they perceived the spoil heap as a local asset that provided informal open space and a vantage point from which they could view the adjacent countryside. Whilst the outsider visiting a traditional industrial area may be appalled by some of the effects of dereliction and pollution, the local landscape may be regarded as normal and acceptable by local residents. Hazardous activities are, however, a matter of specific concern to local communities, especially following a major incident at a local industrial installation, or at a plant with a similar configuration that is located elsewhere.

Community attitudes towards industry change over time. For example, the incident that took place at the Associated Octel plant at Ellesmere Port in February 1994, when a leak of ethyl chloride occurred, led to calls from local residents for this plant, which was established on its current site in 1938, to be relocated. The Associated Octel plant forms part of a large petrochemical complex located on the southern bank of the River Mersey; this complex has provided the southern Merseyside area with much-needed jobs and income. The raised environmental awareness that is evident in many local communities in the UK, coupled to the specific effects resulting from the leak of ethyl chloride, caused the role of the plant to be re-examined by local residents and representatives. A local authority councillor concluded that 'the danger is just too great and it is hampering development because we cannot grant planning permission for any new building on that side of town' (Sharratt, 1994, p. 3). Even in traditional industrial areas, where jobs are highly valued and keenly sought, a major incident can result in a change in social attitudes and values. In the past local communities often gave precedence to the economy in the trade-off between jobs and the environment, but the balance has shifted in recent years and hazardous or environmentally undesirable businesses are no longer tolerated. Such businesses once offered the prospect of jobs at the cost of the environment, but raised aspirations and current legislation have brought about a situation in which environmentally undesirable companies are now viewed as damaging both the economic and environmental health of an area.

Considerable spatial variations exist in social and cultural values, and in the attitude of business towards the environment. These variations are at their extreme when the situation obtaining in less developed nations is contrasted with that in developed countries. Many of the world's most rapidly growing economies are to be found in the developing nations. Economic growth in such nations has often started from a very low base and is relatively unrestricted by social or environmental regulations. The existence of widespread poverty and high levels of unemployment in the developing world, together with the absence of an indigenous industrial base, has left these nations vulnerable to exploitation and they have become the recipients of industries regarded as environmentally unacceptable by developed nations. The operation of such economic activities in the developing world is not only environmentally damaging but it can also lead to a reduction in their potential for economic growth. Pearce (1991) estimates that the developed nations may be losing up to 5 per cent of potential GNP due to environmental degradation, but in the developed world the loss could be as much as 15 per cent. This longer-term loss of environmental and economic value in the less developed world is often ignored by national governments who concentrate their attention on the achievement of short-term gains. Understandably, consumers and citizens in such countries pay relatively little attention to environmental matters and, in any case, there is often little that they can do to influence either the environmental standards set by national governments or the environmental performance of companies.

Spatial variations in social attitudes are reflected in variations in the value that is placed upon the environment in different areas. Such variations may give rise to situations in which the cost to industry of complying with best environmental practice is far in excess of the cost of compensating anyone who is injured or affected by any environmental damage that occurs. However, in some cases, the costs of failing to ensure that the environment is protected can be extremely high and has led to situations in which the overall integrity and financial solvency of a company is in question. Shrivastava (1992a, p. 127) has noted, for example, that 'the Bhopal disaster slowly but steadily sapped the financial strength of Union Carbide. It drained financial resources and adversely affected morale and productivity of the company'. This case may not be typical, but it does demonstrate the consequences for a company of an environmental disaster, even if such a disaster occurs in a developing country. However, while a growing body of evidence suggests that on both environmental and economic grounds sustainable development is the only form of development which should be permitted in both the developed and developing worlds, the developing world is not always in the position to make a choice. Cairncross (1991) has observed that the costs of environmental damage are high in developing countries because exploiting the environment provides a source of income for many people. Primary production is often the mainstay of the economy of a developing nation and the continued production of timber, ores, agricultural produce and other goods either directly erodes the stock of environmental resources, or makes use of other finite resources in order to ensure that output is maintained. The problem in such a situation, which is recognised by the notion of sustainable development, is that developed countries cannot expect the citizens of developing countries to abandon their existing economic activities without either compensation or, more preferably, alternative activities. The true meaning of intragenerational equity is to be found in this recognition.

Changes in the attitudes of citizens towards the environment in developed nations reflects both the immediate problems associated with the operation of advanced economies and the environmental degradation evident in the developing world. Public concern for the environment is a complex amalgam of many different experiences, perceptions and messages. People are influenced by their personal experiences of pollution and hazard – by the visual portrayal of deforestation, environmental degradation, and the extermination of threatened species on television and film – and by a variety of other messages transmitted via the radio and press. Social perceptions as to what constitutes an environmental problem are also conditioned by the level of education and the availability of information, sometimes supplied by companies, on the operation of a particular plant or process.

Surveys of public attitude reveal that there are many differences between countries in the priority given to the environment. Table 4.1 illustrates some of these differences. As can be seen from this evidence, whilst the level of priority given to the environment reflects the extent to which economic growth is perceived to be important, the general trend is towards a desire either to prioritise environmental protection or to attempt to balance the needs of the environment with those of the economy.

Table 4.1   Public opinion on the environment versus the economy (%)

	Priority to environment	Priority to economy	Balance between the two
USA	71	19	—
Japan	36	3	43
Finland	63	6	26
Norway	48	1	49

Source: Adapted from OECD (1991a).

The public attitudes revealed by the OECD survey are mirrored in other studies. A MORI study of attitudes towards the environment (Worcester and

Corrado, 1991) showed that, irrespective of culture and political system, both the public and opinion leaders were of the view that the condition of the environment had deteriorated over a ten-year period. In most countries opinion leaders were more concerned than the public about the deterioration in the condition of the environment (Table 4.2). This would seem to reflect the priority given to the environment in global political discussions.

Table 4.2 Rating of environment in the last ten years (%) (Members of the public and opinion leaders were asked: Do you feel that the environment has become better or worse in the last ten years? The percentage who thought it had become worse is shown in the table)

	Public	Opinion leaders
All countries	55	69
Hungary	68	69
China	49	58
India	63	98
Japan	39	52
Saudi Arabia	41	38
Argentina	76	92
Brazil	52	82
Kenya	44	82
Senegal	60	70
Norway	62	64
West Germany	59	50

Source: Based upon Worcester and Corrado (1991).

At national level in the UK a similar trend of growing concern for the environment can be seen. In Department of the Environment surveys the number of respondents who have indicated that the environment is a matter of specific concern has risen in recent years. The results of the 1986 survey showed that 8 per cent of respondents thought that the environment was an important issue (sixth of eight issues), whilst in 1989, 30 per cent indicated that the environment was a matter of concern; in this year it was second only to concern about health and social service provision (Department of the Environment, 1992a). There are regional and local differences in the public's perception of the nature and causes of environmental problems. Surveys conducted in England, Wales and Scotland in 1989 and 1990 showed, for example, that whilst pollution of rivers and seas was seen by all respondents as a problem of great significance, the environmental threats associated with the development of the countryside were not as important to Scottish respondents as they were to those surveyed in England and Wales (*ibid.*). This growth in concern for the environment is also reflected in the growth of membership of voluntary environmental organisations, for example, the membership of Greenpeace UK grew from 8,000 in 1981 to 397,000 in 1991 (Cairncross, 1991).

The increased importance attached to environmental issues by the public and opinion leaders is reflected in the growing priority given to environmental matters by business leaders and individual companies. A survey of 108 large UK companies, conducted by Coopers and Lybrand in 1990, showed that 87 per cent of companies interviewed thought that environmental issues were important, 41 per cent of companies had an environmental policy and 29 per cent had included environmental information in their annual reports (Coopers and Lybrand, 1990b). Although a later survey, by KPMG Management Consulting in 1992, showed that two-thirds of companies considered that the environment was not a trading issue in the past year, many businesses (44 per cent of manufacturing companies) had already been affected by environmental legislation (KPMG, 1992).

A survey conducted by the Advisory Committee on Business and the Environment (ACBE) provides additional evidence on the importance of the environment. This study examined the benefits to companies from the adoption of environmental policies:

- 65 per cent reported an improvement to their perceived image;
- 61 per cent of respondents had achieved direct financial benefits;
- 40 per cent believed that they improved relations with stakeholders, regulators and the local community;
- 28 per cent had gained a competitive advantage;
- 23 per cent had improved their relations with customers and this had enhanced their chances of survival; and
- 12 per cent had observed an improvement in working conditions.

This study (ACBE, 1993b) illustrates the benefits that may accrue to companies if they take action to understand the perceptions of the public, opinion leaders and other business organisations. The companies in this survey demonstrated a relatively high level of concern for the environment; 68 per cent of companies surveyed had developed environmental policies, compared with the average of 25 per cent reported in other recent surveys conducted by the British Institute of Management and the Institute of Directors. The proactive companies in the ACBE survey also reported that they had gained other advantages from the adoption of environmental policies including improvements in the quality of products and services.

Although the changing views of society have clearly had an impact upon larger companies, small and medium enterprises have been slower to respond. A report from the Cranfield School of Management (1990) has shown that most small companies have no policies or procedures on environmental issues and only 10 per cent have carried out an environmental audit. It is this group of companies that is likely to be most vulnerable to the changing attitudes and preferences of consumers, and to increasing supply chain pressures. Despite the virtual absence of action to date, the majority of small firms surveyed by Cranfield accept that environmental concerns are not just 'a passing fad' (*ibid.* p. 4) – this offers a foundation for the development of environmental policies in such companies.

The growing concern of society in general with regard to the environment is reflected in the attitudes of business. At global, national and local levels this concern has been translated into action, including the growth of voluntary organisations and coalitions of interest and, increasingly, in the enactment of stricter environmental legislation. The legal framework of environmental regulation reflects both the views and aspirations of society, and the strength of political conviction that the environment is an important and legitimate field of intervention. The final section of this chapter reviews some of the more important areas of environmental policy and legislation.

Environmental policy and legislation

Although some companies have adopted higher standards of environmental behaviour in advance of legislation, the threat of legal action is often the single most important influence upon a company's decision to improve its procedures for environmental control and management. In the various studies of business responses to the environment, it is frequently the case that companies seek to anticipate future legal requirements when they specify the criteria for new plant, design new products or develop new services. The increasing implementation and enforcement of policies, such as the polluter pays principle, will result in stricter controls on business, and will make companies more accountable for their impact on the environment.

The legal and regulatory limits that constrain the environmental behaviour of business activities can best be considered as a pyramid or hierarchy of policy and law (Figure 4.2).

International law and agreements

International agreements, whilst not always expressed in the form of binding legislation, exert a considerable degree of influence on the framework of law within which business operates at international, national and local levels. Although some of the current legislation in the UK has its origins in the efforts made to regulate and improve the environmental conditions that were prevalent in the Victorian era, many aspects of current legislation also reflect more recent international conventions and agreements. The World Commission on Environment and Development (1987) provided a useful framework of legal principles for environmental protection (Box 4.3). Certain of these principles have been influential in framing subsequent international agreements, including Agenda 21 which was agreed at the United Nations Conference on Environment and Development held in Rio de Janeiro in 1992.

Agenda 21 provides a further elaboration of some of the basic principles and policies put forward by the World Commission on Environment and Development. It represents a vast work programme for the twenty-first century; this programme was agreed by 179 states at the Rio Conference. Agenda 21 provides a guide for the development and elaboration of government and business policies and, as will be discussed below, it has proved to be

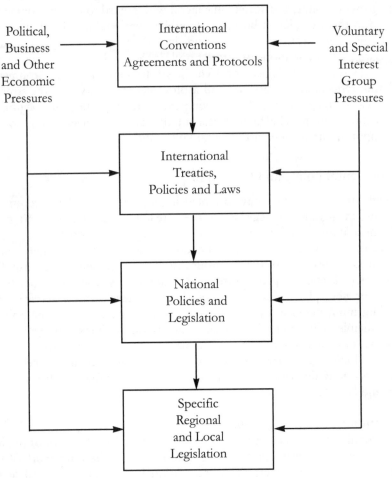

Figure 4.2　Hierarchy of environmental policy and law

influential in the design and development of national policies and programmes of legislation on the environment.

Despite the emphasis placed in recent years on agreements reached at the
Rio conference (these are reflected in Agenda 21) there is a long history of
international agreement and legislation with regard to the environment. Key
issues, such as the pollution of the seas and the regulation of water quality
and rights, have been the subject of a series of specific treaties, conventions
and agreements. These international agreements, which each individual
nation state has to sign before the agreement is brought into force, have
varying degrees of power. In general, the enforcement of an agreement or
treaty is the responsibility of the individual nation state. Examples of the
many agreements, treaties, protocols and conventions that affect the environment include the United Nations Conference on the Law of the Sea (this

Box 4.3 *Summary of the legal principles for environmental protection proposed by the World Commission on Environment and Development*

I   **General principles, rights and responsibilities**
  1. *Fundamental human right* – all human beings have the fundamental right to an environment adequate for their health and well-being.
  2. *Intergenerational equity* – states should conserve and use the environment for the benefit of present and future generations.
  3. *Conservation and sustainable use* – states shall maintain ecosystems, biological diversity and respect the principle of optimum sustainable yield.
  4. *Environmental standards and monitoring* – states shall establish adequate environmental standards, monitor changes and publish data on environmental quality.
  5. *Prior environmental assessments* – states shall make prior environmental assessments of proposed activities which affect the environment.
  6. *Prior notification, access and due process* – states shall inform in a timely manner all persons affected by a planned activity and grant them equal access and due process in proceedings.
  7. *Sustainable development and assistance* – states shall ensure that conservation is an integral part of development activities and assist other states.
  8. *General obligation to co-operate* – states shall co-operate with other states in implementing the preceding rights and obligations.

II   **Principles, rights and obligations concerning transboundary natural resources and environmental interferences**
  9. *Reasonable and equitable use* – states shall use transboundary natural resources in a reasonable and equitable manner.
 10. *Prevention and abatement* – states shall prevent or abate any transboundary environmental interference which could cause harm.
 11. *Strict liability* – states shall take all reasonable measures to limit risk and ensure compensation should harm occur.
 12. *Prior agreements when prevention costs greatly exceed harm* – states shall enter into negotiations on harm which is substantial but far less than the costs of prevention.
 13. *Non-discrimination* – states shall apply at least the same standards for conduct and impacts regarding transboundary resources as are applied domestically.
 14. *General obligation to co-operate on transboundary environmental problems* – states shall co-operate in good faith to achieve optimal use of resources and effective prevention of environmental interferences.

15. *Exchange of information* – states of origin shall provide timely information regarding transboundary resources or environmental interferences.
16. *Prior assessment notification* – states shall provide prior notification and require an environmental assessment of planned activities.
17. *Prior consultations* – states of origin shall consult regarding transboundary interferences with the use of a resource or the environment.
18. *Co-operative arrangements for environmental assessment and protection* – states shall co-operate in monitoring, scientific research and standard setting.
19. *Emergency situations* – states shall develop contingency plans regarding emergency situations and co-operate with concerned states when emergencies occur.
20. *Equal access and treatment* – states shall grant equal access and treatment to all persons affected.

III State responsibility
21. States shall cease activities which breach an international obligation regarding the environment and provide compensation for the harm caused.

IV Peaceful settlement of disputes
22. States shall settle environmental disputes by peaceful means. If mutual agreement on a solution or on other dispute settlement arrangements is not reached within 18 months, the dispute shall be submitted to conciliation and, if unresolved, thereafter to arbitration or judicial settlement at the request of any of the concerned states.

Source: Based upon World Commission on Environment and Development (1987).

includes a wide range of obligations to protect the marine environment), the North Sea Conferences (this concentrates upon the regulation of the environment of the North Sea basin), the Montreal Protocol (on substances that deplete the ozone layer) and a series of agreements on the control of pollution of the River Rhine (see Box 4.4). Cutter (1993) provides a full analysis of the major international agreements and laws relating to these issues.

European policy and legislation
The environmental policies and laws of the European Union exert direct and indirect influence upon the operation of business in the UK. Although the original Treaty of Rome, signed in 1957, made no direct reference to the environment, the European Community (European Union since 1993) has a

---

Box 4.4 *International agreements to control pollution of the Rhine*

In 1963 the riparian countries – Switzerland, France, Germany, Luxembourg and The Netherlands – decided to co-operate in the control of pollution of the River Rhine. An International Commission for the Protection of the Rhine Against Pollution was established and, through a series of agreements and conventions, the riparian states committed themselves to an action programme aimed at meeting four objectives by the year 2000:

- The return to the Rhine of important species no longer present, such as salmon.
- Maintaining a level of water quality suitable for the supply of potable water.
- Reducing pollutant levels in river sediments.
- Improving the health of the North Sea ecosystem.

The various agreements and conventions have also gained the support of the European Union.

Source: Adapted from OECD (1991a, p. 268).

long history of concern for the environment. The initial moves towards the establishment of a community environmental policy were made in the early 1970s. As a consequence of the oil crises of the late 1960s and early 1970s, and the emergence of environmental problems, the community developed a series of policies with regard to the environment. The first environmental policy was adopted at the Paris Summit of 1972 and this was followed by the First Environmental Action Programme in 1973. At the Paris Summit a number of objectives were specified for community environment policy. These objectives sought:

- first, to prevent, if possible, pollution at source and to establish the most appropriate form of action to counter any pollution which does occur;
- second, to introduce an environmental dimension into decision-making and resource exploitation procedures;
- third, to encourage and co-ordinate transnational action to improve environmental standards and to manage pollution and other environmental damage;
- fourth, to ensure that the polluter pays principle is introduced and implemented throughout the community; and
- fifth, to encourage the improvement of scientific and technical knowledge and research.

In 1973 the community published its First Environmental Action Programme.

This set out a number of principles and themes that can be traced to the present day. Most of these principles elaborated in more detail the points agreed at the Paris Summit. Following the First Programme, the community has extended its concern for the environment in four other programmes (adopted in 1977, 1983, 1987 and 1993). It has also incorporated environmental concerns within the revised treaties, thereby establishing a legal basis for community action on the environment. The movement towards the incorporation of environmental issues within the treaties resulted from a growing awareness of the fact that environmental problems are not necessarily confined within national boundaries. This realisation helped to legitimate an active interest in the transnational impact of environmental problems, fuelled by incidents such as the escape of dioxins at Seveso, chemical spillages into the Rhine and the growing evidence of the impact of acid rain.

The scope of the community's concern about the environment is reflected in the *Report on the State of the Environment* (Commission of the European Communities, 1992b). Among its conclusions are

- atmospheric pollution continues to be a problem, particularly in terms of greenhouse gases and urban air quality;
- severe pressures remain on fresh and marine water quality;
- overintensified use of land is resulting in soil deterioration;
- pressure on endangered species and their habitats is increasing;
- development pressures are jeopardising the quality of life in urban areas; and
- systems of waste management are struggling to keep pace with the growing amounts of waste produced in the community.

Many of these concerns were incorporated into the Single European Act 1987. This Act stresses that the community will aim at a high level of environmental protection, while Article 130R sets out the objectives of the community's actions in the environmental field as being

- to preserve, protect and improve the quality of the environment;
- to contribute towards protecting human health; and
- to ensure a prudent and rational utilisation of natural resources.

The article also established a number of principles as the basis for community action:

- That preventative action should be taken.
- That environmental damage should be rectified at source.
- That the polluter should pay.
- That environmental protection requirements shall be a component of the community's other policies.

The Treaty on European Union (the Maastricht Treaty) reaffirms these objectives and principles, but what were previously described as actions are elevated to the status of policies. Maastricht states that community policies should be based on, or take account of

- available scientific or technical data;
- the environmental conditions in the community's regions;
- the benefits and costs of any action; and
- the economic and social development of the community and the balanced development of its regions.

This treaty also reinforces the principle of subsidiarity as applied to environmental actions. Subsidiarity expresses the view that functions should be carried out at the lowest level possible and only transferred by consent to a higher level of government. A further point of importance is that member states of the community are not prevented from introducing more stringent environmental standards, as long as such standards are not incompatible with the treaty, and especially its provisions on free competition.

As a result of the various action programmes, revisions of the treaties and other special measures, there are now some 280 pieces of legislation (Bennett, 1992) covering pollution of the atmosphere, water and soil, waste management, safeguards in relation to chemicals, environmental assessment, protection of nature, biotechnology and product standards. Legislation takes the form of regulations (directly applicable to member states), directives (binding on members states but implemented through different methods in individual countries) and decisions (binding only on the member states, companies or individuals to whom they are addressed). Bennett (*ibid.*) categorises Community legislation as follows:

- *Product standards* – these measures seek to ensure that the free circulation of goods is not hindered by national restrictions and that harmonisation of products takes place 'at a high level of environmental protection' (p. 3).
- *Fair competition by equalising the environmental costs of production* – these measures are designed to reduce disparities in pollution control standards and to enforce high standards of environmental control.
- *Purely environmental in character* – including measures to protect the quality of water, wildlife and its habitats, to prevent the improper disposal of waste or depletion of the ozone layer.

The European Community's Fifth Action Programme on the Environment was introduced in March 1992 (Commission of the European Communities, 1992a). This programme represents the community's response to the challenge of sustainable development and provides the current framework of community action in the field of the environment. Key elements of the programme focus attention on a number of elements: air and acidification, water, soil, waste, quality of life, biological diversity and risk management, and a series of sectors where 'integrated approaches to sustainable development must be adopted in order to change the trends of the past and to safeguard the environment for the future' (Morphet, 1993, p. 13). The sectors of particular concern are

- agriculture, forestry and fisheries,
- energy,
- industry,
- transport, and
- tourism.

The major elements of action proposed in the Fifth Action Programme on the Environment that relate to business are summarised in Box 4.5.

Box 4.5   *Fifth Action Programme on the Environment: issues for business*

The European Union acknowledges that manufacturing industry accounts for 25 per cent of its wealth, but also recognises that the industrial sector is among the principal causes of environmental degradation. A new package of measures is proposed comprising the following elements:

- Strengthening the dialogue between the union and industry.
- Improving environmental assessment procedures.
- Improving the management and control of production processes including integrated pollution control, environmental auditing, effective environmental valuation and accounting, the use of best available technology, and the introduction of market-based pricing systems for consumption and use of natural resources.
- Encouraging life-cycle analysis and introducing ecolabelling.
- Promoting self-regulation.
- Encouraging effective waste management including reclamation, recycling and reuse.
- Increasing public participation and awareness through access to relevant information.

In order to increase and disseminate knowledge and understanding of environmental systems, and to demonstrate better the origins and impacts of environmental problems and the potential for, and progress with, the achievement of sustainable development, the European Union has established the European Environment Agency. This agency, which is located in Denmark, will enhance access to reliable information on the environment and about the environmental impact of goods and services that are produced and sold within Europe. Its role in monitoring environmental progress is likely to expand in future and this will involve the establishment of local monitoring units.

There are many other elements of European Union environmental policy and legislation that are of particular importance to business. A summary of the major areas of European Union environmental legislation has been published by the commission in the form of a guide to aspects of the environment (Commission of the European Community, 1992c). A comprehensive and easy-to-access compilation of the major elements of European environmental policy and legislation has been produced by the EC Committee of the American Chamber of Commerce (1994), and a detailed analysis of the Fifth Action Programme on the Environment has been prepared by Fleming (1993). Other information is available in specialist journals, such as *European Environment* and the *Journal of Environmental Law*.

UK policy and legislation

Although environmental policy in the UK can trace its origins back to the Middle Ages, the true point of origin of current policy and legislation was in the growth of concern during the nineteenth century for matters related to public health and pollution control. Early legislation, such as the series of Public Health Acts that were enacted from 1848 onwards was, on the one hand, extended to protect public health and to secure minimum standards of housing and, on the other, it attempted to provide for the establishment of a system of administration and control. Many of the current-day functions that are discharged by local authorities have their origins in these early attempts to limit and regulate the undesirable environmental consequences of the industrial revolution. It is also the case that a majority of the organisations and agencies responsible for regulating the operation of public and private sector industrial and infrastructure activities have their origins in the nineteenth century. One of the first measures specifically designed to regulate the activities of business was the Alkali Act 1863. This Act created a national Alkali Inspectorate which was charged with the inspection of all manufacturing establishments 'concerned in the production of substances the manufacture of which may involve the release of noxious fumes and smoke' (Bigham, 1973, p. 158).

The Alkali Inspectorate was the predecessor of the current-day Her Majesty's Inspectorate of Pollution (HMIP). This body was established in 1987 with the intention of creating a more integrated approach to pollution control. It brought together a number of specialist agencies, including the Industrial Air Pollution Inspectorate of the Health and Safety Executive and the Radiochemical, Hazardous Waste and embryonic Water Inspectorate of the Department of the Environment (Ball and Bell, 1994). Water pollution and water quality issues outside the remit of HMIP are the responsibility of the National Rivers Authority. This body, formed in 1989, has taken over many of the regulatory powers of the old regional water authorities. Other bodies responsible for environmental matters include local authorities (for planning matters, waste regulation and disposal, public health, noise control and air pollution of a localised nature), the Health and Safety Executive, and the Nuclear Installations Inspectorate. One of the major problems confronting a business is to which of these organisations should it turn for advice and assistance. This issue has been recognised and acknowledged by the present government and the Queen's Speech of November 1993 announced the government's intention to establish a new environmental agency responsible for the regulation of air, water and waste.

In the UK there is an elaborate and often confusing structure of regulation and control with respect to the environment. Companies are obliged to comply with many separate pieces of legislation and, as noted above, to work with a number of different agencies responsible for various aspects of environmental regulation. Three main areas of legislation are of particular concern to business: town and country planning, pollution control and waste management, and the conservation of nature.

Town and country planning legislation regulates the use of land and the activities conducted on land. It is, in Ball and Bell's (1994, p. 182) view a 'good example of a sophisticated anticipatory regulatory mechanism and it emphasises prevention of harm'. However, in Hughes' (1992, p. 105) view 'planning has its limitations as a means of environmental regulation' because it is a 'basically managerial rather than a protective system being primarily concerned with the orderly management of change'. Business comes into contact with the planning system in three main ways. First, in relation to forward planning through the system of development plans. This aspect of planning produces development plans that seek to guide or influence development; structure, local and unitary development plans are prepared at regular intervals by local planning authorities. Guidance is provided to local authorities to assist them in the preparation of development plans through the provision of Planning Policy Guidance Notes and government circulars. Companies who have an interest in the use of land, or in particular aspects of the development plan process, have the opportunity to participate in the preparation of plans. The second way in which business comes into contact with the planning system is in relation to development control. This is the element of the planning system that deals with applications for planning permission. Two aspects of development control are of particular concern to business: that concerned with obtaining planning permission for an operational development, and that concerned with an application for change of use. Third, businesses have a contact with the planning system through the associated procedure for environmental assessment. Although strictly speaking a separate system, the procedure for environmental assessment operates in parallel with the planning system (a more detailed discussion of environmental assessment is included in Chapter 6). All aspects of planning law and policy place emphasis upon the need for planning to reflect appropriate local and regional variations.

Pollution control and waste management are the subject of specific pieces of legislation. Historically, the basis of pollution control rests on the operation of the principle of best practicable means (BPM). This principle was 'first applied in 1842 in an attempt to control smoke nuisances in Leeds' (Ball and Bell, 1994, p. 253). A major difficulty encountered in the application of this principle was the definition of the terms 'best', 'practicable' and 'means'; each of these terms implied a judgement and this led to considerable variations in the application of BPM. Each application of BPM was conditioned by the circumstances and economics of a particular plant or industry. The Environmental Protection Act 1990 (EPA) introduced an alternative concept; that of the best available techniques not entailing excessive cost (BATNEEC).

Part 1 of the 1990 Act introduced a new system of integrated pollution control (IPC) aimed at improving pollution control in relation to the operation of industry. This system of control, as it relates to the most significant polluting processes, is managed by HMIP and is organised through a scheme of authorisation, control and enforcement (Garbutt, 1992). A parallel system for less significant processes is subject to air pollution control (APC) by local authorities. The Act specifies the processes to be regulated through IPC (Part A processes) and by APC (Part B processes); some 5,000 industrial installations are subject to control under Part A, and 27,000 under Part B (Ball and Bell, 1994).

Part 2 of the EPA is concerned with waste management and introduced new powers designed to strengthen control over waste 'from cradle to grave' (*ibid.* p. 315). Waste is defined by the Act as: 'any substance which constitutes a scrap material or an effluent or other unwanted surplus substance arising from the application of any process; and any substance or article which requires to be disposed of as being broken, worn out, contaminated or otherwise spoiled' (quoted in *ibid.* p. 318). Given this wide definition and the problem of regulating the disposal process, the Act classifies waste in two main categories:

* *Controlled waste* – household, industrial or commercial waste, excluding agricultural and mining wastes.
* *Non-controlled waste* – agricultural waste and mineral wastes not controlled for the purposes of the EPA.

These categories supplement the earlier definitions of special wastes and hazardous waste provided by the Control of Pollution Act 1974.

Under the duty-of-care regulations in Section 34 of the EPA, anyone who imports, produces, carries, keeps, treats or disposes of waste must take all such measures applicable to him or her in his or her capacity, and as is reasonable in the circumstances to:

* prevent others from committing an offence in relation to the disposal, treatment or keeping of waste;
* prevent the escape of waste from their control or the control of others;
* ensure that waste is only transferred to authorised persons such as a waste collection authority or licensed waste manager; and
* provide a written description of the waste when it is transferred to enable other persons to avoid committing an offence.

(Eversheds, Hepworth and Chadwick, 1992, p. 5)

The Act defines three types of waste authority (waste collection, waste regulation and waste disposal) and specifies their functions. It also specifies the duties of all persons who produce, manage or dispose of waste.

Quite clearly the law regarding pollution and waste disposal is of central concern to business. The duties involved in complying with the law and the penalties that result from a failure to comply are complex and potentially onerous.

The final element of legislation to be discussed in this brief review relates to the conservation of nature. Many of the areas of law already referred to have a direct or indirect impact upon nature conservation. Explicit protection and regulation is provided by a number of specific measures that are aimed at the protection of individual animals and plants, habitat protection, the use of grants and incentives, and incidental protection (Ball and Bell, 1994). Important legal means for nature conservation include the Wildlife and Countryside Act 1981, elements of the Environmental Protection Act 1990 and a series of acts and regulations concerned with national parks, countryside management and specific species and habitats.

This brief review of the legislation in the UK would not be complete without mention of the local legal powers available through byelaws. This is the final stage in the progression from the global to the local level of regulation, and at this spatial level specific local powers can be established aimed at curbing or controlling localised forms of environment damage. The case in favour of a locally set and variable approach to the definition of environmental standards has been argued by Ball and Bell (*ibid.*); they argue that such an approach allows standards to be set by reference to local environmental quality.

This is further reflected in the position of the common law in relation to the environment. A guiding principle in common law is the 'so-called locality doctrine' that 'asserts the need to take into account the circumstances of the place where the thing complained of actually occurs' (*ibid.* 1994, p. 143).

Conclusions

This chapter has demonstrated the links that exist between the various economic themes discussed in Chapter 3 and the stance taken by political and other policy-makers. It has also demonstrated the considerable influence that is exerted by social attitudes and values on political and policy processes. The final section of the chapter discussed the origins, content and implications of some of the major areas of legislation that seek to control the condition of the environment. The law in one sense reflects the ideals, aspirations and fears of society and, as such, it mirrors the environmental concerns of society and the willingness of citizens to pay for the cost of providing a better environment. For business the messages of this chapter are clear: there is now a considerable degree of political agreement on the need to give priority to the environment and a realisation that sustainable development is essential. Society requires a change in the attitudes and performances of business *vis-à-vis* the environment and is willing to express such desires in political choices and the law. Finally, the legal system both sets standards of performance which it expects business to reach and it specifies remedies should the performance fail to meet the standards set. These remedies are of various types, many of which may have an effect upon the operation of business, including the processes used by a business and the nature of any contamination caused by an industrial process. This latter point, the contamination of an industrial site, could have a detrimental effect upon, for example, the value of a site or premises (Booth and Co., 1993).

5

Organisation, operational matters and industrial structure

The general organisational and operational characteristics of business, together with the overall sectoral structure of economic activity, exerts a considerable degree of influence upon the attitude that is adopted by an individual company towards the environment. Local and regional factors also play an influential role in determining attitudes and business responses.

This chapter examines a number of the more important environmental difficulties and opportunities that are associated with the organisation, operation and structure of business activities. A key concern in this chapter is to identify and assess both current problems and the potentials for future business development. It is equally possible, for example, to consider the need for organisational change in order to meet new environmental regulations as either an additional and unnecessary burden placed upon a business, or as an opportunity to manage better an aspect of company activity that may in future offer potential for growth and leadership. By associating the solution to an actual or potential problem with the creation of new business opportunities, environmentally sustainable business development can be seen as a benefit rather than an additional cost.

In order to analyse and assess the implications for the environment of the organisational operation and structure of business, this chapter considers three areas of concern: the broad organisational pattern and structure of businesses, including the internal distribution of power and responsibility within companies; the main operational characteristics of business and the need to review and assess the way in which a company operates at all levels from the global to the local; and the influence of industrial structure upon sustainable business development, especially at local and regional levels.

These three areas of concern represent the following:

- *Organisation* – the framework within which individual business activities take place; suitable organisational patterns can help to stimulate and support beneficial change.

- *Operation* – the way in which business functions and impacts upon the environment.
- *Structure* – the framework of business organisation beyond the individual company; local and regional sectoral structures display particular characteristics that can help or hinder an individual company to achieve its environmental objectives.

Organisational issues

All businesses are influenced by their organisational structure, and changes to the organisation of a particular business function can provide both a stimulus for management innovation and an opportunity to tackle an old problem in a new way. Traditional business structures may well disguise environmental problems or consign such matters to the domain of lawyers and public relations advisers. These traditional views fail to recognise the potential for positive change that is often associated with the adoption of enhanced environmental awareness and behaviour.

Two examples of the negative influence that is exerted by organisational structure serve to illustrate the problem. In a hierarchical business structure, based upon a rigid division of functions into separate operating units, it is often difficult to recognise any opportunities that may exist for the exchange and recycling of materials between units of production or the possibilities for minimising energy consumption through the integration of production processes. In such situations materials may be purchased by one division independently of the total corporate requirement, and any surplus materials or wastes may be discarded at a substantial cost to the company for their safe disposal. Likewise, in a business that operates through a series of discrete production units it may be difficult for management to recognise the potential that exists to use the waste heat that is generated in one process as an input for other purposes. Such companies are likely to fail to achieve cost-efficient production or to minimise the overall environmental consequences of production.

A second example relates to the desirability of ensuring that all the employees of a company are fully aware of the environmental costs associated with the operation of the full range of business operations. In a rigid hierarchy, there is a danger that a high degree of employee isolation may exist, in parallel with a tendency to view the system of management as offering the only valid solution to all a company's problems. This misses the real message of sustainable business development, that is, that environmental problems can only successfully be resolved if all employees understand the causes and consequences of such problems, and if they are provided with the opportunity to take action in order to redress existing problems and to prevent the occurrence of environmental problems in future.

These examples serve to illustrate three of the major difficulties that confront a business in its attempt to improve its environmental performance:

the problems associated with the structure of the organisation, the difficulties encountered in transmitting key messages to employees and the inadequacy of existing theory.

Organisational structure and management

Smith (1992) has discussed the implications for business organisations of the competitive environment. In developing a business strategy, and in ensuring its implementation, managers attempt to achieve a best fit between the operation of a business and the competitive pressures acting upon it. In Smith's view the competitive environment is primarily concerned with factors such as the barriers to entry, the power of suppliers and buyers, and the economic exploitation of the resource base. The strategic response of the traditional business organisation is aimed at ensuring a satisfactory competitive position and at gaining advantage within a market. This narrow view of the mission of a business excludes the incorporation of many of the objectives that are associated with environmental sustainability.

The mission of a company frequently reflects its organisational structure and it may also exert considerable influence upon the operation of the structure through the selection of, and the choices made by, managers who act as the key decision-makers. The dominance of technocratic and financially driven solutions in business is reflected in the status afforded to technical managers and financial experts. This is not to suggest that engineers, chemists, accountants and other managers are unaware of the requirements of environmental sustainability, rather it reflects the roles that they are required to perform within business organisations.

In order for change to take place, and for environmental considerations to be given the prominence required if such matters are to become embedded within business organisations, there is a need to interrogate and to reformulate the traditional model of business structure. The traditional model, especially as it operates in large transnational corporations, is one that is pyramidal in nature. Within this steep pyramid the dominant influence upon the operation of a company is from the top down. This structure, especially if it is divided into self-contained divisions or business units, can lead to the compartmentalisation of activities and to undue emphasis being placed upon matters such as the operation of individual cost centres. In this model control is exercised from the top.

In a traditional business organisation the responsibility for dealing with environmental matters is often divided between a number of separate divisions, and this can hinder the adoption of the holistic approach which was discussed in Chapter 1. By dividing the many environmental duties and tasks in this manner, it is difficult for a company either to develop an overview of its balance with the environment or to conduct an assessment of how its inputs and outputs relate to each other. In other words, such a company will lack the ability to identify the environmental sources and sinks to which its operations are connected. In addition to the rigidity that is imposed by a divisional structure, the traditional model also discourages any real attempt by individual units to adapt to the particular circumstances encountered in either the local environment or the local business community.

One of the more significant consequences of this mode of organisation is that individual managers are forced into a position whereby they often have to make piecemeal judgements of the environmental consequences of the actions for which they are responsible. Whilst an overall corporate strategic design for the interaction of environmental policies and objectives may be well intentioned, it may lack the ability to provide appropriate responses to the many environmental challenges that confront a company. This is the essential failing of what Davis (1991) calls the machine model of company organisation and management. The machine model, in Davis's view, 'perceived business as an essentially static operation, into which resources of people, money and machines had to be so introduced and controlled as to produce a higher value of the output than input' (*ibid*. p. 109). Although this view of business organisation provides a degree of stability and order, at least within an individual company, it can be found wanting when challenged by changes in attitude and behaviour in the broader world.

Wehrmeyer (1992) has taken this model a step further and he contrasts what he describes as 'prescribed management' with 'tightrope management'. The prescribed manager, like Davis's machine manager, assumes that the world is stable and that little will change in the future to alter this situation. A prescribed manager is allowed little discretion within an organisation and can only operate within strictly defined limits. There is a stark contrast between this situation and that which the tightrope manager experiences. The tightrope manager, in Wehrmeyer's (1992, p. 98) view, 'acknowledges the pluralistic nature of activities and attempts to manage perceived dichotomies'. A tightrope style of organisation and management encourages the incorporation of environmental issues and aims to strike the correct balance between the environmental and the economic aspects of a company's operation.

The traditional hierarchical model of business organisation, as it is applied in large organisations, suffers from three major failings with regard to its ability to deal with environmental matters:

1. Because it operates through a rigid top-down system of policy, control and information it lacks the ability to adapt to local environmental conditions.
2. The division into functionally specific and self-contained units of activity hinders the adoption of a holistic approach.
3. The absence of flexibility to respond to new environmental regulations and to business opportunities weakens the competitive position of divisional units and the company as a whole.

The traditional model is illustrated in Figure 5.1.

Dominance of
Top-Down
Views and
Attitudes

Strategic
Functions and Senior
Management

Rigid
Divisional Structure

Minimal
Interaction With
Local
Environment

Operational Level

Little Opportunity for Inter-Divisional Transfer

Figure 5.1   A traditional model of business organisation

Involving the workforce

Many traditional business organisations suffer from a further weakness, which is partly of their own making, in terms of their ability or otherwise to communicate messages from the boardroom to the shopfloor. As Cannon (1992, p. 209) recognises in a discussion of the environmental challenge facing business, a 'firm's employees determine the effectiveness of all aspects of the company's response to the new expectations'. In a green, or to be more precise a greener, business the organisational pyramid must be shallower than in the traditional model and corporate strategic intent should be transmitted to all employees. Top-level commitment to the achievement of environmental objectives needs to be matched by a clear understanding of the important role that can be played by the workforce in the attainment of such objectives. Bennett, Freierman and George (1993) have described this process as one whereby a company has to harness the environmental know-how of its employees; such knowledge may be gained from employees' experience gained at work, at home or from other sources.

In a company with a shallower organisational pyramid, and one in which the crossfertilisation of ideas and actions between divisions or units is encouraged, there is a greater likelihood that top-down management decisions will be informed by bottom-up workforce knowledge and commitment. Learning from experience offers a company the opportunity to fine tune its environmental policies and to motivate employees.

The CBI (1992) has identified the need for the improved environmental awareness and training of employees as a crucial element in the restructuring of a business organisation which seeks to achieve a higher standard of environmental performance. As the CBI (*ibid.* p. 6) states 'many breaches in consents and authorisations occur as a result of employee error rather than equipment failure'. The CBI approach to training is illustrated in Box 5.1.

Box 5.1 *Key issues in environmental awareness and training: the CBI view*

The major business issues which need to be addressed in an awareness programme are

- energy efficiency,
- ozone-depleting chemicals,
- waste minimisation and recycling,
- raw materials usage and conservation,
- packaging,
- water quality,
- air quality,
- transport, and
- community impact.

Key areas where environmental training is needed include

- strategic arrangement,
- marketing,
- research and development,
- product and process design,
- technical and process operations,
- health and safety,
- purchasing,
- distribution,
- finance,
- office support,
- human resources and personnel issues, and
- public relations.

Source: CBI (1992).

Systems of organisation

Gladwin (1993) has made a plea for the development of an organisational theory of the greening of business. This plea highlights the confusion surrounding the issue of how a business can successfully change its organisational structure in order to incorporate an enhanced level of environmental awareness, and how it can translate this enhanced level of awareness into action. In his discussion of the ambiguity of greening, Gladwin (*ibid.* p. 41) notes that 'greening can't be everything or else it is nothing'. He also considers that in moving towards a practical demonstration of the value of greening, it is vital to understand how greening really works and what the consequences of it happening are. Gladwin reviews the various approaches taken towards greening and characterises these stances as follows:

- *Greening as 'institutionalisation'* – here the business organisation is reformed in order to allow it to conform with the standards expected by the institutional environment.
- *Greening as 'organisational learning'* – through the acquisition of information and knowledge the organisation learns and this learning stimulates changes in behaviour.
- *Greening as 'natural selection'* – organisations adapt in order to survive; such adaptation requires the transformation of organisational structures in response to external pressures.
- *Greening as 'strategic choice'* – rational choices can allow a company to plan and implement new modes of organisation, products, processes and alliances.
- *Greening as 'transformational leadership'* – proactive corporate leadership can stimulate changes in an organisation and the values held by the organisation.
- *Greening as 'organisational evolution'* – rather than waiting for frame-breaking change, organisations can, and will, adapt through incremental change and innovation.

The value of Gladwin's analysis rests in the demonstration that there is no single right or wrong model of an organisation; rather it shows that many options are available to an individual company that wishes to transform its system of organisation. The final choice of an organisational style and system will depend upon the pre-existing characteristics of a company, its chosen future pathway and the conditions prevailing in its particular market-place, industrial sector or locality. Strategies for moving from a present organisational system to one that encourages the expression and incorporation of enhanced environmental values are discussed in later chapters of this book.

A different view of organisational matters is one that considers particular functional issues in business from a systems approach. Such an approach does not seek to explain the implications of the various theoretical perspectives; rather it aims at describing the operation and the limitations of the system. Gray, Bebbington and Walters (1993) have outlined the organisational system within which accountants operate. This system can be viewed at a number of different levels, each level reflecting a particular content of the environment:

- The individual organisation with its system of records and accounts. These records receive, process and transmit information.
- The accountant's operational context which allows for an understanding of the sources and destinations of information and the transfer of information to other activities.

- The broader social context through which the individual organisation may be connected, via a complex web of interactions, to the social world.
- The biosphere which contains society, operational business conventions and individual organisations.

These various levels of activity within an organisation interact in many different ways. In some cases the interaction is obvious, explicit and easily recognised, whilst in other cases the interaction may be accidental, unintended and hidden.

Organisational systems may require substantial adaptation in order to allow them successfully to incorporate the changing aspirations and objectives of a company. If environmental policies are to be implemented it will be necessary to set objectives, targets and criteria, and to ensure that the various organisational systems within a company are adjusted or modified in order to allow for the assimilation of the new requirements. Roome (1992) stresses the need to develop organisational systems that are as simple as possible and flexible in use. The development and implementation of such a system is seen by Roome to be a prerequisite for achieving excellence in commercial and environmental performance.

Operational matters

There are three main areas of concern that a company will have to address if it wishes to understand the ways in which its operations interact with the environment. First, there is the need to understand the impact of its current activities upon the environment. Second, a company will need to consider the methods and procedures that it uses to develop its future strategies, together with the implications of its corporate strategy for future operations. Third, a company should attempt to assess the implications of current and likely future changes in legislation, and the operational parameters utilised by other companies in the same industrial sector or locality.

These three areas of concern may be summarised in three questions:

1. Where are we now and what are the impacts of what we are doing?
2. Where do we want to go in the future and what are the implications for strategy?
3. What does the future hold and what will be the responses of our competitors and of other firms in the locality to new challenges that emerge?

Each of these issues is now considered in more detail.

Environmental policy and the initial environmental review

The first step in conducting a review of the environmental implications of the way in which a business organisation conducts its affairs is to establish a baseline of information and understanding. By establishing such a baseline a company will have provided itself with a means whereby it can assess its current policies and operations in order to ensure that they are working within the parameters of the law or of best practice. A starting point for many companies is to prepare an interim environmental policy statement or to conduct a review of the existing environmental policy. For the purposes of this discussion it is assumed that the company has already prepared an interim environmental policy.

By undertaking a review of its environmental policy and the operational objectives implied by such a policy, an organisation will be able to establish the degree to which its current operations match its aspirations. There is, in some cases, a considerable gap between what a company wishes to do, or thinks it is doing, and what it is actually doing. In other words, the very act of conducting an initial review can reveal any mismatch that exists between the image that a company wishes to project and the reality behind that image. The rhetoric of greening needs to be supported by the reality of business policies and operations that respect the environment.

It is a matter of debate as to the merits of defining an environmental policy prior to undertaking an initial environmental review of the activities of a company. In reality the process is interactive. However, many businesses have found it helpful to draft an initial policy and then to refine it having undertaken a review of its operations.

An environmental policy is a statement of intent that conveys the commitment of a company to achieving and maintaining a specified standard of environmental performance. The policy also presents a public declaration to a company's employees, shareholders, suppliers, customers and other public and private bodies that it intends to conduct its current and future business operations in such a way so as to achieve certain specified environmental objectives. In addition, the policy signals to all the operating divisions and units of a company the standards of performance that are expected now and in the future.

In conducting an initial review of company environmental policy, or in constructing a policy, there are a number of areas that will require investigation and consideration. The Institute of Business Ethics (Burke and Hill, 1990) has identified six key criteria for judging the effectiveness of an environmental policy:

1. The policy should be comprehensive and it should deal with all aspects of a company's impact on the environment.
2. It is important to ensure that the implementation of the policy can be measured.
3. It is vital to ensure that the messages contained within the policy can be communicated to the expected audience.
4. The process of implementation of a policy should be specified.
5. It is important that the policy should reflect the process used for its formulation.
6. There is a need for a policy to be led and managed.

These criteria provide both a test of the validity and of the effectiveness of a current environmental policy and, more importantly, they provide a framework of guidance for the development of policies for the future.

In its guide to good environmental practice the Institute of Business Ethics has defined the characteristics and purposes of an environmental policy statement in the following way:

> they give all the employees in a company from the chief executive officer to the doorman a clear idea of what the company is setting out to do regarding the environment and thus help to create a sense of direction and purpose; they also give a clear signal to the outside world of the standards by which the company wishes to be judged.

(Hill, 1992, p. 4)

This statement encapsulates the role of a policy and, in addition, it expresses the need for a policy to be transparent. Openness is a fundamental requirement if a policy is to be accepted and believed, both within a company and by the wider audience to whom the policy is addressed. This issue of openness, or corporate disclosure, is also an important issue if a company is seeking support from an ethical fund. Many ethical funds require companies both to promise future disclosure and to demonstrate that they are willing to make available information on a range of environmental and social matters.

Defining the limits of an environmental policy is a difficult task. Although many of the companies that have prepared a policy acknowledge a wide range of environmental factors, they frequently fail to encapsulate the full definition of sustainable development. As was discussed in Chapter 1, sustainable development is a wider concept than that of the ecological environment. This is because it also incorporates social and intergenerational equity goals. It is therefore helpful in drafting an environmental policy to attempt to consider the wider role and responsibilities of the company, both now and in the future. The International Institute for Sustainable Development (1992, p. 33) has expressed the challenge of drafting a policy for sustainable development in the following way: 'Drafting a policy statement that is both inspirational and capable of influencing behaviour is challenging and time consuming. However, the benefits are well worth the effort because such a statement helps focus the company's attention on this important issue.' Whilst not all company environmental policies meet the high standards suggested by the institute, many businesses have now made substantial progress. Some examples of environmental policies, at various levels of sophistication and from companies operating in different sectors of the economy, are provided in Box 5.2.

Having reviewed and redefined its environmental policy a company can then proceed to conduct an initial review of its activities. A review of current performance is in many senses similar to an environmental audit, except that its primary purpose is to establish a baseline. As Welford and Gouldson (1993, p. 57) note 'strictly speaking an audit measures the attainment or non-

Box 5.2   *Enviromental policy statements*

Norsk Hydro

Our overriding Mission Statement affirms that

- We will demonstrate a strong sense of responsibility for people and the environment.
- Hydro will be in the forefront of environmental care and industrial safety.

Led by these commitments, we believe that it follows that:

- Care for the environment and the welfare of future generations will be the basis for company policy and decision making.
- We shall set out to fulfil the world's needs for our products, in such a way that we do not diminish the capabilities of future generations to meet their own needs.
- And this means that we must set environmental goals and integrate them into business planning at all levels.

National Westminster Bank

National Westminster Bank is committed to achieving environmental best practice throughout its business activities, wherever this is practicable. We recognise that the pursuit of economic growth and a healthy environment must be closely linked and that ecological protection and sustainable development are collective responsibilities in which governments, businesses, individuals and communities all have a role to play.

Our environmental responsibility programme is based upon continuous improvement, consistent with current knowledge.

Environmental management continues to be a corporate priority, fully integrated into our business. We believe sound environmental practice is a key factor demonstrating effective corporate management. We will seek to educate and train our staff to act in an environmentally responsible manner.

National Power

Five policy principles guide our activities. These ensure that environmental considerations are an important part of whatever we do, in the UK and overseas:

- *Approach* – To integrate environmental factors into business decisions.
- *Compliance* – To monitor compliance with environmental regulations and to perform better than they require, where appropriate.
- *Improvement* – To improve our environmental performance continuously.

- *Accountability* – To review regularly at Board level, and to make public, the company's environmental performance.
- *Responsibility* – To establish a reputation for effective environmental management.

attainment of some target objectives whereas the environmental review simply provides an initial assessment of the environmental performance of the company on which to plan for improvement'. This distinction is important because, whilst an audit implies a regular assessment of performance, the review may be a one-off exercise.

In this book the term environmental review is used to mean a preliminary form of audit. A full discussion of environmental auditing and environmental impact assessment is presented in Chapter 6.

An initial environmental review is likely to focus attention on a number of major areas of activity within a company. Most initial reviews follow a standard pathway:

- The scope of the review should be defined in order to establish which activities are to be included, who should be responsible for conducting the review and how it should be reported.
- Baseline information should be collected, including all material relevant to the operation of a company and its related activities.
- Each activity should be assessed against the information collected during the baseline study and against the current performance targets set by legislation and by relevant professional organisations.
- The information gathered should be evaluated and possible areas for future action should be identified.
- A report should be prepared. This should outline the findings of the review and indicate priorities for further action.
- The report should be presented and decisions should be made regarding future priorities, targets and procedures for monitoring.

This process is illustrated in Figure 5.2.

The initial environmental review may lead to the development of one or more detailed programmes of analysis and assessment that focus attention on particular aspects of a company's environmental performance and on the activities of its suppliers and customers. The review will also provide information that can be used to assess a company's environmental policy statement and to correct any mismatches that emerge between the aspirations of a company and its current performance.

In many cases the initial environmental review will be used to establish a baseline case from which improvements can be monitored and measured as part of an ongoing process of environmental auditing. This process is described in more detail in Chapter 6. The review is also the starting point in

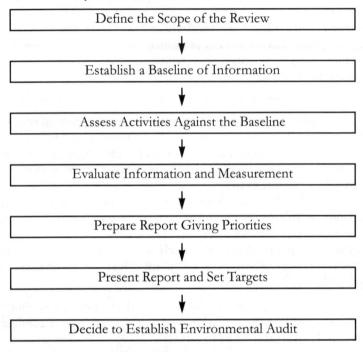

Figure 5.2 An initial environmental review

the development of a comprehensive environmental management system.

One of the most difficult tasks in developing and applying a methodology for an initial environmental review is deciding which activities should be included in the process. It is difficult to provide precise guidance on this issue, because companies use many different processes of production, methods of transport and approaches to training. However, in general, most companies will wish to review the following areas of activity:

- Company policy.
- Methods and structures of management.
- Raw materials inputs.
- Energy use.
- Transport methods.
- Processes and products.
- Land and buildings.
- Wastes and discharges.
- Recycling and reuse.
- Accident and emergency procedures.
- Legal and other requirements and standards.
- Practice within the sector and the locality.
- Staff training, awareness and participation.

- Communication policy.
- Reporting and disclosure procedures.
- Site history and constraints.
- Anticipated and planned changes in the locality.
- Issues related to future environmental policy and auditing.

This list is not exhaustive and it will need to be supplemented with additional information in order to encompass all the activities that are relevant to an individual company.

A number of sources of assistance are available to companies who wish to undertake an initial environmental review. In some sectors of business the relevant industry association has developed procedures that are designed to assist companies who wish to improve their environmental performance. The Chemical Industries Association's Responsible Care programme includes a network of local cells that provide for the exchange of information at local level and for intercompany collaboration. Many local environmental business clubs and forums provide assistance to companies who wish to undertake an environmental review. Business in the Environment, the Groundwork Foundation and a number of consultancy organisations also offer review services.

Future issues and strategies

Two other matters are of particular concern when a company decides to undertake a review of its operations. The first relates to the future intentions of a company and the implications for its corporate strategic policy, and the second relates to the likely evolution of the general, sectoral and local environmental conditions within which it operates. These issues are, in one sense, two sides of the same coin, and the purpose of corporate strategy is to understand the relationship between the two issues in order to inform and guide future company policy. Building a strategy that will allow a company to survive in future market conditions is a complex and difficult task. Although this topic is considered in more detail in Chapter 7, the intention at this stage is to indicate some of the more immediate issues that may result from an initial environmental review.

Most companies have a reasonably sophisticated knowledge of the current market conditions in the sector of business in which they operate, and they are likely to possess an adequate understanding of the legal and other parameters that influence the way in which they conduct their business.

A matter of greater uncertainty for many companies is the likely future evolution of market conditions and the longer-term implications for their business of tightening legal and other controls that are aimed at limiting the occurrence of any negative environmental impacts. Bringing together the likely progress of the market and the increased value (and protection) placed upon the environment allows for interaction to occur between what Smith (1992) calls the ecological and the economic environments. The recognition and acceptance of the importance of the interaction to occur between the ecological and the economic environments is a vital element in the construction of a corporate strategy. The development of a corporate strategy that aims to satisfy both these elements represents an important step towards the attainment of environmentally sustainable business development. However, with the exception of a few larger, often transnational, companies there is little evidence that the simultaneous assessment of ecological and economic futures currently plays an important role in the corporate strategy process.

Strengthening environmental regulations, together with the anticipation of more difficult market conditions in future, combine to make the environment an essential element of business strategy. One of the most noticeable features of the strategic planning undertaken by those major companies who place emphasis upon the environmental implications of their activities is the extent to which strategy aims to move ahead of the regulatory requirements. Examples of company proactivity in this field include the targets set by Monsanto and Du Pont to reduce pollution. Du Pont aims to cut toxic air emissions by 60 per cent over a six-year period and to reduce the emission of carcinogens by 90 per cent by the year 2000. Other examples include the moves made by packaging companies to comply with what are expected to be increasingly stringent regulations requiring the recycling of packaging and a reduction in the type and amount of packaging used.

The International Chamber of Commerce has provided general guidance to companies on the areas of environmental concern that should be included in corporate strategies in order to satisfy the requirements of sustainable development. Most of the major areas of company policy and forward planning are covered by this guidance. The Business Charter for Sustainable Development (see Box 5.3) also includes a number of principles, especially 1, 2, 3, 5, 6, 9, 10, 14, 15 and 16, that are of considerable importance in developing and implementing a sustainable business strategy. The charter was launched in March 1991, and within a year over 900 companies had signed it.

Many other factors specific to an individual company, together with the range of public policies that are directed towards the environment, will influence the choice of the elements to be included within a company strategy. In addition, during the process of developing an environmentally sustainable business strategy it is also essential to take account of a range of possible alternative future circumstances. A strategy should be robust and capable of responding to new challenges and opportunities in a positive manner and this implies the need for it to be informed by, and tested against, a variety of scenarios. The United Kingdom Environmental Foresight Project (CEST, 1993) provides a number of examples of how environmental issues are expected to evolve in the future. As this study indicates, the aim in developing environmental foresight is to allow for the avoidance of problems through the use of anticipation, prior awareness and precautionary action. By avoiding a problem a company can both reduce its costs and safeguard its reputation.

However, foresight on its own is not sufficient to guarantee that a company

Box 5.3   *Business Charter for Sustainable Development*

1. *Corporate policy.* To recognise environmental management as among the highest corporate priorities and as a key determinant to sustainable development; to establish policies, programmes and practices for conducting operations in an environmentally sound manner.
2. *Integrated management.* To integrate these policies, programmes and practices fully into each business as an essential element of management in all its functions.
3. *Process of improvement.* To continue to improve corporate policies, programmes and environmental performance, taking into account technical developments, scientific understanding, consumer needs and community expectations, with legal regulations as a starting point; and to apply the same environmental criteria internationally.
4. *Employee education.* To educate, train and motivate employees to conduct their activities in an environmentally responsible manner.
5. *Prior assessment.* To assess environmental impacts before starting a new activity or project and before decommissioning a facility or leaving a site.
6. *Products and services.* To develop and provide products and services that have no undue environmental impact and are safe in their intended use, that are efficient in their consumption of energy and natural resources, and that can be recycled, reused or disposed of safely.
7. *Customer advice.* To advise, and where relevant, educate customers, distributors and the public in the safe use, transport, storage and disposal of products provided; and to apply similar considerations to provision of services.
8. *Facilities and operations.* To develop, design and operate facilities and conduct activities taking into consideration the efficient use of energy and materials, the sustainable use of renewable resources, the minimisation of adverse environmental impact and waste generation, and the safe and responsible disposal of residual wastes.
9. *Research.* To conduct or support research on the environmental impacts of raw materials, products, processes, emissions and wastes associated with the enterprise and on the means of minimising such adverse impacts.
10. *Precautionary approach.* To modify the manufacture, marketing or use of products or services or the conduct of activities, consistent with scientific and technical understanding, to prevent serious or irreversible environmental degradation.
11. *Contractors and suppliers.* To promote the adoption of these principles by contractors acting on behalf of the enterprise, encouraging and, where appropriate, requiring improvements in the practices to make

them consistent with those of the enterprise; and to encourage the wider adoption of these principles by suppliers.

12. *Emergency preparedness*. To develop and maintain, where significant hazards exist, emergency preparedness plans in conjunction with emergency services, relevant authorities and local community, recognising potential transboundary impacts.

13. *Transfer technology*. To contribute to the transfer of environmentally sound technology and management methods throughout the industrial and public sectors.

14. *Contributing to the common effort*. To contribute to the development of public policy and to business, governmental and intergovernmental programmes and educational initiatives that will enhance environmental awareness and protection.

15. *Openness to concerns*. To foster openness and dialogue with employees and public, anticipating and responding to their concerns about the potential hazards and impacts of operations, products, wastes or services, including those of transboundary or global significance.

16. *Compliance and reporting*. To measure environmental reporting; to conduct regular environmental audits and assessments of compliance with company requirements, legal requirements and these principles; and periodically to provide appropriate information to the board of directors, shareholders, employees, the authorities and the public.

Source: International Chamber of Commerce (1991).

will be immune from future environmental difficulties, or to ensure future success in business. In all cases it is necessary to link strategy to action, and to make sure that good planning is not thwarted by poor implementation. Linking strategy with the key areas of business operation is a priority if a company is to benefit from the adoption of a forward-looking stance.

As this section of the chapter has attempted to demonstrate, the quality of foresight is determined by the breadth of the vision that is employed in its construction. By combining a judgement of the likely future evolution of environmental conditions and policy with an estimation of the possible responses of other businesses in the same sector of activity, a company will be better able to judge its own chances of success. Industry-specific standards of good practice are now emerging, and these standards reflect both the global challenges facing particular industrial sectors and the standards of performance achieved at a local or regional level. This matter is considered further in the following section.

The influence of industrial structure

Change in the environmental aspirations and behaviour of companies results from a combination of circumstances. In some cases a major emergency or shock may provide the stimulus for change whilst, in other cases, the adoption of the principle of sustainable business behaviour may reflect a conscious shift in the central policy stance of a company. The modes of organisation and operation employed by a company also reflect the standards prevailing in a particular sector of industry. No company is an island; pressure exerted through the supply chain reflects consumer preferences, and to retain or increase its market share a company has to operate at the leading edge of good practice.

The definition of good practice varies from country to country and between sectors. Much of the impetus for the stricter environmental legislation that has recently been enacted by the European Union emanates from a desire to create a level playing field of environmental regulation and standards of performance. In the absence of a level playing field, the fear is that a company located in one member state will gain an unfair advantage over its competitors because it does not have to comply with the stricter standards required in other member states. But standards also vary between sectors. Whilst this is partly a consequence of the historic pattern of evolution of a particular industry, it also reflects the varying level of tolerance displayed by national, regional or local governments towards the specific difficulties experienced by an industrial sector. This is not to suggest that different standards are set and applied in an arbitrary manner; rather it reflects the reality that some companies, and some sectors, start from a less favourable baseline of environmental performance.

In the case of an individual industrial sector this baseline is likely to reflect the combination of a number of particular operational characteristics. These may include, for example:

- a high level of dependency upon raw materials that are obtained from mining operations or from sensitive ecological habitats;
- a location in an area of natural beauty or near to a major centre of population;
- a high degree of dependence on long-distance road haulage for the supply of materials and for the distribution of products;
- the need to consume large volumes of water;
- an energy-intensive method of production;
- inherently hazardous or environmentally disruptive production processes;
- an inability to transport its workforce by means other than the private car;
- difficulties experienced in developing or utilising methods for the recycling of waste; and
- problems related to the safe disposal of waste.

The list of problems is illustrative rather than definitive, but it serves to demonstrate the problems that confront some sectors of production.

It is difficult to define with any degree of accuracy the sectors of production that are most likely to experience difficulties in relation to the environmental impacts of their activities. CEST (1990) has attempted to define the sectors that experience the greatest number of interactions with the environment, and these are considered to be the most vulnerable. On the basis of an assessment of the most significant environmental issues, CEST classified 13 of these issues as of particular importance to business:

- The greenhouse effect.
- Stratospheric ozone depletion.
- Acid rain.
- Water quality.
- Heavy metals.
- Volatile organic compounds and smells.
- Persistent organics.
- Air quality.
- Noise.
- Waste management.
- Contaminated land.
- Major accidents and spills.
- Releases from biotechnology.

CEST also identified a number of industries which experience some or all of the 13 environmental problems. Although the number, scale and significance of the interactions between the activities undertaken by an industry and the environment varies from sector to sector, a number of conclusions are applicable to almost all sectors of economic activity:

- Most industries experience a number of environmental problems; 16 of the 22 industries identified by CEST experienced seven or more problems.
- Some problems are common to all industries, especially those related to the use of fossil fuels and transport.
- Some of the problems experienced by an industry are related to each other.

Some of the industries most affected were

- petroleum refining – 13 of 13 environmental issues;
- chemicals –12 of 13 environmental issues;
- pharmaceuticals – 11 of 13 environmental issues;
- petroleum and coal products – 9 of 13 environmental issues;
- iron and steel – 9 of 13 environmental issues;
- electrical engineering – 9 of 13 environmental issues; and
- transport equipment – 9 of 13 environmental issues.

However, other industries, often considered to be somewhat more environmentally benign, also generate a significant number of interactions with the environment. They include:

- agriculture – 8 of 13 environmental issues;
- electricity production and supply – 7 of 13 environmental issues;

- textile and leather manufacture – 6 of 13 environmental issues; and
- wood and paper manufacture – 6 of 13 environmental issues.

In a third group of industries the range of interactions with the environment is more limited, although the impact on a particular facet of the environment may be particularly severe. They include

- gas supply – 5 of 13 environmental issues; and
- printing and publishing – 4 of 13 environmental issues.

Although this evidence is of value, it is somewhat limited in its use because it simply indicates the number of potential interactions between particular industries and the environment. It is important not to be misled into thinking that an activity with relatively few interactions is less harmful to the environment, in terms of its total quantifiable impact, than an activity with a large number of interactions. This is especially the case at a regional or local level where a cluster of individual activities can generate a significant cumulative impact, even though the impacts associated with an individual company may be limited.

Even though the occurrence of pollution, contamination and other forms of environmental damage are now recognised as global problems, it is also possible to identify concentrations or clusters of environmentally damaging industries. In some cases these clusters represent the outcome of the historical evolution of an industry, such as in the case of the dyestuffs industry in West Yorkshire, which is spatially concentrated because of the presence of the textiles industry to which it supplies products and services. Other clusters reflect the desire of public policy-makers to concentrate potentially polluting industries in remote locations. These remote locations, which often house a complex of linked activities, such as the various petrochemical complexes frequently sited at estuarine locations, can become what Blowers (1993a, p. 90) refers to as 'pollution havens', imposing high levels of risk on local populations. The cumulative risks and hazards that are associated with such complexes are subject to detailed environmental and hazard assessments, the imposition of controls on the size and proximity of plants, and a strict planning regime that includes the preparation of contingency plans and the designation of safeguarding zones.

The regional and local distribution and concentration of industries that experience a significant number of environmental problems has changed over time. For example, coalfield areas were once host to a complex of coal-using, processing and associated industries, but those coal-based complexes have become less significant in recent years due to the closure of collieries, the move of steel making to coastal locations and the eventual cessation of other activities such as coke manufacture. By way of contrast, petrochemical complexes have grown in size, and a number of related industries have developed which seek to gain locational advantage from a close proximity to the activities that they supply, or from whom they purchase feedstocks.

In order to measure the spatial concentration of environmental risk it is necessary to consider both the characteristics of a particular industry and the spatial distribution of activities within that industry. A crude measure of the extent to which regions and localities are potentially at risk can be derived from an analysis of the regional distribution of employment by industrial sector. A measure of risk can be developed through the calculation of a location quotient. A higher than national average concentration of employment in potentially polluting industries in a given region (see Box 5.4 and Table 5.1) indicates that the region may be more vulnerable to environmental damage than other regions. Other indices that measure the spatial concentration of environmental risk can be developed by relating the national and regional distribution of industrial plants, or the national and regional distribution of sectoral manufacturing capacity, to the number of particular environmental issues and the level of environmental risk that are associated with particular industrial sectors. This analysis can also be applied to the structure of the economy at a local level.

Box 5.4   *Examples of location quotients for selected industries*

The location quotient for each industry in a region can be derived from the following ratio:

$$LQ = \frac{S2/S1}{N2/N1} \text{ or } \frac{S2/N2}{S1/N1}$$

where S1 and S2 represent the numbers employed in a given sector nationally and regionally and N1 and N2 represent the total number of workers employed in the nation and the region. The resulting ratio illustrates a region's dominance in a particular industry. An LQ above unity indicates that an above-average concentration of employment exists in a region. Substituting actual values for S1, S2, N1 and N2:

$$LQ = \frac{43,514 : 365,700}{1,231,250 : 24,380,000} = 2.36$$

Applying this to selected industrial sectors in some of the regions of Great Britain, the location quotients given in Table 5.1 can be obtained.

It is also the case that, whilst historically some nations and regions have been regarded as 'clean' areas, other nations and regions have allowed 'dirty' activities to continue to function. As Chapman and Walker (1987, p. 256) note, in the USA variations in state regulations prior to the Clean Air Amendments 1970 meant that 'similar industrial plants could face very different pollution control regulations depending on whether they were located in a clean or a dirty area'. In the UK and elsewhere in the European Union, environmental legislation seeks to remove such an option and all economic

Table 5.1 Location quotients for selected industries

Selected regions	Electricity production and distribution	Chemical industry	Iron and steel	Printing and publishing
South East	0.8	0.9	0.2	1.4
South West	1.4	0.5	0.2	0.9
North West	1.0	1.8	0.1	0.7
North	1.0	2.0	–	0.6
Wales	1.4	0.9	8.1	0.5
Scotland	1.1	0.7	0.6	0.7

Source: Department of Employment (1991).

activities are regulated through the application of common standards, irrespective of their location. However, this attempt to set common standards cannot undo the results of over two hundred years of industrialisation and, as a consequence, it is likely that some regions and localities will continue to act as willing or unwilling hosts to concentrations of polluting industries for some years to come.

Although it is not intended in this chapter to examine in detail the operation of specific business activities, it may prove helpful to illustrate some of the environmental problems that are associated with individual sectors of the economy. These sector profiles are offered in order to illustrate the general nature and broad implications of the environmental problems encountered in a particular sector. They are not examples of the problems faced by a particular company. The profiles are based upon a selection of material from company, industrial association and other sources.

Three profiles are provided: the first is of a sector that provides raw materials to a wide range of industrial activities – aggregates; the second is of a process-based manufacturing industry – chemicals; and the third is of a service sector activity – tourism. Each of these brief profiles indicates the major environmental problems confronting the sector and, if available, the costs that are associated with the control of pollution and other environmental problems.

Aggregates
The mining of aggregate construction materials is widespread in the UK and most other advanced and developing societies. As is the case in all mining operations, the industry is concerned with the extraction of a stock resource and is, therefore, reducing the total amount of resource available to future generations. In addition, the mining of aggregates generates a range of environmental impacts that affect both the natural and built environments. Their impacts are experienced both at the quarry or pit, and at a variety of locations remote from the point of production.

A number of aspects of the environment are affected by the mining of aggregates:

- Air quality is adversely affected by dust emissions from all material-handling operations.
- Noise can be a significant problem in some mining operations and at particular points in the cycle of development and production, including blasting and other disturbance.
- Water is used for a number of operations and the discharge of water can cause environmental problems; the flooding of abandoned workings is a further difficulty.
- The lighting of workings can cause disturbance to residents and wildlife.
- Visual impacts are often significant.
- Energy consumption can be excessive, especially in deep pits where a shallow seam of aggregates is covered by a thick overburden.
- Transport to and from a site is predominantly by road and this can cause disturbance to local communities.
- Ecological disruption can be severe and is often total; rehabilitation procedures and techniques attempt to take into account the need to maintain or restore the ecology.
- The built environment and the archaeological heritage are also affected.

Problems associated with the mining of aggregates are not confined to the point of production. Aggregate materials are used in construction operations, and a number of associated activities, such as the preparation of ready mixed concrete, create additional environmental disturbance. A major area of research in relation to the production and use of aggregates is concerned with the minimisation of the need for materials; this includes work on methods and technologies for recycling materials and procedures to minimise the need for virgin materials.

Further information on the environmental problems associated with the extraction of aggregates can be found in reports and surveys published by the British Aggregate Construction Materials Industries (BACMI, 1992), and in books by Roberts and Shaw (1982) and Blunden (1991). The Department of the Environment has also published a series of Mineral Planning Guidance Notes that deal with specific aspects of aggregates production, and the issue of minerals working is included within the UK Strategy for Sustainable Development (DoE, 1994).

Chemicals

It is almost impossible to provide a brief overview of all the environmental issues that are associated with the production of chemicals. The production, use and disposal of chemicals generates a number of environmental problems. These vary in their severity according to the toxicity and other properties of the raw materials used and the nature of the final products. The number of chemicals produced has increased rapidly over the past twenty years; for example the full inventory of chemicals produced and available within the European Union contains over 100,000 substances (DoE, 1994). Spending in the UK on environmentally related measures was estimated at £727 million in 1992 (Chemical Industries Association, 1993).

The major environmental issues associated with the chemicals industry have been identified by Vaughan and Mickle (1993) and include

- the emission of greenhouse gases and substances that cause stratospheric ozone depletion and acid rain;
- the use and release of volatile organic compounds which evaporate readily and contribute to air pollution;
- poor air quality at and near to plants and at a regional scale;
- problems of waste disposal and management;
- hazards, risks, emergencies and the dangers associated with major spills; and
- water quality issues related to the discharge of water following its use in a variety of processes.

In addition, other problems relate to

- the transport, storage and handling of materials;
- the visual impact of chemical plants;
- effects upon habitats due to land-take and the use of particular sites; and
- energy use in a variety of production processes and in the transportation of materials and products.

As in the case of aggregates, the environmental problems that are associated with the chemicals industry are not confined to the processes of production. Almost all other sectors of the economy make use of chemicals and many of the problems noted above are equally valid in relation to all intermediate and final consumers. The chemical industry is aware of the scale and significance of its interactions with the environment, and it has taken steps to limit or reduce the impacts of its operations on the environment in terms of both the production and the use of its products.

Many sources of information are available on the environmental problems that are associated with the chemical industry. The Chemical Industries Association through its Responsible Care programme, which originated in Canada in 1984, aims to improve and enhance environmental standards in the industry (Chemical Industries Association, 1992). Chem Systems (1990) has produced a useful digest of the key issues related to the chemical industry and the environment. Company and other case studies are available in many books and journals, including work by Otter (1992), Essery (1993), Simmons and Wynne (1993) and Wahlstrom and Lundqvist (1993).

Tourism

This sector of economic activity is not usually associated with environmental problems. However, as Elkington and Burke (1989, p. 84) observe, 'Even the transition to a leisure society is having a major impact on the environment, which remains tourism's basic resource'. The cause of the problem is complex but, in essence, it is associated with the desire of an increasingly aware and mobile society to sample, at first hand, the images conveyed by television, books and other tourists. Other leisure activities, as distinct from tourism, generate special forms of environmental problems, such as those associated with the erosion of footpaths in areas of natural beauty.

The environmental problems associated with tourism vary from country to country and between local areas depending upon the characteristics, scale and accessibility of the tourist attraction. In England the major environmental problems have been identified by the English Tourist Board (1991a) as follows:

- Overcrowding which occurs when the numbers of people at a particular location exceed the capacity of the place or the local environment to accommodate them; this problem occurs in both natural honeypots and at sites of historic or cultural interest.
- Traffic congestion disrupts local road use, damages roads and verges, necessitates the construction of visually intrusive car parks and generates atmospheric pollution and noise.
- Wear-and-tear on the natural and built environment can reach alarming proportions; erosion and pollution in environmentally sensitive areas, and the damage caused to ancient monuments are unsightly, costly to repair and diminish the quality of the environmental resource.
- Inappropriate development is often associated with tourist areas, including the pressure for new development to serve the needs of tourists, infrastructure provision and the need to provide additional facilities such as sewage treatment plants.
- Conflicts with the local community and the disruption caused to lifestyles.

Growing awareness of the importance of the environment as the fundamental resource upon which tourism is based has led to increasing efforts to provide guidance to companies, local authorities and other agencies involved in the promotion and management of all aspects of the tourist industry. In *The Green Light*, the English Tourist Board (1991b) has provided a guide to the operation of tourism businesses that combines economic prosperity with environmental stewardship. Further advice and information is available from a range of official and voluntary agencies. The aim of such guidance is to promote sustainable tourist development which avoids the nightmare scene encountered by Douglas Adams on his visit to the island paradise of Bali:

> The narrow, muddy streets of Kuta were lined with gift shops and hamburger bars and populated with crowds of drunken, shouting tourists, kamikaze motorcyclists, counterfeit watch sellers and small dogs. Somewhere not too far from here, towards the middle of the island, there may have been heaven on earth, but hell had certainly set up business on its porch.
>
> (Adams and Carradine, 1990, p. 14)

This need not be the case as is illustrated by the attempt that has been made to establish an environmentally sustainable ski resort in the Nuria Valley of Catalonia (Generalitat de Catalunya, 1992). The ski resort is located in a remote valley; the only access, except on foot, is by a rack railway. In order to protect the environment of the Nuria Valley, a maximum of 2,000 tourists are allowed to visit the resort at any one time. In addition, extensive ecological surveys have been conducted in order to assess the carrying capacity of the resort. This project, which has created over 130 jobs, represents an attempt to avoid some of the environmental problems normally associated with such developments.

Conclusions

This chapter has analysed a number of environmental issues that are related to the ways in which business is organised and which result from the operation of business activities. It has also examined the importance of industrial structure in assessing the scale, location and cumulative effects of the environmental impact of business activities. These three elements (organisation, operation and industrial structure) combine to provide an overview of the way in which business interacts with the environment.

The importance of developing and adopting a holistic view of the entire range of business activities will be demonstrated in Chapters 7 and 8. At this stage it is more important to realise that the organisational, operational and structural dimensions of the relationship between business and the environment are simply the various manifestations of a single set of problems. Further insights and guidance as to how this problem may be better understood is provided in the following chapter.

6

Environmental assessment, auditing and information systems

Understanding the environmental impacts of business operations is an essential prerequisite for the development and introduction of a system of environmental management. It is impossible to manage environmental impacts in the absence of a method for measuring their severity, significance and locational characteristics. Measurement also implies that there will be a need to construct some form of database or information system; this information system can be used to provide the fundamental resource for the establishment of an environmental management system.

It is important at the outset to distinguish between environmental impact assessment (EIA), also known in the UK as environmental assessment (EA), and the variety of methods and procedures used to conduct initial environmental reviews, environmental surveys and environmental audits. Terminology presents a number of difficulties, because there is no single authoritive source or legal definition which encompasses all the terms. In this book the following definitions are used:

- *Environmental impact assessment (or environmental assessment)* is a procedure for predicting, analysing and evaluating the impacts of a proposed action on the environment and ensuring that information regarding these impacts is taken into account in decision-making.
- *Environmental auditing* is a process for checking, on a regular basis, the environmental performance of an existing organisation or activity.
- *Environmental review* is an initial or preliminary form of an environmental audit; it may provide the basis for the adoption of an environmental policy and the introduction of a full system of environmental auditing.

These definitions are also helpful in identifying the roles and purposes that are assigned to EIA and environmental auditing. Although the distinction may be blurred in certain forms of practice, in general the purposes of these methods are as follows:

- EIA is normally undertaken prior to making a decision. It is a preventative form of analysis; it offers an organisation the ability to review its proposals and to avoid taking an action that may have a negative impact upon the environment.

- Environmental auditing is normally undertaken by an organisation as part of its regular cycle of monitoring and evaluation; it is a systematic method for ensuring that information is collected in order to aid the process of management.

It is worth mentioning at this point that both methods are also related to the concept and procedure of life-cycle assessment. This method of assessment seeks to highlight particular activities during the environmental life of a product or project where specific environmental impacts may occur. These impacts can then be addressed and any problems can be rectified through the redesign of the product, process or project. For example, if an impact results from the use of a particular source of raw materials, then alternative sources may need to be identified or the process may have to be changed (Welford and Gouldson, 1993).

Common features of EIA and environmental auditing

Both EIA and environmental auditing attempt to measure and evaluate a wide range of environmental impacts that are associated with an action or an activity. They use units of measurement that are appropriate to the action or activity which is the subject of analysis, although it may also be possible to assign monetary values. By using appropriate units of measurement (number of species, parts per million) these methods avoid the criticism frequently made in relation to cost-benefit analysis, that is, that it is impossible to assign a monetary value to many aspects of the environment. The measurement of actions and activities may, in some cases, also involve an assessment of the relative significance of certain aspects of the environment *vis-à-vis* the action or activity in question. Priorities may have to be set and assigned to the inter-actions that occur between the environment and the various elements or stages that are contained within an action or activity. The assignment of priorities will vary between actions or activities; for example, a proposal to construct a dam is likely to have a major impact upon the volume and flow of water in a river, and in an EIA a high degree of priority may be assigned to the possibility of a reduction in river flow and the implications for water supply. By way of comparison, an EIA of a proposed airport may place priority on the environmental consequences of the loss of good agricultural land and the generation of noise. In a similar manner, whilst an environmental audit of a transport business may place particular emphasis on energy use and the emission of exhaust gases, in an audit of a chemical company, even though road transport is used to move materials and products, it is likely that emphasis will be placed upon measuring process-related emissions rather than the emission of exhaust gases.

The commonality of approach, in terms of the use of appropriate units of measurement, that exists between EIA and environmental auditing can be extended to other characteristics of the methods. Other common features include the roles played by assessment and auditing within a hierarchy of decision-making, the need for adequate baseline information, the relationship of the methods to legal and other requirements, the importance of disclosure and communication, the wider application of such methods, and the importance of ensuring that any analysis takes into account the context within which an individual project or activity will take place.

Although many EIAs have been conducted in order to assess the likely environmental consequences of a particular project, EIA is equally valuable as a method for the assessment of policies, programmes and plans (see Figure 6.1). It has also been suggested that EIA offers considerable potential for the analysis of individual subproject elements and of specific products, such as a motor vehicle. To ignore the role of EIA in the assessment or screening of policies, programmes and plans is to ignore the potential for reducing the need for, cost of, and time taken to conduct assessments. By assessing the environmental impact of a policy, programme or plan, undesirable options can be eliminated at an early stage in the development process, and before any such options emerge as proposals for specific projects. This concern with the strategic dimension of EIA is of long standing (Lee and Wood, 1978; Roberts and Shaw, 1981), and it is currently reflected in calls for the introduction of strategic environmental assessment. The role, features and procedures of strategic environmental assessment are considered in the third section of this chapter.

Environmental auditing also has the potential to play a strategic role in the analysis and assessment of options. At the level of corporate strategy it is possible to filter out policies which have undesirable environmental consequences, and at subsequent stages in the processes of business planning the application of environmental auditing can be effective in screening operational programmes and plans. As with EIA, the use of environmental auditing throughout a business is intended to ensure that an individual process or product is in accord with the requirements for environmentally sustainable business development.

Both methods necessitate the development of a baseline of information and understanding. In the case of EIA this is likely to involve the assembly of existing knowledge relevant to the spatial level at which the assessment is to be undertaken; for example, in order to make a policy decision as to the future form of transport policy, it will be vital to gather information on the current split among the various modes of transport, forecasts of demand and other factors. An environmental audit will involve the gathering of information on subjects such as the sources of materials, the range of production processes and products used, and the generation of wastes. For both methods

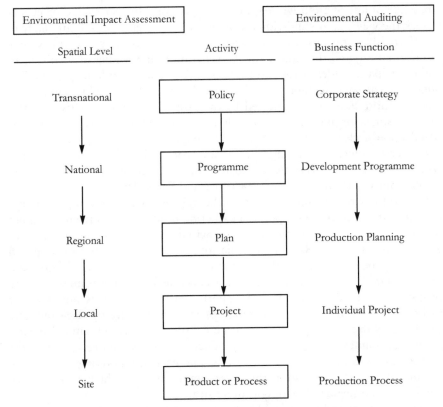

Figure 6.1   EIA and environmental auditing: a total approach

it is essential that this database is kept up to date. The information gathered as part of the process of preparing an EIA, or in conducting an audit at the lowest level in the hierarchy, should be fed into the database. Other relevant externally generated information will also need to be captured at regular intervals, including the implications of changes in legislation and environmental standards.

Current legislation and other regulatory standards provide a starting point for an EIA or environmental audit. Whilst an EIA is required for any major project proposed in the UK, or elsewhere in the European Union, the position is less clear with regard to environmental auditing. Nevertheless, it is important to be aware of the range of environmental standards that currently condition and constrain the activities of a company and to anticipate future limits and standards. In both EIA and environmental auditing, the emphasis is on anticipation and taking action to avoid problems that may emerge in the future.

For EIA and environmental auditing to give of their best, it is essential that the process of preparing the assessment or audit is an open one. Constructing a baseline of information will require extensive consultation, including efforts to seek the views of any individuals, organisations or groups who are likely to be affected by a proposed action. These views can provide a valuable source of information, and they allow for the generation of a feeling of involvement and participation. Ideally the results of an EIA or audit should be presented in non-technical language and should be widely disseminated. This will help to reassure those likely to be affected by the proposed action or activity that a full assessment or audit has been undertaken, and that any decision made is based upon a clear understanding of the impacts and consequences. In the case of environmental auditing, such an approach will also ensure compliance with the need for corporate disclosure and the requirements of a social responsibility audit (Clutterbuck, Dearlove and Snow, 1992).

EIA and environmental auditing can be applied to a wide range of activities. Both methods depend upon the gathering of information from a number of sources; they attempt to assess an actual or proposed action, and to evaluate the extent to which a particular option amongst a range of proposed actions can be seen to be to the mutual benefit of both the organisation and the environment. Early EIAs were mainly concerned with major infrastructure projects, such as dams, roads and airports, but the method is now used to assist in making decisions on a range of investments. Many decisions and functions within a company can benefit from the use of environmental auditing, including those related to product design, the configuration of the technology used in production processes, purchasing, marketing and human resource management. Both methods are vital elements in the construction of any form of strategic policy or corporate strategy.

Environmental auditing and EIA should be undertaken within an appropriate and relevant context. Whilst it may be convenient to assume that all projects or processes have the same impacts irrespective of their location in space, this assumption is both erroneous and dangerous. An individual plant or project is located in a local environment and each local environment displays distinctive and individual features. A local natural and built environment is unique, and it may be valued in different ways by various groups in a community, including residents, other business activities and local public policy organisations. Each of these groups may place a different interpretation or value on the component parts of the local environment, and these differences should be recognised and respected. It is also the case that the local environment will change over time, and this implies that an audit or an EIA should be anticipatory. For example, a factory may have been established in a remote location prior to the development of adjacent land for housing. In the past noise from production processes may not have generated a perceived environmental impact. However, following the development of housing, the current situation may be one in which residents complain about the noise which is generated. Any decision on changes to layout, the use of new production equipment and the siting of extensions should anticipate the future use of land adjacent to a factory. If necessary a safeguarding area of land may have to be purchased in order to comply with anticipated legal requirements and stated standards of corporate behaviour.

Some common criticisms of the methods

As well as sharing many common features, both EIA and environmental auditing have been the subject of a number of common criticisms. These criticisms relate to the precision of the methods, the feasibility or otherwise of allowing for participation, the absence of arrangements for the full disclosure of results, variations in the requirement to make use of EIA and auditing methods, and the extent to which the methods can inhibit good or rapid decision-making.

The degree of precision of an EIA, or an environmental audit, will depend upon the availability of baseline information, the resources available for the conduct of the audit or assessment, the amount of time available to conduct an analysis, and the degree of co-operation offered to the analysts by local and other actors who have a stake in the outcome. The need for a comprehensive and up-to-date baseline of information and understanding has already been discussed and, whilst it is recognised that adequate information is an essential prerequisite for a satisfactory outcome, the reality is often far removed from this ideal. In many areas, ecological and other surveys may be absent, incomplete or out of date. The absence of good information will inevitably affect the degree of precision that can be attained by an EIA or audit. This is not the fault of the method itself, although it does provide a powerful argument in favour of the development of procedures for assessment and auditing that are designed so as to minimise the need for the collection of data and which can produce reasonable results irrespective of the quality of the data available.

Whilst it is always possible to supplement an existing baseline of information by conducting direct surveys, the extent to which additional information can be collected will depend upon the resources available to the assessment team, in terms of both money and personnel. Other constraints include the amount of time allowed to prepare an EIA or audit, and the willingness of local and other actors to make available any specialist information and knowledge which they may possess.

The availability of financial, staff and other resources will also influence the precision and accuracy of an environmental assessment or audit. Given that many of the stages in any assessment or audit will involve the exercise of a high degree of professional judgement, the availability of trained and experienced staff is a crucial matter. Of equal importance is the provision of sufficient time to conduct a full and comprehensive EIA or audit. Co-operation from local and other actors who are likely to be affected by a proposed project or process may prove helpful in ensuring that sufficient information is obtained, and such co-operation may be essential in order to allow an audit or EIA to proceed with an analysis of the key issues, many of which are only likely to emerge through consultation and participation. Many environmental problems are virtually invisible or unseen, and participation by the workforce in an environmental audit, or by the local community in an EIA, is an important factor that may determine the successful application of either of the methods.

Lack of precision may result from all or any of the above causes. However, compared with many other business methods, both EIA and environmental auditing are relatively precise. As Muller and Koechlin (1992, p. 48) observe, 'the standards applied in environmental questions are stricter by far than in other management problems', and that if 'the same exactitude were to be demanded for, say, an investment decision, investment would virtually come to a standstill'.

The extent to which the participation and co-operation of a workforce, or of a local community, can be secured will influence the accuracy and validity of an EIA or environmental audit. One criticism levelled at both EIA and environmental auditing is that they are procedures that allow for the assertion of the values held by the proposer of a project, or which can be dominated by the views of management. This need not be the case, and it is important to ensure that any assessment is carried out in a spirit of openness and full participation. Full disclosure of the method to be used, the criteria for assessment and the form and accessibility of the results can do much to guarantee the participation of all parties. In the USA this is provided for in terms of the public right-to-know principle (Cannon, 1992), but there is resistance to the adoption of this principle in certain other countries.

Considerable variations exist between countries with regard to the extent to which an EIA or an environmental audit is required. As will be discussed later in this chapter, EIA is now a legal requirement in the European Union if a major project is proposed. Determining the threshold above which a project is considered to be significant, and thereby requires an EIA to be produced, is a matter of debate. Environmental auditing is not a statutory requirement in the UK and most other countries but, as was discussed in Chapter 5, Norwegian company law now requires an environmental statement to be included within the annual report. In order to comply with the requirements of British Standard 7750 a company has to utilise a satisfactory form of audit.

The final criticism levelled at EIA and environmental auditing is that the use of such methods can hamper effective management and can delay vital decisions. This criticism has little validity, unless there is a need to achieve immediate cost savings. However, if a project or company is in such a difficult financial position that it can only be saved by pragmatism of this nature, then it is almost certain that the project or company should not continue in its present form.

Intracompany and extracompany dimensions
Given the shared features of EIA and environmental auditing, and accepting that the methods share a number of weaknesses, it is important to consider the position of each of the methods in relation to the operation of business

organisations. In analysing the relationship among a business, the environment and the other characteristics of an individual location, it is apparent that there is a need to consider both the way in which:

- this relationship is analysed and assessed within an organisation; this can be referred to as the intracompany dimension; and
- the relationship between a company and the wider environment can be assessed; this can be referred to as the extracompany dimension.

It is important to recognise the existence of both of these dimensions in analysing the relationship among business, environment and place, and to acknowledge that they reflect a range of broader social concerns. Both dimensions are vital because a business does not operate in isolation from other factors and actors in its immediate environment, nor can it hope to achieve the objectives of environmentally sustainable business development without taking action itself to improve the environment, and encouraging and supporting similar actions that are taken by other companies and organisations in a locality.

In contemplating the construction of premises, or the installation of new plant, it is both logical and cost-effective to use an EIA as a method for testing the sustainability of a project. In addition, it is sensible to prepare an EIA using a format that can provide a baseline for future environmental audits. Equally, an EIA can obtain much useful information from the results of successive rounds of environmental audits conducted at a similar plant located elsewhere.

This distinction between the intracompany and extracompany dimensions of environmental analysis and assessment is made in order to illustrate the importance to business of attempting to pay equal attention to both the internal and external characteristics of the environment. An example of the way in which the extracompany dimension can be assessed is provided by EIA, whilst the intracompany dimension can be analysed through the adoption of environmental auditing. As noted above, the former procedure is now a statutory requirement in the case of major projects, whilst the latter, in its broadest sense, is not.

Environmental impact assessment

On 27 June 1985 the Council of Environment Ministers of the European Communities adopted Directive 85/337/EEC on 'the assessment of the effects of certain public and private projects on the environment' (CEC, 1985). This directive, which is generally known as the European Environmental Assessment (EA) Directive, requires member states of the community to develop and implement procedures and methods for the comprehensive assessment of the environmental consequences of major projects. The directive, which was the outcome of over ten years of negotiation between the Commission of the European Communities and member states, came into force in July 1988 and is subject to detailed monitoring and review. In one sense, the directive can be viewed as an experiment in transnational environmental regulation, while in another sense it represents a logical extension to the long-standing programme for environmental protection and improvement, and the principle that prevention is better than cure.

The origins of EIA

Whilst the directive was an important step forward in the development of a common European programme for environmental regulation, it was based upon over twenty years of experience of the application of EIA both in Europe and elsewhere. Much of the impetus for the adoption of a standard form of EIA within Europe came through a recognition of the benefits that were derived from the implementation of a nationwide approach to EIA in the USA. Following the enactment of the National Environmental Policy Act 1969 (United States Government, 1969), all federal agencies in the USA were required to prepare an Environmental Impact Statement in advance of all major projects. European experience, often built upon the foundations laid in the USA, is more varied. Some member states introduced detailed statutory systems of EIA at an early point in time; for example, the federal government of Germany has required that, since 1971, all measures undertaken by federal authorities should be subject to an examination for environmental compatibility, whilst other member states, including the UK, encouraged the preparation of EIAs outside the requirements of specific legislation (Roberts, Shaw and Adkins , 1980; Wathern, 1988).

This wide experience of the use of EIA, both generally and more specifically in the UK, has its roots in the 1960s. Early experience in North America demonstrated the benefits of undertaking the comprehensive environmental assessment of major civil engineering and other projects. In a number of cases these professional interests in the capabilities of EIA were reflected in the growth of an increasingly powerful and vocal environment lobby. Similar lobbies emerged in many European countries, including the UK, during the late 1960s. The loose coalition of interests that comprised the environment lobby in the UK began in the late 1960s and early 1970s to analyse and contest proposals for the development of major projects. The earliest evidence of increasing concern was demonstrated, for example, in the opposition mounted to the proposed construction of a Third London Airport at Maplin, the mining of potash in the North York Moors, and the development of oil platform construction yards and servicing facilities in Scotland. Doubts also emerged regarding the competence and appropriateness of the traditional means of planning control to deal with these projects.

In Scotland, and to a lesser extent elsewhere in the UK, the experience of having to comply with the stricter national legislation encountered in the USA prompted many oil companies to submit an EIA alongside any application for planning permission for the construction of oil-related facilities. Preparing an EIA had become second nature to such companies, and the practice of EIA was accepted as an integral part of the industry's standard approach to environmental issues. The result was the production of a series of informal EIAs, of many types and related to many different projects. In addition to these practical experiments in the use of EIA, the UK Department of the Environment commissioned a series of research investigations (Catlow and Thirwall, 1976; Clark *et al.*, 1976). These reports, together with the informal EIAs, set the standard for best practice and the debate which ensued. Despite the clear demonstration of the need for a formal system for assessing environmental impacts, which was presented by the aforementioned reports and the informal EIAs, it was not until 1985 that a statutory requirement for EIA (now renamed EA) was introduced. It is this statutory system, implemented in response to the European directive of 1985, that forms the basis for the operation of EA in the UK.

The features of EIA

There are many different procedures and systems of EIA and they utilise a variety of techniques, criteria and methods of measurement. However, in general terms, most forms of EIA can be expected to conform to four basic principles:

1. They identify the nature of the proposed and induced activities that are likely to be generated by an action including alternatives to the action and, if appropriate, alternative locations for an action.
2. They identify the relevant elements of the environment that will be affected by an action.
3. They evaluate the initial and subsequent impacts of an action, including alternatives and alternative locations.
4. They are concerned with the management of the beneficial and adverse impacts likely to be generated.

In proposing the above principles, it is suggested that EIA provides not just a method of analysis but a comprehensive system for identifying, analysing, evaluating and managing the impacts of the introduction and operation of any action, be it a policy, a project or a process. The output from an EIA is a detailed assessment statement which provides an objective basis upon which a decision can be made. The purpose of an EIA is to help decision-makers to make better decisions; it does not, in itself, provide a decision.

It is also important to distinguish EIA from other forms of assessment, such as cost-benefit analysis. This can be achieved by examining the characteristics of EIA and setting them against those of other forms of testing, analysis or evaluation. Whilst many traditional forms of analysis and assessment are often specific to an individual process or project, and normally attempt to utilise measurement criteria that are individual in nature, such as monetary value, EIA measures all the major elements which are encapsulated within a proposed action and relates them to the overall operational environment. It is no longer realistic or possible to claim that individual actions that have an effect on a particular operational environment can be assessed solely by reference to the measurement of their inherent characteristics.

EIA attempts to examine and evaluate a project within the context provided by an existing (or future) operational environment. This implies that a hierarchy of actions exists, and that there are various levels of application of a specific action. In general terms this implies that a specific action, such as a motorway project, should be viewed as an individual element set within a nested set of actions, often occurring in a chronological sequence and generating impacts at different spatial levels. To paraphrase Lee and Wood (1978, p. 102) this offers the possibility of developing a 'tiered system of EIA' within which an 'action at one tier is inevitably conditioned by prior actions at higher tiers'. Such an approach suggests that EIA can be applied through a spatially nested hierarchy. The spatial sequence, or hierarchy, of policies, programmes, plans, projects and process has been demonstrated in Figure 6.1.

An approach such as that suggested in Figure 6.1 indicates the potential and the inherent strengths of EIA as a tool of analysis and assessment. It also indicates the possibility of developing a two-way interaction between the design and implementation of policy and the design and operation of an individual project or product. Thus, for example, national or international transport policy may contain an explicit consideration of the noise aspects of policy options, and this may be reflected in the specification of noise limits which relate to a particular product.

A dynamic assessment system, which incorporates both positive and negative feedback links, provides a powerful tool that may be used both by the community and by those in business. It has the inherent advantage of providing explicit guidance for those who are responsible for the design, manufacture and evaluation of specific projects, and it also allows product assessment to coexist with the operational environment within which products are utilised.

By implication EIA is concerned with assessing the impacts of a specific proposed action upon the environment, and considering a range of alternative actions or products which could be adopted should the projected impact of such actions, or products, prove to be undesirable or unacceptable. It would, for example, be possible for an EIA to suggest that

1. a proposed action is acceptable at the site suggested;
2. a proposed action is not acceptable at the site suggested, but is acceptable at an alternative site;
3. the proposed action is unacceptable at any site; and
4. a modified action may be acceptable at the site suggested or at an alternative site.

These possible outcomes are not mutually exclusive, and there are potential trade-offs between the recommendations. In addition, it is important to recognise that the criteria and standards utilised in preparing an EIA will vary from one country to another, and even between areas within a single country (Murphy, 1981).

The current system of environmental assessment in the UK

It is important to recognise that the broad description of EIA that has been provided above does not equate directly to the system of EA introduced in the UK in response to the EC directive. The more restricted system of EA now in use in the UK does not, for example, readily allow for the comparison of a series of alternative sites for an action or project, unless the proponent of the action has directly provided the possibility of such a consideration.

There were, and still are, many different views and opinions as to the merits of introducing a uniform statutory system for EA in the various member states. In order to minimise any delays in introducing a common European system for EIA, the European Community therefore opted in the directive to require that: 'Member States shall adopt all measures necessary to ensure that, before consent is given, projects likely to have significant effects upon the environment by virtue of their nature, size or location are made subject to an assessment with regard to their effects' (CEC, 1985, Article 2), and that: 'The environmental impact assessment may be integrated into the existing procedures for consent to projects in the Member States or, failing this, into other procedures to be established to comply with the aims of this Directive' (*ibid.*).

The directive recognised the diversity of legislation and procedures that exists within member states, whilst at the same time attempting to ensure that a common approach to EA was implemented. The success or failure of the directive and, by implication, the future development of EA within the member states of the European Union, depends on

1. the *quality* of EAs that are prepared;
2. the structure and *organisation* of the pre-existing procedures for decision-making and assessment; and
3. the *willingness* of member states to adjust and improve pre-existing procedures in order to allow for the specific consideration of the findings of EAs.

In practice, the UK decided to introduce a system for EA that operates in parallel with the normal planning requirements. The operational objective of the EA system is stated in the guide to EA published by the Department of the Environment in 1989:

> Properly carried out, EA will help all those involved in the planning process. From the developer's point of view the preparation of an environmental statement in parallel with project design provides a useful framework within which environmental considerations and design development can interact. Environmental analysis may indicate ways in which the project can be modified to anticipate possible adverse effects, for example, through the identification of a better practicable environmental option, or by considering alternative processes. To the extent that this

is done, the formal planning approval stages are likely to be smoother.
(Department of the Environment, 1989, p. 3).

This positive approach to the value of EA reflects the earlier findings of the House of Lords (1981) who observed that substantial benefits could be gained by developers who utilised EA as part of project design and development, for example, through the avoidance of costly modifications to plant once operational or by reducing delays in gaining approval for a project. British Gas, for example, claimed it had saved £30 million over a ten-year period, mainly because it had achieved quicker authorisation of projects.

The system introduced by the Department of the Environment conforms to the requirements of the EC directive. The directive and the UK regulations (Department of the Environment, 1988) classify projects into two major groups: Schedule 1 (or Annex I) projects for which an EA is required in every case, and Schedule 2 (or Annex II) projects for which an EA is required only if the particular project is likely to give rise to significant environmental effects. The activities classified under Schedule 1 are shown in Box 6.1.

Box 6.1 *Schedule 1 projects*

1. Crude-oil refineries and installations for the gasification and liquefaction of 500 tonnes or more of coal or bituminous shale per day.
2. Thermal power stations or other combustion installations with a heat output of 300 megawatts or more and nuclear power stations or other nuclear reactors.
3. Installations for the storage or final disposal of radioactive waste.
4. Major iron and steel works.
5. Installations for the extraction of asbestos or for the processing of asbestos or products containing asbestos.
6. Integrated chemical installations.
7. Construction of motorways, major roads, long-distance railways and airports.
8. Trading ports and inland waterways which permit the passage of vessels of over 1,350 tonnes.
9. Installations for the disposal of toxic and dangerous waste.

In the case of Schedule 2 projects an EA is required if the project is considered to be likely to give rise to significant environmental effects. The assessment of significance is a crucial matter and it is difficult to define precise screening criteria in order to determine if an EA is required. In general terms three criteria are used to determine significance:

1. Is the project of more than local significance, principally in terms of its physical scale?

2. Is the project located in a particularly sensitive location, such as a national park?
3. Is the project likely to give rise to particularly complex or adverse effects, for example, will it discharge pollutants?

The projects specified in Schedule 2 (see Box 6.2) can be tested by reference to a number of quantified thresholds. For example, a sand and gravel working of more than 50 hectares may require an EA, as will a new manufacturing plant requiring a site in the range 20–30 hectares or above. A particular problem in practice is how to judge the cumulative impact of a number of projects, each of which is just below the threshold size, that are located adjacent to one another.

Box 6.2 *Schedule 2 projects*

1. Major agricultural projects.
2. Extractive industry – peat, deep drilling, coal mining, petroleum, natural gas, ores, bituminous shale, open-cast mining, surface installations, coke ovens, cement works.
3. Energy industry – except those in Schedule 1.
4. Processing of metals – except those in Schedule 1.
5. Glass making.
6. Chemical industry – except those in Schedule 1.
7. Food industry.
8. Textile, leather, wood and paper industries.
9. Rubber industry.
10. Infrastructure projects – except those in Schedule 1.
11. Other major projects.
12. Modifications to Schedule 1 projects.
13. Developments within a description mentioned in Schedule 1, where they are for the development and testing of methods or products for no more than one year.

In the case of a project that is subject to EA the developer must collect and present certain information about the impact of the project in the form of an environmental statement (ES). The information to be provided in the ES includes a description of the project and the major effects upon the environment, including noise, vibration, emissions of pollutants and the production of residues. In addition, the developer is required to indicate the aspects of the environment that will be significantly affected by the project, including: the human population, fauna, flora, soil, water, the climate, the built environment, landscape and the inter-relationship among these factors. Further information is required on measures to prevent and reduce any adverse effects upon the environment. The developer is obliged to provide a non-technical summary of the above information. These conditions place a major responsibility upon the developer, especially in relation to the need to provide the information in a form which is easily understood by decision-makers.

The procedure for preparing an EA is complex and has been outlined by Wood and Jones (1991, p. 2) as consisting of the following steps:

(i)   Determining the need for EA in a particular case.
(ii) Determining the coverage of the EA.
(iii) Preparing the ES.
(v)   Consultation and participation.
(vi) Synthesising the findings from consultation and reaching a decision.
(vii) Monitoring the impacts of a project if it is implemented.

The major output of the process of EA is an ES. This is prepared by the developer and submitted to the competent authority (in the UK this is the local planning authority). Whilst the preparation of the ES is the responsibility of the developer, there are sound reasons why a developer (or a developer's agent) should consult with the local authority at the outset. As the Department of the Environment (1989) indicates, local authorities can offer advice and provide baseline information which may assist in the definition of the project or the choice of site, and this may help to minimise any delays caused by the EA process.

Key issues worthy of particular consideration in the preparation of an ES include

1. the determination of the scope of an assessment; formal guidance as to scope and content is available, but additional special or local factors also occur;
2. the consideration of the need to investigate alternative ways of proceeding with the project and alternative sites for the project;
3. the range of consultations (above and beyond the statutory consultations) which need to be undertaken; and
4. the range of techniques and methods to be employed in preparing the ES.

Given the additional time required to consider and determine an application for a project that requires the preparation of an EA, the period allowed to a UK local planning authority to determine an application is extended from the normal 8 weeks to 16 weeks. In practice this formal period of time may prove to be insufficient, especially if the local authority has not been involved at the outset in determining the specification for an EA.

Preparing an environmental assessment

The procedure for preparing an environmental assessment (EA) was introduced above. However, this presented a simplified version of the methodology which inevitably requires further expansion. In particular, as already indicated, there are many methodologies and procedures available for use by an environmental assessor. Most methodologies make use of an impact matrix that seeks to relate the characteristics of an action or project to the relevant features of the local environment. A typical environmental impact matrix is illustrated in Figure 6.2.

	Dam Construction	River Control	Road Building	Water Emission	Atmospheric Emission	Noise
Soils						
Land Form						
Water Quality						
Air Quality						
Temperature						

Actions Resulting From the Project

Features of the Environment

In each cell of the matrix an interaction can be recorded. The importance and scale of the impact can be indicated, as can the beneficial or adverse nature of the impact.

Figure 6.2   An environmental impact assessment matrix

As is demonstrated in Figure 6.2, the impact matrix can be used to record either a beneficial or an adverse impact. In a simple recording matrix this may be indicated by a plus or a minus sign. It is also possible to record the severity of the impact; is the interaction between the project and the local environment likely to bring about serious and lasting change? As some features of a local environment are of greater significance and value than others, the importance of any interaction can also be noted. Overall, the benefit of using a matrix to record environmental impacts is that it allows for the pattern of interaction to be clearly demonstrated and readily appreciated, especially by a lay audience.

Preparing an environmental assessment is not, however, simply a matter of determining the incidence and importance of any inter-relationships that exist between the features of a local environment and the characteristics of a proposed project. There are a number of other important steps in the preparation of an EA; these are intended to ensure that the actual process of assessment complies with the requirements of the legislation, and to allow for the assessment to be focused on the most important impacts. The procedure commences with the determination of the need for an EA and is followed by the definition of the scope of the assessment, the specification of the characteristics of the project and the identification of the features of the local environment that require consideration. Other important features of the procedure include the need to make provision for public participation, the methods employed for the actual assessment of impacts, and the desirability of considering alternatives to a proposed project. The production of the final ES is followed by a process of decision-making which may approve the proposed project, suggest modifications to the proposed project, or reject it. This procedure is illustrated in Figure 6.3

This outline of procedure describes the overall approach to the use of EIA and attempts to demonstrate, in a general manner, the various stages that are involved in constructing and applying EIA. The specific procedure for EA that is used in the UK is described in detail in the Department of the Environment's *Guide to the Procedures* (Department of the Environment, 1989). More detailed information on the methods available for conducting an EIA is available from a number of specialist texts (for example, Wathern, 1988).

EA in practice in the UK

A major review of the operation of the EA system in the UK has been conducted by Manchester University on behalf of the Department of the Environment (Wood and Jones, 1991). This review examined all known environmental statements submitted between 15 July 1988 and the end of 1989. In addition, it surveyed 24 local authorities who had not received an ES, and it looked in more detail at a number of cases where an ES had been submitted.

The Manchester research team experienced some difficulty in identifying the precise number of statements which had been submitted. The Department of the Environment notifies the *Journal of Planning and Environment Law (JPEL)* on a regular basis of the number of ESs submitted. During the review period some 138 ESs were referred to *JPEL*; one was later excluded. The Manchester team also established the existence of 16 other ESs, bringing the total recorded to 153. Of these, 121 ESs were submitted to English authorities, 13 were submitted in Wales and 19 were in Scotland. Some 13 per cent of ESs were associated with Schedule 1 projects and 87 per cent with Schedule 2 projects.

In total, 107 ESs were submitted to district councils (70 per cent), some 39 (25 per cent) to county or regional authorities, 6 (4 per cent) to urban development corporations and 1 to a national park authority. Voluntary submission occurred in 89 per cent of cases. In 9 per cent of cases an ES was submitted in response to an opinion, and in 2 per cent of cases following a directive from the competent central government department. Some 36 per

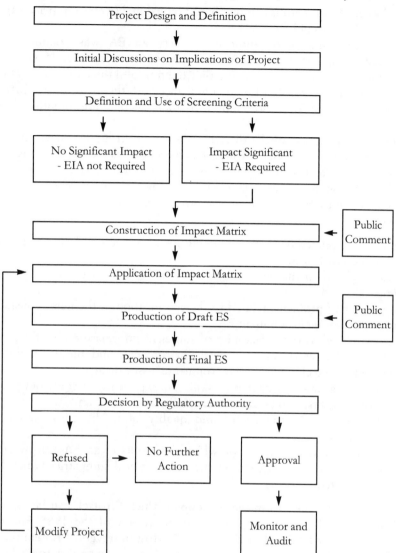

Figure 6.3 An environmental impact assessment procedure

cent of developers were large companies, 54 per cent small companies and 10 per cent local authorities. In 73 per cent of cases consultants were employed to prepare the ES. Some 32 per cent of ESs were prepared for projects located in urban areas, and 25 per cent of projects were located in areas, such as national parks, that are subject to specific forms of environmental regulation and protection.

Of the cases which had been decided at the time of the publication of the

Manchester report, permission had been granted in 22 cases (56 per cent) and refused in 17 cases (44 per cent).

In the case studies of authorities where an EA was conducted, the Manchester team reviewed the ESs. Of the 24 cases reviewed, 15 were considered to be unsatisfactory because they did not fulfil the requirements of the EA scheme and were not in broad compliance with the EC directive. In 10 of the 24 cases examined, the local authority took less than four months to reach a decision.

The implementation of the directive allows for an initial judgement to be made of the extent to which business has responded to the implications of the introduction of a stricter regime of project development and assessment. A number of concerns have emerged from the review undertaken by the Manchester researchers and from the broader experience of using EA. These include

- difficulties related to the precise definition of projects and their assignment to Schedules 1 or 2;
- issues related to the definition of what is considered to be a significant impact;
- a number of problems related to the specification of the items considered necessary for inclusion in an EA;
- issues related to the availability of sufficient information about a project and the characteristics of a local environment, and the availability of methods and techniques for environmental assessment;
- doubts regarding the degree of skill and experience of some developers, and their agents, in relation to their ability to conduct an EA;
- factors related to the extent and quality of public consultation and involvement;
- issues related to the means by which the results of an EA are presented, and the inadequacy of some of the non-technical summaries which have been prepared.

These and other issues form the basis upon which EA itself can be assessed; such matters will figure prominently in the review of the 1985 European directive which will take place during 1994. Most observers of EA expect that the European Commission will press for EA to be extended to include a capacity for strategic environmental assessment (SEA).

Strategic environmental assessment

Project or product-related EIA or EA is seen by some observers as only the tip of the iceberg of environmental assessment (Glasson, 1994). Although the application of EIA is a good example of the use of the precautionary principle, that prevention is better than cure, many problematical projects would not have been developed to the state at which they require an EIA if the policy, upon which they are based, had been assessed for its environmental impact at the outset. In addition, as well as the conventional coverage of EIA, a case has been made for the inclusion of socioeconomic impacts within EIA. These two additional dimensions, strategic assessment and the widening of the scope of EIA, are likely to figure as major issues in the future development of environmental assessment.

Strategic environmental assessment has been described by Therivel *et al.* (1992) as the application of EIA to policies, plans and programmes. These higher-level tiers of the policy process were illustrated in Figure 6.1 and the application of the principles of EIA at these levels can be seen as the next step towards prevention rather than cure. There are two approaches to the development of a system of SEA: the refinement of project EIA and the trickling down of the objective of sustainability (*ibid.*). The former approach, whilst possessing the merit of extending the use of already known and familiar methods and procedures, suffers from a number of drawbacks. These include the inherently responsive nature of project-based EIA – it reacts to proposals rather than initiating them – and this limits the extent to which project-based EIA can satisfy all the objectives of sustainability. Difficulties are also experienced in project EIA when it is faced with having to assess the cumulative impacts of more than one project. Problems also arise with the need to assess alternatives to a specified project. Equally, it is difficult for conventional EIA to consider measures for the mitigation of impacts; to deal with difficult projects rapidly or within a tight timescale; and to incorporate fully the requirement for public participation (*ibid.*). Whilst these weaknesses are not, in themselves, incapable of rectification through revisions to present methods and procedures, they could prove to inhibit the development and introduction of SEA.

A more satisfactory basis for the development and introduction of SEA is offered by using the generic principles of sustainability as a starting point. By using such an approach, which first defines the objectives for the achievement of sustainability, the principles of sustainability can be trickled down through policies, programmes and plans. A first step, at the level of the individual plan, towards the introduction of SEA has been taken in the revised guidance published by the Department of the Environment on the structure and content of development plans (Department of the Environment, 1992b). This guidance requires plans to take environmental considerations into account.

Over the next decade it is likely that, at both European level and in the UK, SEA will become an established feature of the policy landscape. As such, it will prove essential for the environmentally aware business to assess its policies for their environmental sustainability and to ensure that the principles of sustainability trickle down into all aspects of operational programming and business planning.

The translation of these objectives into reality is likely to involve a number of elements:

• A commitment to sustainability and its interpretation in relation to an individual activity.

- The definition of the parameters for the achievement of sustainability.
- The definition of the carrying capacity of an environment within which an activity occurs.
- The preparation of an SEA for all policies, programmes and plans that will have an effect on the environment.
- The assessment of individual projects (or products) within the constraints set by SEA.
- The introduction of monitoring and auditing to trace the consequences of a project (Therival *et al.*, 1992).

The introduction of a requirement for regular monitoring and auditing provides a feedback loop that can be used to inform the future policy process. A knowledge of the impact of past actions can allow for the avoidance of future mistakes. The following section considers how a capacity for monitoring and auditing can be introduced into business procedures.

Environmental auditing

As was noted earlier in this chapter, environmental auditing can be viewed as the intracompany dimension of the linked processes of environmental assessment and auditing. It is chiefly concerned with the regular monitoring and evaluation of the environmental performance of a business.

Environmental auditing is now well established as good business practice. There are many approaches to auditing, but they share a common concern to ensure that a systematic, documented, periodic and objective evaluation is conducted of how well an organisation's systems are performing in relation to the environment when assessed against internal objectives and procedures, and the need to comply with statutory requirements. The point made earlier, that environmental auditing in its broadest sense is not a statutory requirement, needs to be qualified by reference to those aspects of a company's operations, for example, in relation to health and safety matters in the work environment, that are regulated through legislation.

An approach to environmental auditing

It is interesting to note that many companies have sought a form of statutory validation for their audits, initially through extending the coverage of the British Standard on total quality management and more recently through meeting the requirements of the new BS 7750 for *Environmental Management Systems* (British Standards Institution, 1991).

The component parts of a typical environmental audit are as follows:

1. Defining the objectives of the audit – what is required from the audit?
2. Setting the scope and span of the audit – will it relate to the entire company, to a division or to an individual aspect of the company's operation?
3. Defining the baseline – identify the major production activities carried

out by a company (and possibly on behalf of it), the range of supporting activities, the key aspects of the legislation and the broader environmental context within which a company operates.

4. Agreeing on the action to be taken following the completion of the audit – it is important to understand the implications of conducting an audit and to determine what limits, if any, will be placed on its implementation.

5. Selecting the audit team – insiders and outsiders – ensuring that the team has knowledge of, or access to, all aspects of a company's activities and that the workforce knows the reason for conducting the audit.

6. Gathering information and evidence in relation to prespecified requirements and the means of assessment – this will require substantial assistance from staff. This procedure will look at many aspects of the operation of a company including

   - the overall environmental policy of a company;
   - production issues – raw materials, sources of materials, production processes, products and packaging;
   - staff awareness, training and recruitment;
   - energy use;
   - water use;
   - waste disposal and recycling;
   - discharges;
   - the transport of goods and people;
   - accident and emergency procedures; and
   - the adequacy of management and technical control systems.

7. Assessing the performance of all aspects of a company's operations in relation to the objectives of policy and specified targets.

8. Evaluating the audit findings – this is likely to employ many different techniques and procedures, but a non-technical summary is essential.

9. Reporting the findings – there is likely to be a need for interim reports (to individual units) for clarification and further work, and a final report; again a non-technical summary is essential.

10. Developing an action plan – this might, for example, classify outputs and possible actions into:

   - major changes required   at low cost, and
                              at high cost
   - minor changes required   at low cost, and
                              at high cost

At this stage it is important to re-examine company policy and to redefine the objectives and targets of policy. It is also important to look at the time spans required for successful implementation and the need to gain approval and help from regulatory agencies, other companies and advisers.

11. Monitoring is vital; there is a clear need to follow up the action plan and to assess the changing operational features of a company, the industry generally and the scope of environmental regulation.

An outline procedure for conducting an audit is illustrated in Figure 6.4.

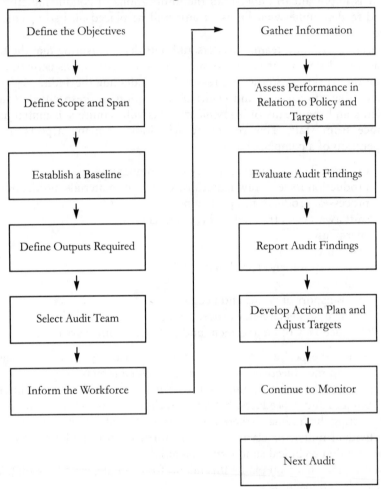

Figure 6.4   Procedure for an environmental audit

The role of environmental auditing

Environmental auditing is now well established, and many companies have undertaken an audit as part of their regular review of company strategy. Other organisations have widened the scope of a statutory COSHH (control of substances hazardous to health) audit to include environmental auditing, or have extended existing procedures that were initially designed to monitor and audit total quality management.

Although not a statutory requirement in itself, environmental auditing is now seen as playing an essential role in the sustainable management of a business. Governments, the International Chamber of Commerce, the CBI and other business organisations consider auditing to be a normal and highly desirable central aspect of corporate strategy. In his introduction to the CBI guidance on environmental auditing, Sir Brian Corby, the CBI President, noted that

> Companies must not wait for restrictive legislation to bring about change. Whilst many companies have a good record, there is a gap between what a business could do to reduce its impact on the environment and what it actually does, which could be closed with better information and instruction.
>
> (CBI, 1990, p. 3)

Environmental auditing is increasingly seen as an essential element in achieving total quality. Welford (1992a) has argued that the concept of total quality management implies the elimination of any negative impacts on the environment. He also suggests that the main elements of a system of environmental management and auditing are

- *team work* – the workforce needs to be involved in any system of auditing;
- *commitment* – a company-wide commitment is essential from the chief executive down;
- *communications* – essential in order to ensure that accurate information is available and that feedback flows throughout a company;
- *organisation* – clear channels of responsibility and reporting need to be established;
- *control and monitoring* – the existence of a system can generate a false sense of security; checks and inspections are vital elements in ensuring compliance;
- *planning* – processes need to be well planned and implemented in order to monitor, record and adjust processes; and
- *inventory control system* – this is essential both in order to minimise costs and to ensure that materials and energy costs are reduced.

Audits for specific purposes

In Chapter 5 one of the many forms of environmental audit was discussed: the initial environmental review. The review was presented as a one-off exercise, conducted in order to allow a company to establish a baseline from which an environmental policy may be established or elaborated. The full environmental audit, which has been illustrated above, can be viewed as a general-purpose approach to auditing that is applicable to most business situations.

However, many companies have also discovered that an audit is required for a particular purpose, or to assess a specific aspect of operation. Owen (1993) has illustrated the need for such audits by reference to the range of procedures used by British Petroleum. The different forms of audits used by BP include

- *compliance audits* – these are designed to allow a company to check its performance in relation both to statutory requirements, and to voluntary codes and internal standards;
- *site audits* – spot checks may be required at individual sites, including sites to be acquired;
- *activity audits* – in some cases it is important to examine activities that cross the boundaries between activities within a business;
- *corporate audits* – a full audit of an entire business sector;
- *associate audits* – examining the activities of companies associated with the business; and
- *issues audits* – these concentrate on specific issues or topics such as energy use or the consumption of scarce raw materials.

The use of specific forms of audit is growing rapidly. One of the clearest examples is found in relation to the acquisition of companies, or of sites and premises. Given the potentially expensive and time-consuming problems that are associated with having to clean up a business operation or site that fails to comply with statutory or other regulations, many companies now seek assurance through an environmental audit that the prospective new acquisition does not harbour unknown environmental problems.

Legal practices, consulting engineers and management specialists offer a range of auditing services that are designed to provide a client with the assurance that a potential acquisition is free of any major environmental problems. The services offered by such organisations range from searches and inspections of public registers in order to identify land which may be contaminated to a full assessment of the environmental implications of the activities of a company.

Environmental auditing schemes

Two main schemes for environmental auditing have been introduced in recent years: the European Eco-Management and Audit Scheme and the British Standard 7750 on environmental management systems. Although the two schemes differ in terms of their details of approach, they are, in Welford's (1992b, p. 26) view, 'completely compatible and it is up to firms which scheme to choose although there is no reason why both cannot be simultaneously adhered to'.

The European Union scheme was introduced in the form of a council regulation on 29 June 1993. The scheme has the following objectives:

1. The establishment and implementation of environmental policies, programmes and management systems by companies, in relation to their sites.

2. The systematic, objective and periodic evaluation of the performance of such elements.
3. The provision of information on environmental performance to the public.

Key elements in the scheme include the definition of an environmental policy, the setting of targets for achievement within a given time, the provision of plans and systems to achieve the targets, the auditing of progress made, the reporting of the results of an audit, and the setting of new targets for the next time period (*ibid.*).

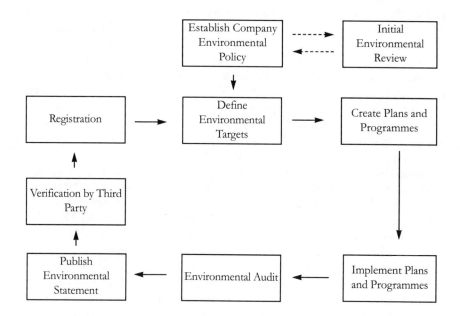

Figure 6.5   European Eco-Management and Audit Scheme

Within the cycle of auditing, illustrated in Figure 6.5, particular attention should be paid to the following environmental effects:

- Controlled and uncontrolled emissions to the atmosphere.
- Controlled and uncontrolled emissions to water or sewers.
- Solid and other wastes, particularly hazardous wastes.
- Contamination of land.
- Use of land, fuels and energy, and other natural resources.
- Discharge of thermal energy, noise, odour, dust, vibration and visual impact.
- Effects on specific parts of the environment and ecosystems.

The effects of a company's activity upon the environment can, in Tanega's (1994) view, be seen to imply that certain decisions should be taken in response to specific environmental issues:

- *Critical* – threatening loss of life, property, environmental catastrophe or the production of hazardous waste.
- *Major* – tending to make environmental objectives fail.
- *Minor* – falling short of an intended function but not necessarily causing a failure of an environmental objective.
- *Incidental* – having no unsatisfactory effect.

An important element in the European scheme is the role played by an accredited environmental verifier. The role of the verifier is to confirm that all stages in the scheme have been complied with and that the information presented in the audit report is accurate. The verifier should be involved in all stages of the audit and can also be used as a source of additional information.

The Eco-Management and Audit Scheme is applicable to both public and private organisations. A guide to the scheme for local government has been prepared by CAG Consultants (1993). The local government scheme provides a useful context for the development of an approach to auditing at local level, and it can be used to guide local economic development procedures. As such, it is of relevance to small and medium enterprises who are members of a local environmental business club or forum.

British Standard 7750 was introduced in 1992 with the intention of enabling an organisation 'to establish procedures to set an environmental policy and objectives, achieve compliance with them, and demonstrate such compliance to others' (British Standards Institution, 1992, p. 3). The scheme shares many of the features and characteristics of the European scheme.

The British Standard requires the establishment of a baseline of company environmental policy through the preparation of an initial environmental review, the assessment and recording of the environmental effects of an organisation's activities and the regular audit of policy and operations. Auditing is at the heart of the environmental management system suggested by BS 7750 in order to 'assess the compliance of the system with the Standards' requirements' and to ensure that management activities and procedures 'meet those requirements' (Gilbert, 1993, p. 50). The British Standard system is illustrated in Figure 6.6.

Environmental auditing in the future
As has already been discussed in Chapter 5, an environmental audit is a vital element in the development of a capability to assess the impact of a company's operations upon the environment. It is likely that commercial and legal pressures to adopt environmental auditing will become more intense and, as a consequence, companies will have to incorporate methods for the regular auditing of the environmental effects of their activities within their standard operational procedures. In some industries and sectors of the economy it is already clear that companies now regard environmental auditing as a normal and essential part of the portfolio of management methods.

Figure 6.6   BS 7750 environmental management scheme

Gray, Bebbington and Walters (1993) stress two points with regard to the current and future use of environmental audits:

1. It is essential to ensure that terminology is clear and that the objective of auditing is stated in an unambiguous manner.
2. It is vital to treat environmental auditing as a serious matter; an audit by itself is little use, it needs to be matched by a commitment to action and a change in attitudes and behaviour.

An environmental audit provides a means of ensuring that future problems can be avoided. It is a proactive and powerful management tool, and it implies the need for an evolutionary approach to be adopted to the continuous raising of the environmental performance of a company. In the view of one observer, environmental audits, and the management systems of which they are an essential component, 'cannot be seen simply as a competitive edge, they will in time become a means of survival' (Welford, 1992b, p. 26).

Environmental information systems

In the introduction to this chapter it was noted that it is important to identify or establish sources of information and knowledge upon which systems and procedures for environmental assessment and auditing can be based. Whilst systems of assessment and auditing generate substantial quantities of information that can be used in subsequent exercises, the initial starting point in any system will be to assemble the necessary data. Having established a system it is equally important that the database is kept up to date.

A substantial part of the information required in order to conduct an environmental audit and assessment is likely to be available from the internal records of an organisation. However, it is likely that much of this information will be dispersed throughout the organisation and it is unlikely to be available in a readily usable form. In the case of the development of a specific project (or new plant) the parameters and characteristics of the project (or plant) will be known and this information can be used to develop a project (or plant) specification report. The information contained in such a report can be used to inform and calibrate the horizontal axis of an environmental impact assessment (as shown in Figure 6.2), or to specify the operational characteristics of a company, or part of a company, that will be the subject of an environmental audit.

An important task is to ensure that any information that is collected and held in a database is available in a form that is compatible with external sources of information. For example, specified international units of measurement should be adopted if possible and efforts should be made to convert historic data to current units of measurement.

In constructing an environmental information system, it is equally important to be aware of the availability of the major sources of information that are held by external organisations, such as government departments, local authorities, regulatory agencies, nature conservation bodies, local amenity groups, business organisations and research organisations including universities and commercial research bodies. An overview of the information that is available from such sources can be obtained from publications such as the Department of the Environment's *The UK Environment* (Department of the Environment, 1992a) and the *European Environmental Statistics Handbook* (Newman and Foster, 1993).

It has been noted that any information system should be organised in a manner that is compatible with similar systems that are used by other organisations. A basic element of organisation is the use of a spatial or geographic method of data referencing. A geographical information system (GIS) relates individual items of information to a specific set of spatial co-ordinates, allowing information to be mapped and manipulated in a way that allows for the environmental effects of an activity, or proposed activity, to be presented or simulated. Modern GIS methods allow data to be collected, analysed and compared over time and between places. Many GIS data and information systems are based upon the pooling of information that is held by various organisations present in a locality. This common user approach implies that individual organisations have to accept a degree of disclosure of information in exchange for access to other information that they may require. A pooling arrangement also implies the need to harmonise the methods used to collect data, the units of measurements utilised, and the formats employed for the recording of data.

The major elements of an environmental information system are illustrated in Figure 6.7. As can be seen from this figure, the major component parts of a system are

- information internal to an organisation;
- published external sources of information;
- unpublished external sources; and
- sources derived from legislation and regulation.

An organisation's individual information system may be linked to other systems or may be freestanding. A more comprehensive business environmental information system has been developed by the International Institute for Sustainable Development (1992).

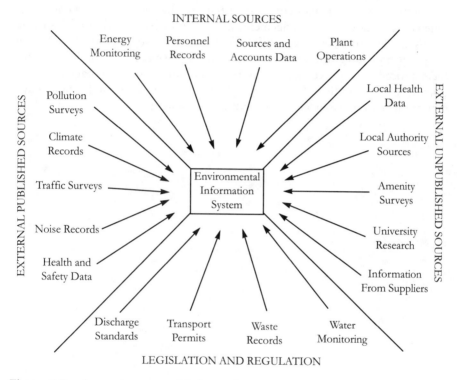

Figure 6.7 An environmental information system

Conclusions

In this chapter attention has been focused on procedures and methods that allow for the assessment and auditing of the environmental standards and performance of business and other organisations. Such procedures and methods provide an organisation with a capacity to understand the way in which it operates, the effects of its operations upon the environment and the alternative ways in which it can respond to any undesirable consequences.

By adopting EIA or environmental auditing an organisation can better understand its ability to bring about change and it can develop a proactive capacity that will allow it to avoid any undesirable environmental effects in future. These methods and procedures have, until now, been mainly applied to specific projects, or to the operation of particular items of plant and equipment. However, it is likely that they will become commonplace in the future. Increasingly, companies and public bodies are applying the principles of environmental assessment and auditing to the development of their policies, programmes and plans. The adoption of strategic environmental assessment and auditing aims to avoid the emergence, in the future, of projects, products and processes that are environmentally unsustainable.

Prevention is better than cure. Organisations that wish to avoid costly and time-consuming errors of judgement, and the possible rejection of their proposals on environmental grounds, would be well advised to consider the adoption and integration of environmental assessment and auditing within their procedures for corporate strategy and operational management. An essential element in the adoption of such an approach is the establishment and maintenance of an environmental information system.

7

Environmental strategies, systems and operational practices

Having outlined the origins and characteristics of environmental problems in the first part of this book, and having identified and assessed the major environmental issues associated with economic and business activities in the second part, in this and the following two chapters attention is focused on organisational matters and the development potential of environmentally sustainable business. This chapter concentrates upon matters related to the development of a corporate environmental strategy and associated management systems and procedures. Chapter 8 examines the potential for the development of green business opportunities and businesses, while Chapter 9 considers the role of business in the development of environmentally sustainable local and regional economies.

This chapter covers a wide span of material: the construction of a corporate strategy; the role and key features of an environmental management system as a mechanism for implementing strategy; human resource management issues including environmental training; and a number of operational issues related to purchasing, marketing and other business activities. The intention of the chapter is to provide an overview of how an environmentally sustainable business organisation may be developed and managed; further information on all the topics covered in this chapter is available in the texts that are cited as references. Although the coverage provided in this chapter of the range of internal management issues is somewhat brief by comparison with other texts, it is the aim of this chapter to introduce a range of topics rather than to duplicate material covered elsewhere in the existing literature. Indeed, the role of this chapter is to provide a foundation for the discussion of business development in Chapter 8, and of local and regional development in Chapter 9.

Within this chapter emphasis is placed upon the desirability of constructing and implementing environmental strategies and systems that satisfy the internal requirements of an individual company and also contribute to the ability of an individual sector of industry to achieve the broader objective of environmentally sustainable economic development. A similar role may be performed by strategy through identifying the role of an individual company in supporting a local or regional programme of environmental improvement. This somewhat broader than normal interpretation of the role of environmental strategies and systems is especially important for small and medium enterprises. Many small companies lack the in-house expertise and the resource base of larger, especially multinational, companies and as a consequence they may have to rely upon other organisations in the same sector or locality to provide a source of expertise and experience in the field of environmental management. The primary role of an environmental business forum or club is to act as an information exchange and as a broker in the transfer of environmental knowledge and experience between companies in a local or regional area. Industry and professional associations perform a similar function within particular industrial sectors.

In constructing and implementing strategies and systems that are aimed at enhancing the environmental performance of business, it is important to recognise and acknowledge that it is unlikely that a company will be able to change its business practices or mode of operation overnight. Most changes will be incremental and will be built upon established practices and procedures; indeed in many instances this gradual approach is preferable to a wholesale change and is likely to result in a more lasting improvement. As was stated earlier in this book, rapid changes, or quick fixes, frequently lack substance and, in addition, they run the risk of provoking a response that is inappropriate to the needs of a company and to the requirements of the area in which a company is located. However, this cautionary note should not be regarded as a reason for inaction or for delaying a change in company policy and procedure in the hope that a miracle technology will materialise that will allow a company to continue to operate its business as usual. Business as usual is no longer an option that is open to a company, whilst end-of-pipe technologies often prove to be an inadequate answer to pressing environmental problems and may generate as many problems as they solve. The alternative is to move to a proactive mode of business strategy and operation that places emphasis upon the need to respect the environment.

Corporate strategies for the environement

Irrespective of the sector of the economy in which a business operates, it is unlikely that an activity will be either totally environmentally sustainable, or unable to improve further its environmental performance. A corporate strategy for the environment is an essential prerequisite for the improvement of environmental performance.

The standard model of environmental regulation assigns a passive role to business (Barrett, 1992). In this model it is assumed that business responds to changes in regulation. However, business can both help to shape regulation and, more importantly, it can use corporate strategy to anticipate legislation and thereby gain a competitive advantage in a current or future market-place where environmental concerns will be given greater weight than in the past.

The construction of a corporate strategy that gives prominence to environmental concerns is little different, with one important exception, from standard methods of strategy formulation. The exception to the general model is the weight given to the ecological environment relative to the competitive environment. Smith (1992, p. 7) has argued that the biggest hurdle to overcome in resolving the competitive and ecological tensions within strategy is 'the search for a short-term solution and the requirement for an almost immediate financial payback on investment'.

Key issues in strategy building

This introduces the first issue that has to be resolved in the development of an environmentally orientated business strategy, namely the need to extend the time horizon of a conventional strategy in order to reconcile the environmental and financial objectives of a company. A financially driven corporate strategy almost inevitably tends to emphasise the need to minimise the payback period on an investment. However, whilst this may be satisfactory in a static regulatory climate, it offers little assistance to a company that is seeking to anticipate future environmental pressures and standards. Such a company would wish to avoid being 'locked into obsolete, environmentally malign technology and processes' (Gray, Bebbington and Walters, 1993, p. 155) and would prefer to retain a degree of flexibility in order to be able to respond to future changes.

One method available to solve this dilemma is to introduce environmental screening into the strategy process at the outset and to apply the screening criteria to all subsequent investment decisions. Alcan has introduced such a procedure and requires all capital investment proposals to include an environmental statement; in addition, Alcan makes substantial investments in order to meet current, anticipated and company environmental standards (*ibid.*). As was discussed in Chapter 5, many other companies have developed environmental policies that place emphasis upon the screening of investment and on proactive investment in advance of statutory requirements.

The second issue encountered in constructing a corporate environmental strategy is the need to determine the range of environmental factors that should be taken into account in setting the parameters for current and future action. Almost inevitably this will require the setting of priorities following a review of all the elements of the environment that interact with a company. Some of these interactions will be immediate and direct, such as the consumption of raw materials, energy and water, whilst others will be secondary in nature and will include the inputs used by suppliers and the final end use of products.

A guiding principle in determining the scope of a review of environmental interactions is to start with a broad overview of all possible interactions, and then to focus on the key areas of the environment that are affected by current, and will be influenced by anticipated future, company operations. A multi-level appraisal of the interaction between the operation of a company and the environment should be updated and supplemented at regular intervals in order to ensure compliance with legislation and the best available scientific knowledge.

A third issue to be taken into account in constructing an environmental strategy is the extent to which an individual business establishment can exercise control over its environmental effects. A branch plant of a multi-national enterprise may have little freedom of action to influence its operations because it is required to perform its functions in a manner dictated by the corporate headquarters irrespective of local environmental conditions. This influence from above could prove to be either negative or positive. Greater local autonomy may be required if a particular establishment is to conform with specific national or local legislation, or if it is to perform a positive role in a local environment. In some cases the influence of a foreign parent company can assist by requiring a local establishment to operate at a standard in advance of the relevant national requirements. Sandoz Chemicals (UK) is the UK operating division of a major Swiss company. Following a major environmental incident in 1986, which caused extensive pollution of the Rhine, the company upgraded its environmental policies. These policies are now applied to all Sandoz operations and they require each individual plant to comply with local legislation and, in addition, to operate at the higher level of environmental protection required by the group (see Box 7.1).

The extent to which a company has the ability to take action on certain environmental matters, such as the use of fossil fuels in the generation of electricity or the transport modes used by suppliers, is often extremely limited, especially in the short term, due either to contractual obligations or to the absence of alternatives. Creating a window of opportunity to renegotiate supply contracts, find alternative suppliers and develop new procedures is an important element in the construction of a corporate environmental strategy.

The final major issue to be considered in the construction of a corporate environmental strategy is the extent to which a business organisation is willing or able to alter its own internal culture. Whilst it may be possible to change suppliers, install new plant and equipment, introduce an environmental management system and apply strict environmental criteria in determining all future investments, it is equally vital to ensure that all employees, from the boardroom to the shopfloor, understand the need for, and are committed to, the achievement of the agenda for action that may result from a corporate environmental strategy.

Davis (1991) emphasises the need for a company to match vision with values. By this he implies that a corporate vision is of little relevance unless shared values are inculcated and implemented in all areas of a company's operations. Vision without shared values is unlikely to produce the desired results. Changing the corporate culture through enhanced procedures,

---

Box 7.1 *Sandoz Chemicals: principles for environmental protection*

Sandoz Chemicals (UK) has developed and adopted a number of principles for safety and environmental protection. These principles apply throughout the Sandoz Group. They include the following:

1. Safety in all parts of our works as well as the protection of the surrounding area and the environment are of top priority for Sandoz management.
2. The relevant local legislation is always binding.
3. The Group Department for Safety and Environmental Protection may also lay down additional regulations which go beyond local legislation and which are valid for the entire Group.
4. Questions of safety and environmental protection are to be treated with the same thoroughness and scientific professionalism as are applied to research and development.
5. An activity may be carried out only when a standard of safety for man and the environment, corresponding to the state of the art, can be guaranteed.
6. The responsibility for the application and realization of these principles is borne by all company employees at all levels.
7. Employees should receive the education and training in safety and environmental protection required by their task.
8. The observance of these principles is to be reviewed regularly.

---

training and communications is an essential element in the construction and implementation of strategy.

Developing a corporate strategy

The first stage in developing a corporate strategy is to prepare a 'scoping' report. This will provide an indication of the nature and scale of the tasks to be confronted. This report provides a baseline upon which policy can be constructed and judged. A scoping report may take the form of an initial environmental review (see Chapter 5), but it will also need to be informed by a comprehensive appraisal of the factors external to a company which are of relevance in constructing the strategy. Elkington, Knight and Hailes (1991) have identified five items and questions that should be addressed in a scoping report:

1. Which areas of a company's activities produce, or may produce, unacceptable environmental effects?
2. What actions are underway in order to minimise or prevent these effects?
3. Do these actions meet current legal and other standards?
4. What is the current state of development of the various internal environ-

mental systems and how do such systems compare to those in place in other organisations?

5. What is the likely progress of both internal and external trends which may have an impact on a company's environmental performance?

The answers to these five questions provide the basis for an assessment of the environmental condition of a company, combined with a view of the likely future progress of competitors, legislation and industry-wide standards.

Having determined the current state and environmental condition of its activities, together with a projection of the likely future evolution of the market-place and the regulatory systems within which it operates, a company is in a position to determine how it should construct its corporate environmental strategy. At this point it is possible to identify two possible pathways that can lead towards the formulation of a strategy:

1. A top-down approach which seeks to identify future conditions and attempts to equip the company to work within such conditions; this approach is anticipatory, but is somewhat responsive in relation to particular anticipated future conditions.

2. A bottom-up approach which identifies the areas of strength within a company that comply with current and anticipated future market and legislative requirements, and which seeks to develop these or new areas of strength; this approach is also anticipatory, but it is somewhat inflexible and is incremental in its basic nature.

Both the macrolevel (or top-down) and the microlevel (or bottom-up) approaches possess weaknesses and merits. A strategy that seeks to combine the strengths of the two approaches – a mesolevel approach – is aimed at maximising the current and anticipated future strengths of a company, whilst minimising the risks that are inherent in adopting an incremental approach. This 'minimax' solution to the development of a corporate environmental strategy is in accord with the established principles of strategic planning, relying as it does upon multilevel scanning of key features and events both within and outside an individual company. Ansoff (1987) typifies such a strategy as one which seeks to combine a number of factors in order to establish a preferred strategy; this strategy may encompass both incremental and discontinuous change.

In order to assess the major components needed to create a meso–level strategy, it is necessary to understand the methods used to construct both macrolevel and microlevel strategies. The macro approach places particular emphasis on predicting the development and outcome of events external to a company; this scan of the external horizons can be achieved through the building of scenarios. There are many methods and procedures available to build a scenario of the future; a common feature of many of these methods is an attempt to build a coherent picture of the future, having discarded those elements considered unlikely to materialise or to have an impact on the individual organisation. Godet (1993) has identified three approaches to building a scenario:

1. *Possible scenarios* – everything that can be imagined.
2. *Realisable scenarios* – all that is possible, taking account of constraints.
3. *Desirable scenarios* – those which are possible, but not all necessarily realisable.

These various approaches to building scenarios are all capable of encompassing environmental futures and, irrespective of the approach or method used, the very process of building a scenario will help to identify and illustrate the challenges likely to confront a company in the future. Scenario building can also play an important role in the construction of a microlevel strategy.

Godet (*ibid.*) and many other writers have discussed the merits of constructing a 'desirable' scenario that indicates the situation an organisation wishes to achieve in the future. As long as the desirable scenario is based upon a realistic assessment of the development of environmental trends into the future, it can provide a useful set of targets to which an organisation can aspire. In effect the desirable scenario is planning in reverse; rather than following present trends in an incremental fashion, the organisation can set its objectives and then work backwards towards the present. This reverse pathway can help in the identification of the steps that are required in order to achieve the desired goals; it is also likely to reveal options at various points between the present and future states. Since the overall direction of change is a more important matter than the identification of a direct routeway from the present to the future, such options provide situations of choice and may indicate alternative ways forward.

Scenarios can be of considerable assistance in developing a corporate mission statement and in informing the process of framing and implementing a strategic vision or visions. However, scenarios, missions and strategies should not be superimposed upon an organisation; in Mintzberg's (1994, p. 114) view 'strategy making is not an isolated process', rather it is 'a process interwoven with all that it takes to manage an organization'. Furthermore, Mintzberg argues that strategies, and especially those for the environment, are best left as broad visions, rather than forming the basis for detailed plans. Given the rapid advances that have taken place in recent years in terms of our knowledge of the environment, this is a valuable and well informed view.

The standard process of moving from a scenario to a corporate strategy involves the determination of priorities, the identification of the resources likely to be involved in developing strategic priorities, the definition of an action plan or plans, the communication of choices and policies throughout the organisation and to those in the external world who interact with the organisation, and the implementation of plans. All this should take place within the context of continual scanning of changing conditions in the external environment. In addition, it is vital to ensure that the progress of strategy is monitored, and that the results of monitoring are applied through a process of continuous review. The strategy process is illustrated in Figure 7.1.

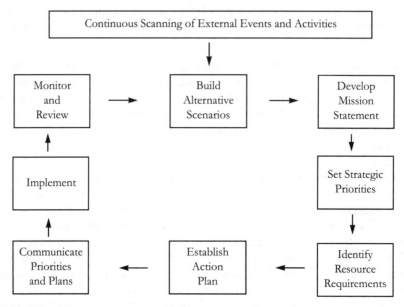

Figure 7.1   The corporate strategy process

Corporate strategies for the environment

A corporate strategy for the environment cannot and should not be constructed separately or in isolation from a conventional corporate strategy. As is the case in many other aspects of business strategy, it is essential to ensure that the environmental dimension is integrated into the overall process of strategic vision and implementation. However, the realisation that environmental concerns are of equal significance to many of the more conventional aspects of a business may necessitate a change in corporate attitudes and behaviour. The emergence and acceptance of new ideas and forms of thinking, such as product stewardship, which implies the adoption of a 'comprehensive ecological view of a product throughout its lifecycle' (Roome, 1992, p.13), suggests that a corporate strategy for the environment is likely to differ from a conventional strategy in a number of ways:

- It implies a commitment by an organisation to a changed set of values.
- It suggests that a long-term view is necessary, especially in relation to the determination of an appropriate payback period in relation to an investment.
- It requires a holistic view to be taken of the costs and benefits that are associated with a variety of operations and actions.

- It involves the introduction of appropriate management systems that are capable of ensuring that environmental objectives and priorities are implemented and met.

In addition, a corporate environmental strategy needs to consider the response of the organisation to a number of important environmental issues and questions. Although the responses to these questions may not result in an immediate change in current corporate policy, there is a likelihood that changes will occur in terms of detail and in methods of implementation and management. The International Institute for Sustainable Development (1992) has suggested a number of key issues that a company should address in developing its strategy for the environment. These include the following:

- *Accountability* – the sustainable enterprise should recognise the full scope of its accountability, both internally and externally.
- *Financial capacity* – an environmental strategy should be affordable and opportunities to obtain financial benefits from the adoption of enhanced environmental practices should be identified.
- *Customer pressure* – the requirements of customers and final consumers should be identified and the demand for more environmentally acceptable goods and services should inform the strategy.
- *Competitive opportunities* – it is important to identify the competitive advantages that can be obtained from the adoption of enhanced environmental attitudes and values.
- *Public policy* – rising environmental standards should be monitored and appreciated in the forward planning of production methods and products.
- *Strategic self-interest* – companies that currently rely upon scarce natural resources, such as tropical hardwoods, will have to consider the future availability of supply and their own survival.
- *Management awareness* – few managers are well equipped to understand and manage environmental issues and this situation requires attention and the development of awareness and training programmes.

These and other issues will need to be confronted and acted upon if a 'transformation strategy for sustainable development' (Davis, 1991, p. 28) is to be developed and implemented. The key to a successful corporate environmental strategy is likely to be the acceptance of the need for change and the adoption of the principle of stewardship in relation to all aspects of a corporate behaviour. Such a change in stance requires, in Davis' (*ibid.*, p. 29) view, an adjustment to be made 'in the shared values and in the vision of most commercial enterprises'.

The approach to corporate strategy implied by the adoption of changed values is one that recognises environmentalism as a 'major new transformative force facing corporations' (Shrivastava, 1992b, p. 19) and it is a force that cannot be ignored. Environmentally sensitive companies will need to change their products, and their methods of production and operation in order to meet the challenges which are now gaining force. The corporate strategy provides an entry point to this approach, but it needs to be matched by systems of management that will allow new priorities and aspirations to be realised.

Environmental management systems

Chapter 6 introduced the basic approach and structure adopted by the European Eco-Management and Audit Scheme (Figure 6.5) and the British Standard on environmental management systems (Figure 6.6). Both schemes offer an approach to the environmental auditing of an organisation's activities that is set within the context of a broader system of environmental management. Whilst the schemes can be viewed as offering a basic approach to the creation of a method of auditing, the real value of any auditing system is only likely to be realised if the overall philosophy that is implied by an environmental management system is adopted. This broader approach to the use of environmental management systems forms the substance of this section of the chapter.

The systems of environmental management that are represented by the two schemes share a number of common origins and objectives. Both the schemes demonstrate a concern with the creation of a capability within companies that is intended to allow them to become proactive with regard to environmental matters. Additionally both schemes advocate an approach that allows for environmental targets to be set and for these targets to be tested on a regular basis against the performance of the company in relation to all aspects of its organisation and operation.

These common features extend further to include a shared view of the value of setting down specified policies, processes and procedures with regard to environmental issues and to those activities that impact upon the environment; the need to develop a method of recording and registering environmental targets, incidents and the results of monitoring; and the desirability of establishing a regular, open and widely available method for reporting the outputs of the system.

In addition to these general features, there are two other common matters which deserve particular attention. The first concerns the likelihood, especially in the case of small companies, that a system of environmental management will be grafted on to a pre-existing system for total quality or general management. The second issue relates to the importance of ensuring that the existence of an environmental management system does not lead to complacency; over-reliance upon the ability of a system to solve problems can create conditions under which operational failure can occur without any warning.

The features of environmental management systems
Most organisations possess a number of long-established procedures for

managing a wide range of operations and activities, including those that interact with the environment. However, in many organisations it is likely that some of these separate systems are inadequate, out of date or they fail to inter-relate to each other. The aim of developing and implementing an environ-mental management system is to bring together these separate or disparate elements of existing policy and procedure and, through the addition of new areas of competence, to create an integrated system that encompasses the entire span of responsibilities, operations and individual roles in a company. Gilbert (1993, p. 9) has put the case for developing an integrated approach of this nature in the following manner:

> How do you currently manage sales, purchasing, expenses, tax law, personnel, product design and performance? You do not leave these to chance, you would not survive in business if you did. So you take control, you define the requirements and put a system in place to meet them. There is nothing new, therefore, in extending a management system like this, to address the environmental issue.

The most important feature of an environmental management system is its circular and all-embracing form. As has been illustrated in Figures 6.5 and 6.6, environmental auditing is a key element within an environmental man-agement system, and the requirements of the audit demand a high degree of regularity and consistency of operation over time. Whilst it is not essential to operate the major auditing and assessment element of an environmental man-agement system on an annual basis, an audit which is less frequent is likely to run the risk of failing to identify and evaluate the implications of any potential or actual difficulties. Indeed, an efficient and effective environmental management system should possess the ability to recognise a problem at the time of its initial occurrence or, in the case of more sophisticated systems, prior to its occurrence. A further reason for suggesting that the major auditing and assessment element of an environmental management system should operate on an annual cycle is the desirability of meshing the environmental management system with the other annual review and auditing procedures that exist in most organisations. By using a common timetable for all its review and auditing procedures, a company will be able to compare the relative performance of the full range of activities within its portfolio. This meshing together of the various management systems allows for the identifica-tion of actual or potential areas of interaction between the operational units of a company, and for the design and implementation of new policies that seek to maximise the positive elements of such interactions. For example, a particular weakness or failure in environmental performance or procedure may require investment in new equipment and the provision of additional training; the environmental management system will need to interact with both the purchasing and the training systems in order to ensure a satisfactory outcome, and these needs should be reflected in the annual budget cycle.

An important feature of an environmental management system is that it cuts across traditional areas of responsibility, function and departmental organisation. Greeno and Robinson (1992) argue that the traditional approach to resolving a problem, which is normally undertaken within an individual department or a particular facility, is an unsuitable model for the resolution of environmental difficulties. This is because many environmental problems have their origin elsewhere in an organisation or, in some cases, such problems may reflect a deep-seated weakness in the overall structure of a company. Although an end-of-pipe solution may resolve an individual immediate problem, little is to be gained by adding a further series of *ad hoc* solutions when what is really required is a total redesign of production strategy.

It is possible to identify three basic approaches to the development of an environmental management system: rethink, redesign and incremental improvement (*ibid.*). Each of these has its merits and its place, but the level of overall satisfaction delivered by each of the approaches varies considerably. A series of incremental improvements can yield rapid rewards but, as noted above, the sum of such improvements may not resolve fundamental problems and, over time, such an approach may prove to be costly in comparison with the additional returns that are generated. The redesign of one or more elements of a company's operations offers the likelihood of a more satisfactory solution and may also achieve cost savings over the long term. By rethinking its entire operation a company is likely to achieve a superior solution. Even though this may necessitate the renegotiation of contracts with suppliers and customers, the overall return will prove to be beneficial.

Irrespective of the approach adopted, the development and implementation of a environmental management system will follow a similar pathway. Gilbert (1993) has identified the four major elements of what he calls the 'improvement loop'. These are 'think', 'plan', 'do' and 'measure'. Extending this framework, the development of an environmental management system should follow the following steps:

- Review and assess the major environmental problems facing an organisation and decide what needs to be done, in what order action should be taken and how such steps can be expressed in company policy and objectives.
- Design and plan the action to be taken, prioritise the tasks and identify who should be responsible and what resources will be required.
- Implement steps to attain the improvements identified and the new procedures needed for their achievement.
- Monitor and measure the improvements achieved through an environmental audit and other methods of assessment.

This cycle of environmental improvement is illustrated in Figure 7.2

Welford and Gouldson (1993) argue that an environmental management system should conform to the general characteristics which any management system should encompass. An environmental management should be

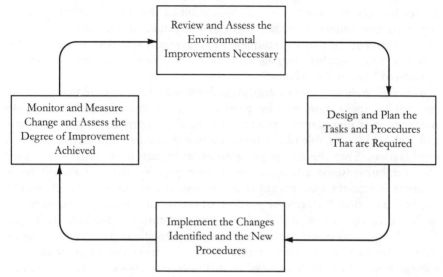

Figure 7.2   The environmental improvement process

- comprehensive, covering all the major activities and operations of an organisation;
- understandable by everyone involved, both inside and outside the individual organisation; and
- open to review and underpinned by a commitment to a continuous cycle of improvement.

An essential element in this approach is clear and adequate communication; each individual member of staff should be aware of what is desired and of the importance of monitoring, and staff should be involved in the process of review and assessment. This is reflected in the view expressed by Davis (1991) that an autocratic or paternalistic management style is unsuited to achieving the full participation of the workforce required by an environmental management system, and that instead an orchestral style of management is needed in which managers have an adequate knowledge of the capabilities and limitations of employees.

In developing an environmental management system a company will follow a process that aims to

1. Decide what is needed and what decision-making structures are required in order to achieve the objectives agreed upon;
2. Define the actions to be taken and who should be responsible;
3. Do what is required;
4. Determine and document the results and outcomes; and
5. Demonstrate the achievement.

These 'five Ds' provide an outline indication of the main elements of most approved environmental management systems and, in addition, they reflect the requirements of many total quality management systems; the relationship between total quality management and environmental management is considered later in this section.

Although policies, actions and procedures may follow a common format, the precise application will be particular to an individual enterprise. An environmental management system must fit the requirements of a company and it should be capable of full integration with the overall functioning of an organisation. Even though an environmental management system may start life as a burdensome additional or bolt-on process, the aim should be to integrate it into the mainstream of a business as soon as possible. A parallel can be drawn here between the position of equal opportunities issues some 10 or 20 years ago (when such matters were sometimes considered as an additional and unnecessary burden, often in a tokenistic manner) and the more recent introduction of environmental issues. In order for an environmental management system to be successful, it is necessary to accept the importance of the environmental dimension in all aspects of the operation of an organisation, and to ensure that environmental concerns pervade the company and become embedded in all processes of decision-making. In the same way that the personnel manager evolved into the human resources director, the environmental manager or director should be given the status necessary in order to achieve the responsibilities that are associated with ensuring that appropriate policies are developed and implemented in every part of an organisation.

An illustration: BS7750

There are a number of environmental management systems now in place, but the one most likely to prove popular with UK companies is that provided by British Standard 7750 on environmental management systems. The system builds upon the experience gained in the design and implementation of the British Standard for total quality management (BS5750) and also seeks to conform to other emerging international standards for environmental management. It follows the broad pathway outlined above in the improvement loop, which is illustrated in Figure 7.2, and it provides a standard process that can be followed by most companies, large or small.

The requirements of BS7750 are that a company should

- define and document its environmental policy. This policy should be relevant and appropriate to its activities and should be understood by the entire workforce. In addition, the policy should be publicly available, should include a commitment to the continual review and improvement of environmental performance and should allow for the setting of environmental objectives;
- create an organisation that allows for the definition of responsibility,

authority and the inter-relations of the key personnel who manage the company's activities. This implies that management responsibilities should be assigned and that a management representative should be appointed who has responsibility for the requirements of the standard, that staff should be kept informed about their roles and be given adequate training, and that the potential consequences of departing from agreed operating procedures should be classified;

- establish and maintain a register of environmental effects. This should relate to all legislative, regulatory and other policy requirements. In operational terms the register should relate to all emissions to the atmosphere and to water; the management of wastes; contamination of land; the use of land, water, fuels and energy, and other natural resources; noise, odour, dust, vibration and visual impact; and effects on specific parts of the ecosystem;
- establish and maintain procedures to specify its environmental objectives and targets. The objectives and targets should both comply with, and go beyond, the targets set by legislation and other regulations, and should be consistent with environmental policy;
- establish and maintain an environmental management programme in order to set targets for each element of the organisation, these targets should be defined in detail and procedures agreed for their implementation;
- prepare an environmental management manual that collates the policy, objectives, targets and the programme. Full documentation should be established and reviewed at a regular interval;
- create and implement procedures to ensure that control, verification, measurement and testing are adequately co-ordinated and effectively performed. Procedures for corrective action in the case of a failure to meet specific targets should also be specified;
- ensure that a system of records is maintained that can demonstrate compliance with the environmental management system. Audits, reviews and other records should be stored and maintained;
- establish procedures to ensure that audits are undertaken according to an audit plan; and
- review the operation of the environmental management system. A management review should include the results of audits.

This brief description of BS7750 outlines its major features; further details may be obtained from the British Standard itself (British Standards Institution, 1991). A detailed discussion of, and guide to, BS7750 has been prepared by Gilbert (1993).

Introducing an environmental management system
The approach to introducing an environmental management system can be considered in relation to three major issues: the implementation of the pro-

cesses and procedures defined in a standard system, such as BS7750; the tactics used by a company for the gradual introduction of a greater general concern for the environment; and the possible addition of environmental considerations to a pre-existing system or procedure, such as a system of total quality management. The first of these matters has already been discussed at length; the method of implementation of an environmental management system is that prescribed by the system in question, and the speed and success of implementation will depend upon the degree of commitment displayed by an organisation in relation to the achievement of the higher standards of environmental performance specified by the system. The other two issues are now considered in more detail.

Many companies have adopted a formal system of environmental management following the earlier introduction of an environmental agenda within the company. In some cases this agenda may have taken the form of a campaign to raise the environmental awareness of employees, suppliers and customers. This is certainly the case in those companies who took early action to enhance their environmental performance. Many such campaigns tend to focus on a restricted range of issues, such as energy saving, recycling or waste management. The advantage of this approach is that it allows and encourages experimentation, and it may also promote a greater sense of ownership of the eventual environmental policy or management system amongst the workforce and others connected with a company.

The next step, having achieved this heightened sense of environmental responsibility, is the incorporation of environmental targets and procedures within an existing system of total quality management. Questions of total quality and environmental responsibility are often linked; Gladstone, Morris and Haigh (1992), for example, inter-relate environmental issues with total quality management by reference to the supply of energy. By linking quality procedures with environmental concerns, a small or medium enterprise is able to introduce environmental management procedures, whilst avoiding excessive cost and the disruption of existing management procedures. Such a strategy for the gradual adoption of an environmental management system also allows a period of time for the education of customers and suppliers. The Holdene Group has adopted such an approach; their approach has been to incorporate environmental procedures in the pre-existing company procedures manual. An extract from the Holdene manual is presented in Box 7.2.

Obstacles and benefits

It is likely that the introduction of an environmental management system will have to confront and overcome a number of obstacles. Based upon the experience of developing and applying total quality environmental management in the USA, Bennett, Freierman and George (1993) have identified a number of such obstacles:

Box 7.2 *Environmental procedures as an addition to an existing procedures manual: the Holdene Group approach*

The existing procedures manual has been subject to review and additions have been made in order to incorporate environmental objectives and policies. Some examples are provided below:

I   Installation procedure – Environmental note:
'Unless requested by the customer to remove, all major packaging is retained by the customer.'
II   Retail sales – Environmental note:
'All packaging of goods, where not supplied by the manufacturer, is obtained from the warehouse store of recycled packaging.'
III   Engineering stores – Environmental note:
'All scrap electronic components are to be returned to Holdene stores for recycling.'
IV   Stores procedure – Environmental note:
'In the process of receipt of goods, clean re-usable packaging ie cardboard boxes, ESD envelopes and foam packaging is collected in box storage area for re-use in storage and shipment of goods.'

- The absence of a perceived reason to pursue an enhanced policy or system of environmental management.
- A lack of involvement in environmental issues by the senior management of a company.
- The dominance of short-term views.
- An absence of employee involvement in the process of improving environmental quality.
- The lack of reliable data and information on company environmental effects and performance.
- A limited view of the customer which excludes the wider range of stakeholders in a company.

These obstacles can be overcome by the measures described earlier in this section, to the benefit of both the individual company and the wider group of stakeholders, including suppliers, customers, shareholders and the residents in the area where a company is located. Bennett, Freierman and George (*ibid.*) suggest three direct benefits may emerge from the adoption of an environmental management system:

1. Improved customer satisfaction, especially in terms of an improved relationship with the wider group of stakeholders.
2. Enhanced organisational effectiveness through the introduction of improved procedures and better methods of communication.

3. Improved competitiveness related to the changing aspirations and preferences of customers, a reduction of costs in some areas of production, the development of new products and markets.

Attempts to identify the costs and benefits that are associated with the adoption of an environmental management system have tended to focus on the direct costs of having to alter methods of production, identify alternative sources of raw materials and make adjustments to other operational factors such as the transport of goods. However, a more comprehensive assessment might include a wider range of issues such as the enhancement of the image of a company or the potential and actual savings that are possible in relation to energy and raw materials consumption. In their assessment of the benefits of adopting a more systematic approach to environmental matters, Gray, Bebbington and Walters (1993) point to the benefits to be gained through the disclosure of environmental and other data. The benefits include, amongst others, a possible positive effect on share price, a reduction in any fears that might exist concerning a company's activities and a proven desire to demonstrate stewardship and environmental responsibility.

Beyond an environmental management system
Although it is now accepted by many writers on environment and business that the introduction and adoption of environmental management systems represents an important step forward in the establishment of the environment as a central feature in company strategies and policies, environmentally sustainable development implies the need for the further extension of concern to include all the impacts and effects of a product or process. The International Institute for Sustainable Development (1992) has, for example, suggested that it may prove possible to develop techniques for measuring the environmental and social costs, or benefits, of a wide range of corporate activities that are not currently considered in existing environmental management systems.

One approach to the incorporation of the wider costs and benefits of improved methods of production is through the use of life-cycle analysis. Although life-cycle analysis has been described by Gray, Bebbington and Walters (1993, p. 165) as 'the potential Holy Grail of environmental decision-making', its fundamental characteristics are relatively easy to comprehend. At its most basic, life-cycle or cradle to grave assessment implies tracing the life-cycle of a product from the initial exploitation of natural resources, through processing and production, to its use and final disposal. However, in practice, it is frequently difficult to determine the boundaries to a life-cycle assessment, and to identify all the stages and substages through which a product passes.

Although establishing a procedure for life-cycle assessment can often prove to be a complex and complicated affair, the benefits that emerge from such an analysis may prove to be revealing. For example, what might be considered to be a harmless or benign material or component might itself have been produced in a manner that is far from sustainable. The use of life-cycle assessment requires co-operation from suppliers and consumers, but it can also yield benefits for these collaborators by indicating the environmentally undesirable nature of those elements of the production system for which they are responsible.

Welford and Gouldson (1993) have outlined the major stages of a life-cycle assessment:

- The definition of the scope and objectives of the assessment. This includes the need to close the life-cycle by defining the links in the supply chain that will be considered, and determining those elements of the environment that will be investigated.
- An inventory analysis should be prepared. This should include all the materials and energy inputs into a product, the stages of production, the distribution and use of a product and its final disposal.
- Impacts should be determined by establishing the environmental effects of each of the areas identified in the inventory analysis.
- An impact assessment will attempt to measure the scale and severity of the environmental effects associated with a product.
- An improvement analysis represents the positive output of a life-cycle assessment. At this stage emphasis is placed upon the identification of ways of redesigning a product, adjusting the methods for its production and considering alternative approaches to its use and final disposal. A range of feasible options can be developed and tested.

Life-cycle assessment is a relatively new method and its application, to date, has been limited. One organisation that has attempted to apply life-cycle assessment to the full range of its business operations is The Body Shop (1992). This organisation has tracked product ingredients and packaging in order to assess the implications for the environment. This assessment has traced products from their sources through to reuse, recycling and disposal.

Although an environmental management system provides an important means of integrating a number of procedures and processes aimed at enhancing environmental quality and presents them in a single package of measures, the danger of a systems approach is that it can generate an atmosphere of complacency. As in any other management system, an environmental system may be subject to the failure of one or more of its component parts. In addition, as Welford (1993, p. 29) argues, it may fail to result in 'the significant step up in environmental performance which the world needs'. The advantage of life-cycle assessment is that it takes a wider view and relates all the operations connected with the production of a product to the objectives of sustainable development.

Some aspects of operational practice

The final section of this chapter examines the impact of environmental policy

on a number of selected areas of business practice. These examples are presented in order to indicate and illustrate the range of tasks associated with the
achievement of an environmentally sustainable business. Each area of operational practice is, however, connected to many other aspects of a business and,
whilst the enhancement of an individual area of practice can lead to a considerable improvement in company environmental performance, it is clearly the
case that the whole is greater than the sum of the parts. Three examples are
provided: education and training, purchasing and marketing.

Education and training

In a number of companies the initial impetus for environmental change has
come from within the workplace. Community-based environmental improvement projects may have encouraged employees to introduce, for example,
schemes to reuse waste materials, collect drinks containers, improve the visual
appearance of the area around a factory or launch schemes for the sharing of
cars. Some of these voluntary efforts to improve the working and community
environments have eventually resulted in the creation of company-sponsored
projects to extend the scope of such schemes and, in some cases, the company
has taken over the running of the schemes.

   In other cases the primary impetus for the improvement of environmental
performance has come from senior management. Often this change in attitude
and management style has occurred as a result of a growing awareness
amongst managers that enhanced environmental attitudes and actions are
increasingly necessary in a society where customers, consumers and financial
institutions require companies to place an increased emphasis on environmental matters.

   Irrespective of the direction from which the pressure for change originates,
it is unlikely that the process of introducing enhanced environmental policies
and practices can progress very far without the provision of education and
training. A change in the culture of an enterprise almost inevitably implies a
need to modify the ways in which many tasks are discharged, and may also
change the nature of the tasks themselves. No company would contemplate
the purchase and introduction of new plant or machinery without providing
adequate education and training to ensure its safe and efficient operation, and
the introduction of a new environmentally sound method of production or
organisation should be regarded in a similar manner. An additional consideration that has been acknowledged by many companies is the need to ensure
that employees understand, accept and share the company's new environmental aspirations. Presenting and communicating an environmental policy is
an essential first step in raising awareness and in introducing training.

   Sadgrove (1992) has suggested that the design and provision of environmental training should be considered in the form of a pyramid; this could
start by examining global problems that may be familiar, such as the incidence
of pollution, and then focus on the industrial sector, the business, the
workplace and, finally, upon the individual task discharged by an employee. It

is helpful to consider the training requirements of individuals in relation to this pyramidal form because, by doing so, a company can demonstrate to an individual employee the important role that he or she plays in achieving the collective environmental improvement that it seeks. In addition, this process of training exposes the company's proposed strategy for improving its overall environmental performance to scrutiny from those who know and understand the operational realities of processes and procedures at first hand.

The mobilisation of the experience and enthusiasm of a workforce in improving a company's environmental performance can be based upon a specific issue or experience. Sells (1994, p. 76), for example, draws upon his experience of working with asbestos and concludes that a company's stance on risk and environmental issues should be to ensure that 'responsibility must be overt, proactive and farsighted'. This learning through experience, however, needs to be set within the context of a commitment from senior management. Such a commitment, whilst implying that enhanced environmental policies need to be 'championed within an individual organisation' (Gray, Bebbington and Walters, 1993), also implies that the company's intentions must be communicated to all employees and that the workforce is provided with the training that is necessary for them to take effective action.

Gilbert (1993, p. 99) identifies three components of effective communication in relation to the introduction of environmental management: 'know the desired response, know the level of leadership interaction required, and know the complexity of the information'. These guidelines for effective communication suggest that the most important characteristic of an environmental awareness and training programme is that it should be appropriate to the needs of the individual organisation. There is little point in introducing a higher level of complexity than that which is required, and there is even less point in adopting a training scheme that cannot be delivered.

A final observation on the development and implementation of environmental awareness and training relates to the potential that exists for companies to collaborate, through a local environmental business forum or an industrial association, in the provision of training programmes. Many small and medium enterprises lack an in-house capacity to offer training, and collaboration can provide a basis for both sharing the training resources that are available and for learning from one another's problems and experiences.

Purchasing

Lockyer, Muhlemann and Oakland (1991) identify five Ps related to the functions of production and operations management: product, plant, processes, programmes and people. For an environmental management system to be effective it is important to add a sixth P to this list – purchasing.

By introducing environmental screening procedures at the start of the production chain, a company can avoid many of the problems that it might otherwise encounter. Ensuring that raw materials and energy flows reach acceptable standards can help to reduce the need for costly, and possibly ineffective, end-of-pipe solutions. Such screening can also help to reduce the negative public relations image that is associated with certain materials. In addition, by using what Winter (1987) describes as 'demand power', suppliers may also benefit by switching to materials, or sources of materials, that are more environmentally acceptable.

Life-cycle analysis and environmental management schemes place considerable obligations upon companies to check the inputs to their operations. One method to ensure that inputs meet a required environmental specification is the supplier audit. Purchasing managers traditionally require suppliers to meet a number of specifications; cost and quality are the most obvious examples. However, other factors, such as the country of origin, method of production and scarcity of a raw material, are equally important. A supplier audit can help to ensure that a company does not unknowingly present itself with a problem.

Having stated its environmental policy a company can subsequently embark upon a review of its purchasing policy. At the simplest level a company may require a supplier to demonstrate the origins and method of production of the products that it provides; this could take the form of asking a supplier to certify that the products meet the requirements specified in an eco-audit. This may imply that a customer will have to educate its suppliers (Gray, Bebbington and Walters, 1993). The process of supplier education and training is similar to that encountered in the development of a new technical or scientific product specification. Through developing a list of approved suppliers an individual company can assure itself, and its customers, that it is meeting its obligations; such a list should be kept under review.

Criteria that may be used for environmentally sustainable purchasing include considerations related to a wide range of factors. However, understanding the flow of materials through a supply process is likely to involve a consideration of both the origins of raw materials and the processes that are used for their transformation. Typical questions relate to the use of energy and water in the production process, the use made of the various modes of transport and the operating conditions within a supplier's factory. In addition, a supplier audit will need to consider the alternatives to a product that damages the environment and the possibility of substituting one product for another (Sadgrove, 1992).

Although there are few hard and fast rules for the introduction of an environmentally responsible purchasing policy, certain basic principles can be identified:

- It is important to identify the sources of the materials used.
- Identify and evaluate the production processes used by suppliers in the transformation of materials.
- Require suppliers to introduce an environmental management system that meets a standard specification or, better still, request suppliers to conduct a life-cycle analysis.

- Purchase goods and materials that carry some form of eco-audit certification.
- Work with an established industry-wide scheme for ensuring that production meets an accepted specification.
- Identify the expected life of a product and the extent to which it can be recycled or disposed of safely.
- Assist suppliers in the establishment of a system of environmental education and training.

By applying these principles a company can ensure that it minimises any environmental risk that may be associated with a given source of supply of a product or raw material.

Local or industry-specific purchasing organisations may be able to offer assistance to individual companies. In addition, companies may be able to obtain information from their customers on supply practices in other sectors of economic activity, or with regard to the experience of their suppliers in other countries. Larger companies may have already started to introduce stricter environmental criteria in other markets, and the learning experience of such companies can help to accelerate the process of enhancing environmental practice elsewhere. Wheeler (1994) illustrates how The Body Shop has transmitted its policies in such a way as to accelerate the process of learning amongst suppliers and customers.

Marketing

Having established environmentally sound policies, practices and products there is every reason why a business organisation should wish to communicate its achievements to its customers. At one level this is the obvious first step in marketing the difference that exists between an environmentally conscious business and a conventional company. However, it is not always apparent to customers that an environmentally responsible company has something different to offer. This section of the chapter considers some general aspects of marketing, whilst Chapter 8 examines the requirements of market research and development associated with new products.

Given the rise in public awareness and concern about the environment, it is important that a company should aim to develop a marketing strategy that provides open and explicit information about its achievements in the environmental field, and that it should seek to gain a competitive advantage by communicating these achievements. The development of environmentally orientated product portfolios that are aimed at meeting both established and emergent consumer demands is one of the most important current marketing challenges (Welford and Gouldson, 1993). However, it is vital that a company should avoid making false claims or overstating its case; much green marketing in the past has been little more than the application of a veneer of respectability and the adverse response of consumers to false claims can do much to damage the existing reputation of even a well respected business.

Peattie (1992, p. 90) has identified 11 key issues in developing what he calls a 'green marketing concept'. They are as follows:

- *Widening the market concept* – this points to the need to develop an all-embracing marketing concept, total marketing, and to relate the whole business to the views and desires of the customer.
- *Holistic management* – the entirety of the business should be considered in relation to the environment.
- *Balancing efficiency and effectiveness* – much conventional marketing theory is concerned with achieving effectiveness over efficiency, irrespective of the means employed. However, in a green marketing strategy the means are as important as the ends and this requires a balance to be achieved between effectiveness and efficiency.
- *Understanding customers* – this implies the need to generate a better understanding of changing customer desires and behaviour. As consumers adopt enhanced environmental attitudes their patterns of consumption change. This should be recognised and acted upon.
- *Balancing needs and wants* – new concepts of the customer reflect changing needs and wants over time. Consumers often have conflicting desires and understanding such conflicts, and ways of resolving them, is an essential part of green marketing.
- *Redefining satisfaction* – customers are now more concerned about the content and method of production of a product or service than in the past; they are also concerned about the disposal of products. This cradle-to-grave concern is reflected in the degree of satisfaction that a product offers to customers.
- *A long-term view* – many environmentally friendly technologies and products have a longer payback period than conventional goods; the customer needs to understand this.
- *A 'less is more' philosophy* – green marketing aims to generate customer satisfaction whilst maintaining profit; this may be achieved by reducing overheads, minimising packaging, by using fewer raw materials or energy.
- *Re-evaluating the value chain* – the environmental value of a product is partly determined by relationships within the supply chain. Green marketing needs to be aware of these relationships and to communicate the objectives of policy to suppliers and distributors.
- *Changing company culture* – traditional corporate values emphasise factors such as competition, market share and profit, whilst green marketing implies partnership, conservation and the assertion of environmental preferences. This may require a change in company attitudes and culture.
- *Shades of green marketing* – companies should appreciate the differences that exist in the degree to which they can market their products or services as green.

These issues provide the principles of green marketing. They are helpful in determining the stance that a company adopts in relation to the entirety of its operations, and they will also determine the speed at which a company can develop its environmental marketing strategy. Peattie (*ibid.*) recognises both the opportunities and obstacles that are presented in moving towards environmental production and marketing, and suggests that marketing practice will vary considerably between companies depending on their size and the industrial sector in which they operate. As has been discussed earlier in this chapter, whilst it is relatively easy to adapt some products in order to meet stricter environmental criteria, other products may require extensive redesign, or replacement by less environmentally damaging alternatives, in order to meet customer expectations. Equally, smaller firms may be able to bring about a change in policy or production methods more rapidly than a large multinational corporation.

The holistic approach to the marketing of environmentally sound products that is advocated by Peattie (*ibid.*) is also echoed by other writers such as Winter (1987) and Charter (1992). They advocate building a marketing strategy on the foundations of a clear corporate commitment to the adoption of enhanced environmental attitudes, and gearing such attitudes to changing market requirements. Given that ecological factors are becoming more important and influential in current society, a company that wishes to remain competitive should reflect such factors in all aspects of its operations. Translating these changed attitudes into a marketing strategy implies that increased attention should be paid to a range of environmental and technical issues. Building upon Winter's (1987) analysis, such issues should include

- the characteristics, design, method of production and environmentally proactive features of a product;
- the use of environmentally friendly packaging materials and the minimisation of packaging;
- communicating the attitudes and behaviour of a company in relation to the environment and ensuring that all claims are true;
- distributing products in a manner that minimises environmental costs and maximises recycling opportunities;
- ensuring that customers appreciate the method of calculation of any increased costs that may be associated with the production of environmentally acceptable products;
- implementing procedures to ensure that all employees are sensitive to ecological issues and providing necessary information and training;
- adapting the company structure to take account of environmental policies and appointing an environmental co-ordinator to be responsible for all environmental questions; and
- monitoring environmental control and performance and providing incentives for achieving environmental targets.

The development and implementation of an environmental marketing strategy represents the eventual output of the various changes in stance, policy and behaviour that have formed the substance of this chapter. As Beaumont, Pedersen and Whitaker (1993, p. 137) observe, 'competitive advantage will only accrue if there is a set of committed and responsible policies and actions that go beyond individual products and services to cover all an organisation's activities'. Environmentally conscious marketing mirrors the entire span of a company's behaviour and, as such, it represents an important interface between the internal strategies and structures of a company and the desires and attitudes of consumers.

Some other key issues

As was suggested in the introduction to this chapter, the process of adopting environmentally responsible attitudes and methods of business behaviour is potentially a vast and complex topic. Some of the major challenges that confront companies have been outlined, including the development of corporate policies and strategies, the establishment of environmental management systems, and a selection of operational implications as they relate to human resource management, purchasing and marketing. Many other aspects of business behaviour are also affected by the environmental challenge.

One of the main messages to emerge from past and present attempts to introduce a greater level of environmental consciousness in business is the need to adopt a holistic approach. Tinkering at the edges of an environmental problem may alleviate an immediate concern, but such an approach is unlikely to result in any lasting improvement and could make matters worse. The implication is clearly that a company should pay equal attention to the environmental implications and impacts of all aspects of its operations (such impacts may be indicated by an environmental audit or through the application of life-cycle analysis) and the company should ensure that action is taken to rectify any deficiencies that become apparent. Many environmental accidents result from an incomplete understanding of the breadth and depth of the environmental implications of business operations; ignoring one link in the chain of responsibility may undo years of progress and could damage a company's reputation now and in the future.

Conclusions

This chapter has demonstrated the importance of basing an environmental strategy upon a foundation of knowledge and understanding about the nature of a business. It has also examined the requirements and features of the environment within which a business functions. Whilst a strategy will inevitably reflect the pre-existing structure and operation of a company, it will also bring about changes in structure and ways of working. As with all aspects of corporate business strategy it is essential that an environmental strategy should encompass all aspects of a business, and that it should be subject to regular monitoring and review.

In order to ensure the effective implementation of strategy it is necessary to introduce an environmental management system or systems. Although a number of alternative systems are available, they share certain common features and characteristics. Chief amongst such common features are the importance of ensuring that provision is made for monitoring and review and the desirability of achieving a standard of environmental performance that is recognised and acknowledged by an external validation body. Life-cycle analysis offers a procedure for extending the scope of an environmental management system.

Many aspects of business behaviour are affected by the adoption of enhanced standards and practices in relation to the environment. Effective human resource management is an essential precondition for achieving a higher standard of environmental performance and employee education and training is a fundamental prerequisite for the introduction of an environmental management system. Purchasing and marketing are also important elements in achieving the objectives of a corporate environmental strategy.

The following chapter will discuss the benefits that may accrue to a business organisation that has followed the pathway of improvement suggested in this chapter. Notwithstanding the additional business opportunities and benefits that may emerge over time, the basic message of this chapter is that improving the environmental behaviour of a company is an essential element in ensuring business survival. Although additional business opportunities may emerge as a company moves towards the achievement of the objectives of sustainable development, the fundamental responsibility of a management team is to ensure the survival of the company, and to achieve this implies adopting the attitudes and approaches that have been outlined in this chapter.

8

Environmental business opportunities

It is a popular perception that compliance with stricter standards of environmental performance implies additional costs. However the reality is that reduced operating costs and new business opportunities can result from the adoption of stricter standards of environmental behaviour. The commonly held perception that care for the environment implies additional cost has been challenged in a number of ways: through a series of governmental and private sector investigations and surveys, in a number of research exercises and inquiries, through proven reductions in cost in those companies that have developed new products and services, and through the creation of new business ventures. Even though cost savings are possible, it should be stated that for many companies the adoption of higher environmental standards will cost more, at least in the short term. However, it is also important to recognise that, for some companies, the cost of not adopting and implementing enhanced standards of environmental behaviour may be a reduction in market share or the eventual failure of the company.

This chapter outlines and assesses some of the main areas of potential for reducing costs and for stimulating business growth, and it illustrates them by reference to a number of case studies. The intention of the chapter is to indicate possible areas of benefit and to relate such opportunities to the development of company strategy. It also provides the basis for the following chapter which considers the role of environmentally sustainable business in the development of local and regional economies.

The considerable size and significance of the potential market for goods and services produced by environmentally aware methods and by environmentally responsible companies represents a major business opportunity. In a recent report from the House of Lords Select Committee on the European Communities, the size of one major element of the rapidly expanding eco-industry was estimated at a worldwide value of £130 billion (House of Lords, 1993). This estimate relates to a single sector of the environmental market: the environmental protection industry. The market value of other sectors of economic activity, together with the cost savings associated with environmental improvements, have to be added to the baseline figure in order to gain a total view of the vast size of the potential market.

Given the rapid growth in recent years in the size of the market for environmental products, and taking into account the inexorable progress of environmental legislation, which itself contributes to market demand, there is little doubt that the increased level of commitment that business now exhibits in relation to the environment has the potential to be translated into new business opportunities. In some sectors of the economy an absence of concern for the environment, and the adoption of a 'business as usual' attitude, has already resulted in a fall in demand for goods and services. There is considerable evidence that the positive response of business to the needs of the environment, which is displayed by companies who are operating in areas of public concern or hostility, is indicative of the growing sensitivity of business to the demands and implications of the environmental agenda. Diversification strategies in some sectors – the tobacco and chemical industries are classic examples – have been driven by the search for new products, or ways of producing existing products that are more acceptable in terms of human health and environmental quality.

In an increasingly competitive and hostile market-place, companies cannot afford to ignore the environmental implications and consequences of their operations and products; neither can they afford to be labelled by investors as operating in a manner that ignores the opportunities available in the market for environmentally friendly products. Pressures from business customers, investors, regulatory bodies and consumers have combined to make the search for new business opportunities a necessity rather than an option. To ignore such business opportunities is to disregard one of the main sectors of business growth during the late twentieth and early twenty-first centuries. Business growth can go hand in hand with improved environmental performance, and the development of a company can, and should, be planned in such a way as to allow for improved environmental performance to result in an associated improvement in financial performance.

In earlier chapters of this book reference has been made to various methods and procedures that can be used by companies to help them to identify weaknesses in the environmental structure and performance of their business. Environmental impact assessment, environmental audits, life-cycle analysis and other techniques can help to isolate the reasons for environmental underperformance and can also be of assistance in correcting any weaknesses that are identified.

Eco-controlling is the name given by Schaltegger and Sturm (1992) to an adaptation of life-cycle analysis that can be used to help to assist managers to identify problems, set targets, and monitor and review progress. By understanding the flow of materials, including the input and output of resources and wastes, through the processes of production and use, a company can better understand the environmental impacts that result from its operations. Figure 8.1 illustrates this approach by reference to pollution and energy use.

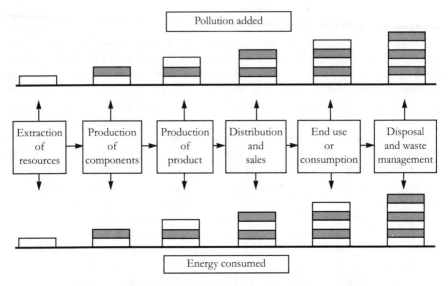

Figure 8.1   Life-cycle analysis and production flows

Source: Adapted from Schaltegger and Sturm (1992)

This method of analysis also allows for the identification of the major areas of environmental difficulty that need to be resolved in order to reduce the consumption of resources and to minimise pollution and waste. In addition, the method can be used to isolate those areas in the processes of production and use where attention needs to be focused upon the substitution or elimination of processes (or products) that are detrimental to a company's environmental portfolio. This method of ecological accounting is seen by Schaltegger and Sturm (*ibid.*) as enabling the

- reduction of the negative ecological effects of existing products;
- setting of benchmarks for product development; and
- creation of an ecologically orientated product range.

The following sections of this chapter consider a number of aspects of improved environmental performance. First, an indication is given of the ways in which concern for the environment can yield savings and cost reductions. The second section examines the opportunities that exist for the introduction of new or improved products and services. The third section considers the potential for the creation of new businesses and business ventures. A final section outlines the ways in which a business can incorporate these new ways of thinking into a strategy for its future development.

Cost savings and efficiency gains

This is the first and most direct implication of improved environmental behaviour for the overall performance of a business. At the simplest and most immediate level not consuming a resource, or consuming less of it, can result in a direct reduction in the costs of production. If by reducing or minimising a resource input a company can also eliminate a stage, or a number of stages, in the production process, then additional savings can be identified and associated with the environmentally preferred solution. Production that is both lean and clean can benefit a company in many ways: potential areas for achieving savings include a reduction in the input of resources and materials, the minimisation of energy consumption, a possible reduction in the requirement for production plant, the need for fewer buildings, less need for pollution control equipment, improved process and product control, the minimisation of waste and the reduction of waste disposal costs, and a reduced call upon the many specialist services that are associated with attempting to contain and maintain a potentially environmentally damaging production operation. A number of other savings are possible, including those related to purchasing, transport, distribution, servicing and other operations.

The issue of environmental efficiency is directly related to the overall efficiency of a business operation. If a company uses more natural resources than it needs to, or if it disposes of waste materials that could be recycled or sold as a feedstock to another company, then it is also operating in a manner that is economically inefficient. The costs that are associated with inefficiency show up in the profit and loss account, and may appear in the balance sheet (Muller and Koechlin, 1992). For example, there are very real costs associated with the excessive consumption or use of obvious items such as raw and semi-finished materials, energy and water supplies, transport and waste disposal facilities. In addition to these more obvious items, there are many other operations and services that can be perceived of as environmental charges or costs. Such additional items include excessive insurance premiums, authorisation and inspection costs, and higher interest rates. Poor environmental performance is likely to lead to increasing costs, and in order to reduce expenditure over the medium to long term it is necessary to adopt a positive attitude towards the environmental content of business operations and to develop a commitment to a programme of action that covers all aspects of a company's operations.

Some concepts and principles upon which an improvement in both economic and environmental efficiency can be based were expressed in Chapter 1 (Box 1.1). These ideas – discriminating development, conserving resources, maximising the four Rs, establishing creative work, maximisation of non-material growth and self-directed personal investment – reflect a number of basic assumptions and beliefs about the nature and content of environmentally sustainable business development. John Davis (1991) argues that the adoption of such concepts implies that the economic assumptions that underlie an environmentally sustainable business activity should reflect

- not only the efficient use of resources but also a number of social and environmental goals;
- the desirability of satisfying all basic human needs;
- the need for communities to become more self-reliant;
- the limitation of intertrading to those goods and services that are naturally maldistributed;
- the value of activities that do not involve financial transactions; and
- the need to consider the interests of future generations.

In addition, Davis also argues that an individual business activity should seek to operate in a manner that reflects a number of important concerns, including

- its desire to provide goods and services to meet the needs of a defined sector of the market;
- the importance of continuity;
- the well-being of all stakeholders;
- the desirability of enhancing the quality of the environment wherever possible and contributing to ecological balance;
- the need to minimise waste and resource consumption;
- the important role played by innovation and improvements in quality; and
- the desirability of adopting a long-term perspective.

Changed attitudes and beliefs are, however, only likely to be of any real significance if they are translated into improved behaviour and performance. Enhancing the environmental performance of a company often implies taking a series of small steps rather than a giant leap forward. The cumulative effect of a succession of modest, but well funded and consistently supported, improvements in environmental performance is likely to generate a greater overall impact over the medium to long term than a few grand initiatives. The emphasis here is on the need for improvements to be well funded and consistently supported; as has been observed elsewhere in this book, it is unlikely that the current environmental problems that face a company can be solved overnight.

This philosophy of environmental improvement based upon the cumulative effect of many small steps is one that is appropriate to most companies and business organisations. It also provides the basic philosophy that underpins the emergence of local environment and business clubs or forums. Appropriate action and the evaluation of the experience of local small, medium and large enterprises can form the basis for establishing what constitutes good practice in a sector or a locality, and encourage the development of a method for the dissemination of good practice that allows local companies to benefit from the experience of their neighbours. Given the limited number of trained and experienced environmental specialists working within, or for, business, it is all the more important to share experience. In addition, few small and medium enterprises can afford to employ the range of specialists necessary in order to develop and implement a full programme of environmental measures. Some examples of good practice related to the minimisation of waste and the reduction of costs are provided in Box 8.1. A further discussion of the operation of local environment and business clubs, forums and networks is included in the final section of this chapter.

Box 8.1   *Cost saving and environmental improvements: some case studies*

Warwick International Specialities Ltd
Warwick International manufactures small and intermediate quantities of fine chemicals. Through the installation of a number of new processes it has managed to reduce both environmental emissions and recurrent costs. Gaseous emissions need to be cooled and were previously managed by the circulation of water on a once-through basis – this was wasteful and costly. A new enclosed cooling water system has been installed to facilitate re-circulation. This new system has reduced annual water charges by £11,000. A further innovation is the introduction of an aqueous hydro-bromic acid scrubber that increases the time that bromide can be used; expected savings are in the region of £50,000 per annum.

Pickersgill-Kaye Group Ltd
Pickersgill-Kaye manufactures locks, handles and valves. The company has undertaken a series of environmental improvements, especially related to energy consumption. A power-major lighting control system, installed in the machine shop, has reduced energy consumption by over 20 per cent; the payback period for the investment involved was 16 months. Other energy saving measures have resulted in a total reduction in consumption of some 11 per cent; an annual cost saving of almost £9,000.

Orcol Fuels Ltd
Orcol recycles waste oil; treating 36 million gallons per annum the company collects and reprocesses oil which is then supplied to a range of industrial customers. The previous method of treatment left a thick liquid sludge that had to be disposed of at a specialist licensed landfill site at a cost of £350 per tonne load. A new decanter-type centrifugal extractor has now been installed to extract liquid from the waste material. The remaining solid material has a low oil content and can be disposed of at a normal landfill site. The initial investment of £50,000 has resulted in an annual saving of over £46,000. The savings have been gained from reduced waste disposal costs, reduced transport use and increased income from the sale of reprocessed oil.

BSD Lye Spencer Steel Service Centre

BSD Lye Spencer is part of the distribution network of British Steel plc. The company spends a considerable amount each year on timber used for the manufacture of pallets and separators. Alternative materials, such as plastics, have been used on an experimental basis, but have not proved to be successful. A pallet recovery service has now been introduced. As the average pallet costs £7 to produce, a 25 per cent rate of recovery yields a considerable saving. The annual expenditure on timber has been reduced by over £5,000.

Joshua Tetley and Son Ltd

Joshua Tetley is a major brewer. The company consumes some 15 million kWh of electricity per annum. Some 30 per cent of this is used in refrigeration. A refrigeration diagnosis expert system has now been introduced. This system can perform several functions related to the efficient operation of the plant and it can also identify problems and generate possible solutions. The new system has led to a major improvement in the efficiency of the refrigeration processes and a significant reduction in energy use. The initial cost of the system, including training, was £16,750. Within nine months energy consumption had been reduced by almost 30 per cent, a saving of over £18,000 within a payback period of less than nine months.

Source: Leeds Environmental Business Forum (1993).

A number of areas of business activity offer considerable potential for cost savings, and some of the cases outlined in Box 8.1 illustrate this potential. In more general terms the priority areas for investigation are likely to include

- raw materials consumption and the environmental soundness of the materials used;
- water consumption and disposal;
- transportation;
- packaging;
- the production process in its entirety or individual processes used;
- waste management and disposal; and
- the use and condition of land and premises.

The remainder of this section considers some of the ways of reducing costs in relation to these areas of investigation. In certain of the priority areas of investigation a direct relationship exists between two or more aspects of business operation; for example, it is likely that a company that wishes to reduce its consumption of new raw materials – through an overall reduction in the level of materials consumed or a switch to reclaimed or recycled materials – will also be interested in minimising its disposal of waste materials to landfill. Thus, in this example, one company's waste may become a feedstock for another enterprise, and the waste from the second enterprise may also be recycled in order to provide a source of supply for a third company. Intertrading in waste materials can help to create a virtuous chain of supply. Equally, the search for potential savings in the use of energy is likely to be associated with an investigation into the efficiency of the use of company transport.

Raw materials

Reducing the consumption of raw materials is the most immediate and obvious way of achieving cost savings. By reducing its consumption of materials, a company can both minimise its purchasing and reduce its overall inventory. The effects of a reduced level of consumption are twofold: first, there is a continuing cost saving in terms of the purchases required in order to feed a production process and, second, a reduction in the level of purchasing will have a proactive impact upon the need to maintain stocks or inventories of raw materials. Welford and Gouldson (1993) identify a number of cost savings that are associated with the control of inventory:

- Less capital invested in inventories.
- Avoidance of obsolescence or deterioration.
- Less storage space is required.
- A reduction in the problems of storing hazardous materials.
- Minimisation of stock control costs.

By reducing raw materials inputs, or identifying the possibility of using fewer materials in order to attain the same level of output, a company can simultaneously reduce expenditure and also achieve its environmental objectives. An alternative to reducing the input of new raw materials is to use reclaimed or recycled sources of materials. This can be achieved in various ways. For example, Easibind International produce a range of binders and office materials using recycled polypropylene, whilst a number of paper and card manufacturers make extensive use of collected and recycled paper and board.

One of the major difficulties that is encountered by companies in switching to a reclaimed or recycled source of materials is identifying a supplier. Several national directories are available that list the major firms. However, many smaller enterprises would prefer to obtain their supplies from a locally based organisation. In order to assist firms in the search for a local supplier, a number of specialist manuals are now available. *The Leeds Waste Manual* (Leeds Environmental Business Forum, 1994) provides detailed information on waste management and recycling opportunities in the West Yorkshire area.

Energy and water

Minimising energy and water consumption is an obvious and direct way of achieving both environmental goals and cost savings. Initial environmental reviews, environmental audits and life-cycle analysis techniques, which have been discussed elsewhere in this book, can all assist in the identification of savings. Potential energy savings are likely to be found in relation to four aspects of a company's operations:

1. The construction of buildings.
2. Heating and lighting.
3. Production processes.
4. Transport.

An energy or water consumption audit is the normal technique adopted in order to identify possible savings. Figure 8.1 has illustrated one method of charting the excessive use of energy and water. More direct methods of investigation can reveal major areas for potential savings. For example, it has been estimated that the replacement of incandescent lamps by compact fluorescent can produce a 50 per cent reduction in delivered energy consumption (Lowe and Olivier, 1993). Equally impressive reductions in water consumption have been achieved by some companies. For example, Thorntons, the confectioners, instituted a water monitoring and efficiency survey and, as a result, the use of water at their Thornton Hall factory was reduced by 30 per cent and the cost of discharge consents for effluent fell by 25 per cent (Hill, 1992).

Although substantial savings can be achieved in existing factories and offices, even better results can be obtained by designing new buildings, or converting existing premises, in accord with best practice. Sainsbury's has systematically reviewed all aspects of store design since the late 1970s and has arrived at the concept of a low-energy store. By designing a supermarket that captures and recycles the heat from lighting, refrigeration and other sources, and by using advanced methods of construction and energy control, the modern store only uses 60 per cent of the energy used by a similar store built in the early 1980s (Sainsbury's, 1992).

Other advances in design and control technology can provide further savings, but in many instances the most direct and effective savings can be achieved through the application of simple and immediate methods – switch off the light and turn off the tap. Staff awareness and training in these simple methods of energy and water conservation can yield significant results.

Additional incentives to improve energy and water saving can be introduced through the accounting process. Gray, Bebbington and Walters (1993) advocate the introduction of codes within the chart of accounts for each source of fuel, the allocation of consumption to cost centres and the separate consideration of energy and other savings as part of the appraisal of any proposed investments.

Minimising the need for transport, and selecting transport modes that use less energy, can also yield positive results in relation to both the environment and the economic efficiency of a business. There are many ways of increasing the efficiency of transport, including the minimisation of journeys, ensuring that vehicles do not run empty, using vehicles that have a longer life expectancy and use less or cleaner fuels, encouraging staff to use public transport and providing facilities for the storage of bicycles. A more radical option, but one which is gaining favour amongst service sector companies, is to encourage staff to work at or from home. Homeworking, especially with the added dimension of a neighbourhood support centre that can provide office technologies and social contact, is now a viable alternative to the daily grind of the journey to work, and is especially beneficial in rural areas where tele-cottaging has developed rapidly in recent years (Clark, Burall and Roberts, 1993).

Waste management

The growth of concern for the environmental impacts of business, together with increased economic pressures to minimise or recycle waste, has coincided with the recent reinforcement of legislative controls over the handling and disposal of waste materials. As was explained in Chapter 4, the Environmental Protection Act 1990 has placed strict and specific obligations on the producers and handlers of waste. It is clearly in the best interests of a company to minimise waste and to ensure that as much waste as possible is recycled. By reducing the amount and flow of waste materials a company can avoid certain direct costs, such as the provision of premises for the storage of waste and the need to pay waste contractors to dispose of unwanted materials.

By reducing waste at source a company can benefit in a number of ways. Through monitoring and identifying the sources of waste it may prove possible to reduce the initial input of materials; this in itself may give rise to improvements in the production process. Further benefits from minimising the production of waste include a reduction in the overall level of risk and liability, encouragement for the development of cleaner production technologies, a reduction in operational risk and hazard, and the minimisation of the labour inputs associated with the handling of waste.

These direct internal savings can be extended through an investigation of the potential for selling all or part of the waste that still remains after basic waste minimisation measures have been applied. New businesses have emerged in recent years that offer a waste removal, sorting and recycling service; further details of such business opportunities are provided in the following sections of this chapter. However, at this stage, it is important to consider the potential that exists for reconsidering the composition of waste and redefining unwanted materials as a product rather than as a residual. Some of these products may be basic materials; for example, a market exists for elaborate packing materials such as those used to transport computer equipment, and these can be sold back to the original suppliers of goods, whilst other waste materials, such as used oil, can be sold to specialist reprocessors. No company can afford to continue to ignore the possibility of selling its more specialist waste products or, even worse, to continue to pay the high and rising costs demanded by waste contractors for their disposal.

Although examples exist of the ways in which improved waste management and the minimisation of waste have led to efficiency gains, many of the examples given in the literature relate to the ways in which waste strategies have been introduced by large companies, such as 3 M's Pollution Prevention Pays (PPP) programme or Dow's Waste Reduction Always Pays (WRAP) initiative. The vast majority of small and medium enterprises find it costly and difficult to devise or introduce such programmes; their requirement is for a locally available, often co-operative, scheme. Localities vary both in terms of their structure of industry and the availability of waste recycling services. A locality with a concentration of small engineering firms may find it worth while to support a shared service for recycling metal waste, whilst a textile area may be able to support a new specialist business that collects and recycles fibre or fabrics. This is not a new idea; the true definition of shoddy is not an inferior product, rather it is a fabric made from shredding old or waste cloth, or which is made from the waste materials generated by textile manufacturers at the better end of the market.

These examples of potential gains from the better management of materials flows and greater efficiency in the operation of a company, minimising the consumption of raw materials, reducing the consumption of energy and water, and managing waste more effectively, illustrate the ways in which a company can link its economic objectives with its environmental goals. However, as noted earlier, not all schemes will produce immediate cost savings. In some cases an initial investment will take some time before it yields savings or, for example, different energy investments have varying paybacks over time; increased draught-proofing pays for itself very rapidly, whilst a new heating system may only justify its initial cost after five to ten years. Notwithstanding these variations in the time taken to realise gains, most companies will gain an immediate advantage by reducing the wasteful use of resources and their production of waste. This immediate advantage can also confer enhanced environmental awareness and an improved public image. Royal Mail North East now disposes of its damaged and disused wicker baskets and hessian sacks, via the Action Resource Centre, to the Meanwood Valley Urban Farm; the wicker baskets are used as rubbish bins and for storing animal fodder, whilst the hessian sacks are used as animal bedding and for covering compost heaps. Royal Mail gains from reducing its disposal costs and from an improved public image, the community gains from the provision of materials that can be used by the urban farm (Leeds Environmental Business Forum, 1993).

New products and services

As was noted in the introduction to this chapter, a large and growing market exists for more environmentally friendly goods and services. There are four different sources of growth in the market for more environmentally friendly goods and services. These sources of growth relate to

- existing companies wishing to expand their business activities by redesigning and relaunching existing products, or by adapting their methods of production;
- new businesses, including the formation of specialist companies;
- inward investment that attracts existing environmentally aware businesses from other countries or regions; and
- specialist advisory and consultancy services that offer signposting, design and management services in support of other economic activities.

The first of these sources of growth is considered in this section. The other three sources are discussed in the following section which is concerned with new business opportunities and ventures.

It is important to recognise that many of the companies seeking to achieve environmental improvements operate on a twin-track model; they continue to offer their existing products and services produced in a conventional manner whilst, at the same time, they are developing new products, services and methods of production. Whilst this twin-track approach offers the opportunity for a gradual transition to occur between old and new products and production methods, it can also result in internal tensions and conflicts of interest between managers in a company. A research and development manager may be sure that given sufficient time an environmentally acceptable product will prove to be viable, but will the accountants provide the necessary breathing space?

The product not the process
Cairncross (1991, p. 193) has identified the dilemma that faces many companies: 'the better companies get at reducing their waste, the clearer it will be that the problem is the product, not the process'. This implies that companies need to consider the overall impact of their products upon the environment, preferably from the cradle to the grave. However, in many companies the immediate response will be to focus on what they make or supply, and how they produce a product. This section considers the adaptation strategies of companies, whilst the following section examines the opportunities for the introduction of new products and services. Although this distinction is somewhat artificial – because many companies are seeking to move from existing products, through improved products, to new products – there are certain distinct differences between these two stages in the evolution of a business. These differences relate to the scale and implications of the operational changes that are involved, to the consequent requirement for new investment, and to the need for changes in company structure and behaviour.

If the root cause of an environmental problem lies with the product rather than the process, then the final solution has to relate to the design and manufacture of the product itself. As has been demonstrated in the previous section, although many environmental and cost savings can be obtained through improved methods of production and through the enhancement of ancillary operations, the characteristics of a product which is environmentally unsound cannot be altered substantially by end-of-pipe solutions. Although such solutions may reduce an immediate problem at relatively low cost, they cannot, and do not, provide a lasting response and may in time result in an increase rather than a decrease in costs.

Some examples exist of products where a change in specification can produce an immediate improvement in environmental performance. For example, whilst the elimination of lead additives in petrol has reduced some of the environmentally harmful effects of the internal combustion engine, it is also apparent that technical substitution and innovation in engine design should be regarded as an essential part of an overall solution. The cradle-to-grave view that is offered by an analysis of the overall life-cycle of a product provides a framework for the identification of those component parts of a product, or elements in a supply chain, that represent the environmental highs or lows in the profile of a product's manufacture and use. This reflects the need to consider a product in its setting and to assess the key factors in its environmental performance through a comprehensive and integrated analysis.

Case studies

A case history of a company that has chosen to adopt a holistic approach to the development of its product line has been provided by Carruthers (1993). Her study of Reckitt and Colman's environmental policy demonstrates the need to consider the characteristics of a product as the key item in achieving an improvement in the environmental performance. The two main environmental issues related to the manufacture of household cleaning products were considered by the company to be the use of phosphates and the degree to which the ingredients used are biodegradable. Following extensive research and environmental screening, a new Down to Earth product range was introduced in 1991. The new range of five products did not use phosphate and substituted oil-based surfactant with vegetable-based material in order to improve biodegradability. In addition, packaging materials were selected that minimised any environmental costs. In Carruthers' (*ibid.*) opinion the launch of the new range, backed by an extensive advertising campaign, resulted in substantial market growth. By 1993 'Down to Earth was claiming 46 per cent of the total £10.8 million green detergents, washing-up liquids and fabric conditioners market and the brand was valued at £8 million in the UK' (*ibid.* p. 22). The company has also embarked upon a process of customer education, has developed a method for assessing the environmental soundness of its suppliers, and now intends to achieve BS7750.

This case study demonstrates the desirability of adopting a total approach to altering a product range. Identifying a market niche is only the start of the process; product development, design, packaging, consumer education and supply chain analysis are all equally important elements in moving from the present situation to a desired future state.

Many other cases of product development, adaptation and substitution can be identified. A classic example is the development by AEG of a washing machine designed to be as environmentally benign as possible. Blair (1992) outlines how the challenge of producing a more environmentally acceptable washing machine led to a fundamental redesign of the product. Modern washing machines spin clothes dry at very high speeds. This, however, causes additional vibration and stress which necessitates the use of additional materials in order to provide stability. By redesigning the machine, including the employment of electronics to control the spin and the distribution of the wash load, AEG have been able to reduce vibration without the need to resort to additional materials; indeed the redesigned product uses 20 per cent fewer materials than the original machine. By redesigning the washing machine AEG has reduced its recurring need for raw materials and it has introduced a product that has enabled the company's market position to be transformed. 'From a relatively adverse position at the beginning of the 1980s, AEG's green washing machine and the organisation's commitment to quality created a successful business repositioning in the top price niche of the market' (Beaumont, Pedersen and Whitaker, 1993, p. 145).

The third case history relates not to the manufacture of a product but to its degree of recyclability. The motor car is considered by many to have a greater impact upon the environment than any other product manufactured on this planet (Ekins, Hillman and Hutchinson, 1992). Motor manufacturers have taken a number of steps to ensure that the negative environmental impact of their product is minimised, and many of them have instituted procedures, such as life-cycle analysis, in order to identify the major problems associated with its production and use. One of the most important of the problems that has been identified is the question of the final end use and disposal of a car. Given that cars, like most manufactured consumer products, have a fixed life span, it is important to ensure that the product is designed in such a way as to allow for the maximum degree of recycling to occur.

Traditionally there are a number of obstacles to the effective recycling of motor cars. These include the absence of economies of scale in collection, the great variety of materials used in car production, contamination of the components and the low quality of many recycled products (Gouldson, 1993). German legislation has obliged manufacturers to develop new designs and procedures in order to ensure effective recycling, and the result is the recent establishment by Volkswagen of an integrated system of recycling, including the establishment of a purpose-built recycling centre at Leer in East Frisia. At this plant scrap cars are disassembled and the parts are type sorted:

- Fluids are collected and sent for reprocessing.
- Steel parts are shredded and alloys are smelted.
- Batteries are dismantled and recycled.
- Plastics and rubber are reprocessed by specialist companies.

Other companies are following the lead set by Volkswagen; BMW operates a pilot recycling plant at Landshut in Bavaria and other manufacturers are introducing recycling initiatives. A joint venture has been established in the UK by the Rover Group in association with the Bird Group. This joint venture, which is assisted by the government-sponsored Environmental Technology Innovation Scheme, differs from other recycling programmes, which concentrate on own makes, in that it aims to offer a recycling facility that can be used to process all common makes of cars.

Gouldson (1993) has identified four factors that distinguish the attempts to recycle automotive components from other recycling initiatives:

1. The industry is of sufficient size to ensure the development of viable dedicated collection, dismantling and recycling facilities.
2. Manufacturers are increasingly utilising recycled parts and materials in their products.
3. Manufacturers are in a position to be able to generate a market for recycled materials through their purchasing policies.
4. Planned obsolescence followed by collection and recycling means that manufacturers are in effect loaning materials to customers for the life-cycle of the car.

Design that is orientated towards the use of recycled materials, easy disassembly and enhanced robustness is an important response to the manufacture of a product which is inherently environmentally unsustainable. By making cars more acceptable to increasingly aware and sophisticated consumers, the major motor manufacturers are embarking upon a pathway of development, and the enhancement of product image, that has been dominated in the past by measures of performance, such as top speed and rate of acceleration, that are now considered to be less desirable attributes than previously. A green league-table of car performance is now available which includes measures of performance such as the extent to which a car can be recycled (*Autocar and Motor*, 1991). Box 8.2 illustrates some of the features of this green performance analysis.

As can be seen from the preceding case studies, in the development of new or modified products emphasis is placed upon design that respects the environment. The term design is used here to express a range of functions related to the development of a product: research, market testing, the physical design of the product, packaging and the methods used for its production, distribution, use and eventual safe disposal. Design for and with the environment is a crucial element in achieving higher standards of performance, and it is seen as a worthwhile goal for manufacturers, retailers and consumers alike (CEST, 1993). Life-cycle analysis enables a company to examine a product in the round, from the production of materials through the manufacturing process to consumption and reconsumption. In addition to these considerations, it is important to ensure that the product is fit for its intended purpose, that it is robust, economic in use and capable of repair should a component part fail.

Some of the most important issues that designers should address in the

---

Box 8.2 *The environmental performance of car manufacturers*

Many motoring organisations and automobile journals provide information on the performance of motor cars. The features that are traditionally emphasised in these evaluations normally include factors such as top speed, acceleration and fuel economy. In June 1991, *Autocar and Motor* reviewed the environmental performance of the major car manufacturers in their 'Green guide to car makers'. The resulting league-table of performance of the top ten manufacturers also included a brief commentary on the content of the environmental policy of each company. In terms of the points awarded for environmental performance the best performing companies were as follows:

1. VAG Group (19 points)– engine technology, recycling of cars, plant operation, research and development.
2. BMW (18 points) – research and development, engine technology, recycling of cars.
3. Mercedes (17 points) – engine technology, some recycling, plant operation.
4. Saab (16 points) – research and development, engine technology, some recycling at plants.
5. Volvo (15 points) – engine technology, some recycling of parts, city filters on cars.
6. PSA Group (13 points) – engine technology, recycling of cars, plant operation.
7. Ford (12 points) – engine technology, research and development, plant operation.
8. Renault (11 points) – plant operation, engine technology, some recycling of cars.
9. Fiat (10 points) – engine technology, plant operation, recycling of cars.
10. Vauxhall, Mazda, Mitsubishi and Nissan (all 9 points) – variety of policies.

Source: Adapted from *Autocar and Motor* (1991).

development of products that are more environmentally acceptable include the following:

- Assess the origins and means of production or preparation of the materials used; the consumption of non-renewable resources should be avoided and the use of recycled materials should be encouraged.
- Avoid the use of environmentally damaging or hazardous materials and substances.

- Products and production processes should be designed to minimise waste in the production process and to avoid the use of hazardous materials.
- Energy consumption in the process of manufacture should be minimised and the product should be energy efficient.
- Avoid animal testing.
- Emissions during production and in use should be minimised or prevented.
- Minimise the weight of the product.
- Products should be quiet in use.
- Durability should be a major concern in the design process.
- Design products in order to facilitate repairs and servicing.
- Packaging should be minimised and should be reusable.
- Transport requirements should be kept to the minimum.
- Design products that can be easily disassembled and recycled.
- Products should meet national and international environmental and safety standards.

Although some of these suggestions are also likely to result in cost reductions, this will not always be the case. ICI Agrochemicals, for example, state that taking environmental considerations into account in the development of a new compound has added 10 to 15 per cent to project budgets (Gray, Bebbington and Walters, 1993). However, the true cost in the long term of not engaging in environmentally responsible product research, development and design could be far greater. As in all business decisions, the immediate cost implications need to be measured against the potential longer-term gains; a net cost in the first instance could ensure the profitability or survival of a company over the long haul.

There is also the problem of measuring any environmental improvement that is brought about by the redesign and modification of products. Measuring performance is difficult, but methods such as life-cycle analysis do offer insights and provide a partial solution. Equally there is the question of how to assess the relative environmental impact of an improved product that entails additional processing during manufacture. Cope and James (1990) have suggested that it may be necessary to construct two environmental impact measures: one would attempt to identify the first order impacts that are associated with the production process, whilst the other would attempt to measure the environmental impacts of the product itself. A company might attempt to transfer environmental impacts from the process of production into the product, or vice versa, thus resulting in no overall improvement in the state of the environmental account associated with the product.

Technology has an important role to play in the design and development of more environmentally acceptable products and in the processes used for their manufacture. New materials, together with advances in methods of recycling and reusing existing materials, have resulted in improvements in both design and production. Clean production allied to environmentally benign design can produce a dramatic improvement in the overall environmental balance sheet of a particular product. Blair (1992) illustrates the way in which this double environmental bonus can be achieved. He cites the case of the substitution of paint by powder lacquering, whereby parts that were previously painted are now treated by a powder lacquering process. In this process powder is sprayed on to an electrostatically charged part. The part is then treated at high temperature. Any surplus powder not adhering to the part can be reclaimed and reused. The resulting product is also more attractive and durable.

A final consideration of importance in relation to product design is related to consumer perceptions, demands and the acceptability of a product. Product improvements are most likely to originate from changes in business attitudes, technical advances or consumer demands. Sadgrove (1992) illustrates the influence of consumer perceptions and behaviour by reference to the results of a Mintel survey of food purchasing. In their research Mintel discovered that 23 per cent of people surveyed said that they avoided purchasing food produced by factory farming methods. As Sadgrove (*ibid.* p. 140) notes, it 'only takes one TV documentary' to change consumer attitudes.

Consumer attitudes towards products would appear to be influenced by a number of factors. Although some consumers are aware of, and take into account in their purchasing decisions, the sources and method of production of a product, the main environmental factors that appear to influence consumers relate to the performance of a product in use. Peattie (1992) has identified seven major factors related to the environmental performance of a product:

1. energy efficiency,
2. resource efficiency,
3. contribution to waste and pollution,
4. product safety,
5. product life-span,
6. reusability, and
7. recyclability.

In addition to these features, Peattie also identifies a number of supplementary characteristics that appear to influence consumers. These include the

- availability of environmental features, such as the fitment of catalytic converters to cars;
- removal of environmentally unacceptable or unsafe features, ingredients and materials, as in the case of CFC-free aerosols;
- use of green naming or badging in order to create an environmentally friendly image; and
- design of a product in order to give it an appearance that projects and reinforces its environmental qualities.

Designing and manufacturing a product in a more environmentally acceptable manner, and ensuring that the final product is regarded by customers as meeting their perception and definition of what is acceptable, is, however, only the start of the process of market research and public relations. These issues are considered further in the following sections of this chapter.

New business opportunities and ventures

Many of the advances in company thinking and behaviour that have been discussed in the preceding sections of this chapter can lead to an improvement in the financial performance of a business, and some of these advances may also result in the generation of new business opportunities and ventures. The previous section examined the development, redesign and diversification of existing products and methods of production; this section considers the creation of new companies, the attraction of inward investment and the provision of new services.

It is now an established fact of business life that the environment is of fundamental and growing importance to the profitability of a company. Until recently many companies concentrated their efforts on the development and implementation of improvements to existing products and associated production processes. The lessons gained from these experiments in sustainable business development are of considerable importance in moving towards more comprehensive and long-lasting solutions. James (1992) has argued that these earlier developments allowed companies to become less defensive in relation to the environmental challenge. Success in attaining their initial environmental targets, however modest in the first instance, provides companies with the self-confidence that is necessary to support further advances. Furthermore he notes that 'it is not too fanciful to imagine the next century as one of environmental capitalism in which environmental production and enhancement is not only a major operational issue and a substantial market, but also a central objective for both business as a whole and individual enterprises' (*ibid.* p. 135).

The environmental challenges that will confront twenty-first century companies are likely to emanate from a number of sources. Bennett, Freierman and George (1993), for example, identify six major sources of pressure that will drive the search for new products and services and the development of new businesses:

1. Pressure to report a double bottom line which reflects both traditional and environmental cost factors.
2. Greater research and development demands, including the need to consider products from the cradle to the grave. This will help to avoid costly problems and meet raised regulatory requirements.
3. Growing internal pressure as employees modify their own behaviour and

implant environmental values, developed initially in the community and through education, in the workplace.

4. Pressures exerted by a more educated and vocal public that demands higher standards of environmental performance.
5. New and strengthened regulatory requirements that seek to establish a more level playing field and to protect the quality of the environment from local to global levels.
6. New demands for information from all the stakeholders in a company.

These pressure can be satisfied by existing companies in the short to medium term through strategies of adaptation, but in the medium to long term the emphasis may switch to the provision of new products and services offered by new or reformulated enterprises.

Three specific issues related to these new business opportunities and ventures are considered in this section: market analysis and development; ethical investment; and the development of new manufacturing and service ventures, including inward investment.

Market analysis and development

Understanding the forces that drive the development of the market for goods and services is a fundamental task for any business. To ignore, or fail to satisfy, new market demands is a sure way of running a business into bankruptcy. As Muller and Koechlin (1992, p. 43) observe, 'new firms will never miss the opportunity of pointing out that their products and production process are more acceptable from the ecological point of view than yours. If you don't make your products obsolete, your competitor will'. Although this lesson may take time to penetrate the inner recesses of some boardrooms, the message is clear.

As has been argued in the preceding section of this chapter, many expressions of consumer preference have traditionally been related to the environmental performance and characteristics of products. However, these product-related perceptions and preferences are now becoming more sophisticated and are extending to encompass broader concerns for the environment. Customers now ask wider and more penetrating questions about finished products, about sources and methods of production of materials and components, and about the structure and policies of the companies who manufacture or provide goods and services.

Evidence has been presented elsewhere in this book (see Chapters 2 and 4) that illustrates the increased value that the public now places upon the environment. Compared with previous eras of economic history, consumers are now better educated and informed by television, the press and other media about the current and likely future condition of the environment and about the importance of treating environmental resources in a sustainable manner. The cumulative result of these new consumer preferences has been to change the way in which public bodies, including governments, view the environment, and to change the attitudes of many businesses with regard to their environmental responsibilities. Ignoring these new trends in consumer perceptions and preferences is no longer an option for a company that wishes to remain in business.

Market demands for more environmentally acceptable goods and services, and the degree of respect for the companies who supply them, are signalled in various ways. Market research prior to the development or launch of a product, and during the period of its availability, can provide direct information on customer preferences. Other less direct evidence can be obtained from investors and the various institutions who provide advice on the availability of investment capital. Industry organisations and associations, local environmental business forums and chambers of commerce can provide information on sectoral, local, national and international trends. Government departments and agencies, including overseas trade missions and commercial intelligence services, can offer advice on domestic and foreign markets. Specialist providers, such as green consumer groups, conservation organisations and specialist environmental research services, offer a range of information. The media acts, in part, as a mirror of the attitudes of citizens and can, in addition, be a powerful force for shaping consumer preferences. Regulators and environmental agencies supply a range of monitoring and performance information. Academic research is constantly adding to our knowledge both of the environment and of patterns of social behaviour. Conferences, seminars, trade fairs and business briefings allow companies to compare their portfolios of activity and their environmental performance with other players in the market. Finally, but of great importance, companies can monitor and evaluate their own environmental performance and can generate insights into the processes of market formation and change.

Understanding the dynamics of market change is a complex and difficult task, but it is becoming more rather than less important in the search for new business opportunities. Moving from the present position to a future state in the absence of good market research and analysis is likely to prove to be a fraught and risky journey. The responses available to a company may be limited, but strategic choice, even with a limited range of options, needs to be informed and anticipatory. Peattie (1992) has outlined some typical initial responses of companies when faced by strategic choice with regard to the environment:

- *Head in the sand* – the problem will go away if it is ignored.
- *Defensive* – attempt to discredit the environmental evidence.
- *Lip-service* – present a green image without any real attempt to implement new policies.
- *Knee-jerk reactions* – apply environmental policies without any real planning or understanding.
- *Piecemeal* – tinker with the problem and ignore the need for a holistic approach.

- *Green selling* – sell existing products or services under a green banner without any real attempt to change the nature of the product or service.
- *Green marketing* – attempt to influence customer behaviour through a range of marketing initiatives.

Such responses are likely to prove to be inadequate or to provide, at best, a short-term and partial solution. In order to respond in a more measured and lasting manner a company needs to address questions related to emerging market preferences through the development of a comprehensive and integrated assessment of future choices and strategic possibilities.

This process of strategic intelligence gathering and analysis is the mechanism most likely to yield the information that is required in order to make long-term strategic choices. Anticipatory strategic thinking offers a way of identifying possible market areas where there is a chance of developing new business opportunities and ventures.

Ethical investment

Consumer preferences provide an important mirror of current market conditions and they may, in addition, offer an insight into possible future market choices. A related, but different, mirror of market conditions is provided by the views and preferences expressed by the investment community. Investment institutions, including banks, pension funds, insurance companies and general investment fund managers, are major financial and environmental stakeholders in their own right, and they also represent the opinions and preferences of the general public. It is estimated that some 10 per cent of the British equity market is now subject to some form of ethical screening (James, 1992) and most ethical funds make use of some form of environmental assessment or audit in constructing their portfolios.

The growth of ethical investment can be seen as a response to a number of consumer and business pressures. Environmentally and socially aware consumers increasingly prefer to place their savings, pension payments and other investments with financial institutions that can demonstrate an explicit concern for the ethical behaviour of companies. This is not to suggest that the managers of ethical funds ignore financial performance; indeed many ethical funds perform as well, or better than, the stock market as a whole. From an analysis of the performance of green funds in the USA, Norway, France and The Netherlands, Joly (1992, p. 132) concludes that 'green equities sell at a premium to the market'. In the UK one of the first of the ethical funds was the Friends Provident Stewardship Fund. This fund performed well throughout the late 1980s, an achievement described by *Money Management* as excellent (Sadgrove, 1992). Other important funds include the Merlin Jupiter Ecology Fund and the TSB Environmental Investor Fund.

As has been noted elsewhere in this book, a number of banks and other financial institutions have started to introduce environmental criteria into their standard terms of lending. The use of environmental criteria is illustrative of a growing awareness amongst financial institutions that the past, present and future environmental performance of a company can make a significant difference to its actual or anticipated financial performance. A number of factors have led to this greater concern with the environmental performance of a company, including:

- the desire to ensure that a company does not have any hidden environmental problems that could cause its performance to falter;
- the need to confirm that the bank or other investor will not inherit any environmental liabilities should the company go into liquidation;
- the fear that the introduction of tighter regulatory controls will result in the need for costly investments in the future;
- the desirability of reducing the cost of environmental risk insurance premiums; and
- the desire to identify and support those areas of investment that are likely to produce future growth, such as investments associated with the market for environmentally friendly goods and services.

A positive assessment in relation to these and other factors, including the environmental record of a specific company or sector of industry, can provide an opportunity for the development of a new business venture aimed at developing goods or services in response to established and emerging market demands. The provision of funds to support new ventures and innovations that relate to the supply of environmentally enhanced goods and services will normally be subject to rigorous scrutiny. A number of organisations provide financial institutions with access to information on the environmental performance of companies. Some of this material is readily available in reports and regular bulletins, such as those published by ENDS and UK CEED, whilst other information can be supplied on request by specialist organisations and consultancies including the Ethical Investment Research Service (ERIS), ECOTEC and the Jupiter Tyndall Merlin ethical investment trust.

The funds that are available from financial institutions to support ethical investment can enable an existing company to change its portfolio of activities, or can be used to support a new venture. Gray, Bebbington and Walters (1993, p. 194) note that these funds can be used to support investments made 'on other than purely financial grounds'. Given that some new ventures are likely to be more risky than conventional business activities, such funds represent an important source of support and advice. In order to gain access to ethical funds an organisation has to be willing to provide evidence of its current operations and future intentions. The Merlin Research Unit produces information that is used to guide the investment decisions of Jupiter Tyndall Merlin. At the first stage in the investigation of a company emphasis is placed upon a precautionary assessment; the minimum requirements for the inclusion of a company on the 'approved list' are

- 'that it is operating without excessive harm to the environment'; and
- 'that it is producing socially useful products' (Moss, 1992, p. 294).

Once a company is placed on the 'approved list' a fuller, stage two, investigation is conducted. This more rigorous assessment places emphasis on the management of a company, on the environmental effects of the processes that it employs and on the products or services which it produces. It is interesting to note that Jupiter Tyndall Merlin also require companies to meet tough financial criteria. However, in practice they have found that many companies who demonstrate good environmental performance are also attractive investment propositions on more normal financial criteria. Moss (*ibid*. p. 297) attributes this to the fact that 'managers in industry who are alive to an issue such as the environment, are likely to be performing well in other areas'.

New manufacturing and service ventures

Having identified a gap in the current or future market-place that offers an opportunity to develop a new product or service, and having established that funds are available to support such a venture, the prospective environmental entrepreneur can begin to move towards the development of a new business. As was noted in the preceding section of this chapter, there are three major sources of new environmentally-sound business ventures:

1. New manufacturing companies.
2. New services.
3. Inward investment.

It was also noted earlier that some existing businesses may choose gradually to abandon their current portfolio of activities and, in effect, re-establish themselves as new environmental ventures.

The areas of search for new manufacturing opportunities and ventures are dispersed throughout the entire spectrum of economic activity. An estimate of the size of one sector of the potential market for environmental goods was quoted in the introduction to this chapter, but this estimate of a worldwide market worth £130 billion represents only a small part of the total global market. A broader indication of the diverse and complex nature of the wider market for environmental products has been provided by CEST (1990) (see Table 2.3). The opportunities in these sectors alone represents a market worth £140 billion in the UK between 1991 and 2000, whilst the size of the market elsewhere in Europe has been estimated at £860 billion and, in the USA, £1,060 billion (*ibid.*).

There are few sectors of economic activity that are likely to remain untouched by the development of environmentally sensitive businesses. From agriculture to financial services, it is possible to identify many business development opportunities (see Box 8.3). Gradual evolution towards a new business may be the pathway to the future that is selected by some ventures, whilst other businesses will be established in order to exploit a particular niche in the market, or to develop commercially a specific innovation. Diversity rather than uniformity is an important characteristic of environmental business ventures, and this diversity also reflects the range of potentials and possibilities that are present at local and regional level. For example, there are some ventures, such as specialist waste reprocessing, that require a minimum catchment area or population size in order to ensure viability; this condition is likely to favour the growth of such companies in urban rather than rural areas. A further general characteristic of many environmental business ventures is the influence exerted by a company's internal environmental requirements upon the eventual product or service that is offered to the market. In some instances the presence of a seemingly insoluble environmental problem can stimulate a company to develop a new product or source that both meets its own immediate in-house needs and produces the foundation for a new venture. Deep-shaft effluent treatment technology was initially developed by ICI in order 'to reduce the biological oxygen demand of liquid effluents prior to their discharge to drains or waterways' (Fields, 1992, p. 103). This technology has proved to be successful and more than fifty plants have now been built world wide to treat a wide range of industrial and municipal effluents.

Box 8.3   *Areas of search for environmental business ventures: some examples*

Although the inclusion of an environmental dimension in business planning and the provision of goods and services is an important matter for all companies, existing companies and new enterprises have developed new business ventures that are aimed at specific sectors of the environmental market. Some examples include the following:

Forestry – improved methods of felling and phased replanting aimed at the development of sustainable forestry, and the more complete use of forest products such as bark for manufacturing garden products.

Chemicals – development of substitute materials and alternative methods of production, improvement of waste management and pollution control equipment, biotechnology products.

Motor vehicles – improvements in engine performance, redesign of components in order to reduce the consumption of materials and to enable more extensive recycling, development of alternative power sources, use of advanced materials to reduce weight of cars.

Mechanical engineering – new environmentally sound products for other industries especially pollution abatement and control equipment, technologies for minimising waste during production, the development of recycling equipment.

Energy equipment – development of more energy efficient conventional energy generation equipment, introduction of advanced sources of renewable energy technology, development of a wide range of energy efficient equipment.

Waste management – improved collection and sorting procedures, development of new technologies, improved methods of collection and disposal, developing markets for waste products.

Research services – introduction of energy and environmental auditing and assessment services, development of environmental data and information services, environmental accounting, life-cycle analysis, technology audits.

The market for environmental goods and services is one that is characterised by rapid change and development. This reflects the progress of technical and scientific innovation, the constant identification of new environmental problems and challenges, and the influence of increasingly rigorous legislation. Because the market for environmental goods and services is subject to rapid change, some companies may be reluctant to develop new products. Such companies fear that they may not be able to recover their investments in research and development or new production technology before a product becomes obsolete. Although this is a problem in some sectors where scientific and technical progress is especially rapid, it should not deter the majority of companies from investigating opportunities for the development of environmental goods and services.

One way of reducing uncertainty in relation to new environmental investment is to enter into a joint venture with a company located in a country that already has a sizeable environmental business sector, or to attract such companies to invest in a less developed national or regional market. The advantages of direct foreign investment, or joint ventures with overseas companies, are that the costs of research and development have already been met, and that the goods and services to be provided have been tested in the market-place. The general advantages and disadvantages of foreign direct investment are well known (Collis and Roberts, 1992) and are not discussed here; but in relation to environmental ventures three specific matters are of particular importance:

1. The possibility of technology transfer.
2. The creation of new marketing opportunities.
3. The spreading of any risks that may be associated with entering a new market sector.

Equally important are the opportunities presented to companies to export new innovations to an already established overseas market. Even if a home market is not yet large enough to support a new environmental business, there is no reason to delay the establishment of a new venture if a market can be identified elsewhere. Indeed, given the high costs that are often associated with the development of some new products, there is every reason to consider the global opportunities as well as the requirements of local and regional markets.

Service activities support both indigenous and inward manufacturing ventures and, in addition, many services are provided directly to customers. As in the manufacturing sector, some environmental services are, and will be, supplied by existing companies, whilst other established and emergent market demands have stimulated the creation of new ventures. Many major legal, accountancy and management consultancy practices have developed new areas of environmental expertise and advice in order to support manufacturing and other service ventures. Other major areas of development are associated with the provision of technical advice, environmental assessment and auditing, waste management and recycling services, transport services, retailing, and green advertising and marketing. Although some environmental service companies operate at a global level, many new ventures have been created in response to local or regional market demands.

Case studies

The innovations discussed in the preceding paragraphs can be illustrated by reference to a number of case studies. Some of the examples which have been cited earlier in this book indicate the variety of business responses to the opportunities that have emerged for the development of environmental goods and services, and some additional examples are provided below.

Blueminster Ltd is a small research-based company, initially founded as a chemical consultancy. The company has developed a number of new technology products that meet the stricter environmental conditions of the 1990s. One of Blueminster's most important new ventures has been the development of a water-based adhesive; this adhesive can be used to replace solvent-based substances in a variety of production and other applications.

Easibind International Ltd produces a range of stationery and packaging products. In association with the World Wide Fund for Nature, the company has developed a new range of binders and document packaging systems. The WWF collection is manufactured from recycled polypropylene waste; the company claims that the cost of production is no greater than for conventional products. An additional environmental benefit is obtained by the donation of part of the proceeds of sales to the World Wide Fund for Nature.

Precious Metal Industries Ltd is an established company in the precious metal trading sector. A new business venture was developed five years ago to process the growing amount of electronics waste materials such as circuit boards, clippings and components. PMI collects metals present in the waste and then disposes of any residual materials in a responsible manner.

Powerstream plc is a new venture concerned with the manufacture, installation and further development of hydro and wind power. In developing renewable energy projects the company takes responsibility for all stages, from surveying potential sites through the design and manufacture of generating equipment to installations and the sale of the power generated.

Aquaterra Environmental Consultants Ltd was founded in 1991 and is jointly owned by GZA Geoenvironmental Technologies and the Carl Bro Group. The company provides a range of specialist environmental services in relation to the analysis of contaminated land, groundwater pollution, the evaluation and design of remedial alternatives, environmental audits, environmental risk management, regulatory compliance and related issues. By drawing upon the international experiences and resources of its parent companies, Aquaterra combines an understanding of local and regional conditions with extensive scientific and consultancy expertise.

B&Q is a major retailer of do-it-yourself and associated products. During the past four years the company has developed and adopted a series of environmental policy initiatives and has, in association with suppliers, established a number of new ventures including the production of alternatives to the use of peat, the encouragement of sustainable timber production and the introduction of a range of substitute and alternative materials. The company introduced a supplier environmental audit scheme in 1991. Since then 30 per cent of suppliers have complied with the conditions of this audit.

Fairweather Green is a small specialist waste paper collection and recycling company. Established in the early 1990s, the company specialises in the sorting of confidential waste paper; its client base of over 160 companies includes legal practices, banks and other financial services companies. When it was first established Fairweather Green operated from a small garage, but by offering a personalised collection and sorting service the firm has grown considerably since its establishment and is now expanding its services to include the processing of other forms of industrial and commercial waste.

ECOTEC Research and Consulting Ltd is a specialist consultancy that offers a range of economic development and environmental services. The company has developed its environmental policy and pollution control division in order to provide a range of expert services, including the establishment of the POLMARK database which holds information on the environmental technologies of over 6,500 European companies. ECOTEC also provides a range of other specialist services in the environmental field as well as offering consultancy facilities that can be used to research the interface between the economy and the environment.

These case studies are illustrative rather than typical. Whilst some of these new ventures are aimed at satisfying international and national market demands, others are locally based and depend upon a relatively small network of clients. One common feature in all the cases is the commitment which is displayed to the achievement of the highest standards of environmental performance at all levels in the company and, in the case of manufacturing concerns, in relation to the local communities that act as hosts to the production of materials, the manufacture of products and the distribution and supply of goods and services. By establishing a link between global aspirations and local requirements, these new ventures serve to illustrate the importance of developing a business response to the environment that is rooted in the needs of individual localities and regions.

Environmental business opportunities and company strategy

Although much of what has been discussed in this chapter requires little further explanation, there are a number of general issues that deserve additional attention. Questions related to general company strategy towards the environment were discussed in Chapters 5 and 7, and an important conclusion from this discussion was the need for a business strategy to be built upon a clear knowledge and understanding of current and likely future market conditions. This prerequisite for building a successful strategy is even more important if new products and business ventures are contemplated.

Three specific issues require particular consideration in relation to the development of new products and services and in the generation of new business ventures:

1. The need for long-term planning and vision.
2. The definition and construction of strategic partnerships.
3. The importance of good presentation and public relations.

Long-term planning and vision

Many of the environmental opportunities that have been discussed in this chapter are unlikely to be realised immediately or in the near future. Although some investments that are aimed at achieving cost savings and efficiency gains may have short payback periods, other innovations may not pay back the initial costs for some years, if ever. In relation to the introduction of new products and the development of new business ventures, it is even more difficult to reach any general conclusions regarding the length of the payback period that should be used for the evaluation of an investment. The only general rule that can be suggested is that any appraisal should incorporate an assessment of what the consequences for a company will be if the investment does not proceed. Investing in the improvement of a company's environmental performance may be costly over the short to medium term, but it could help to ensure survival over the long haul.

Whilst some environmental business opportunities are likely to be opportunistic, the majority will require careful planning and implementation. However, this requirement for informed and comprehensive assessment should not be allowed to diminish the power of a corporate commitment to the environment or to cloud a strategic vision of what is necessary in order to gain and hold a competitive advantage. Traditional definitions of short, medium and long-term planning horizons are of little assistance in relation to environmental matters. Developing and introducing a new biotechnology, investing in an alternative to the internal combustion engine or establishing a facility for the sorting and recycling of industrial waste are typical short to medium-term projects in the business and environment field; but in such cases the medium term may be fifteen to twenty years. Such timescales should not be viewed as excessive, nor should a longer than normal planning horizon present a well managed company with any particular problems. Successful companies, and especially those of Japanese origin, are well acquainted with the merits of establishing a long-term strategic vision for a company and using this as a sounding board for the evaluation of shorter-term investment proposals.

Alleviating or solving the present array of environmental problems that confront businesses is not an easy or short-term task. Changing course after almost two hundred years of continuous industrial growth will take some time, and this supports the case for decision-makers to utilise a longer than normal time horizon. It is not suggested here that all companies should adopt the 250-year planning horizon that is used by Matsushita (the parent company of Panasonic) in its forward planning, but they will need to think at least five to ten years ahead if they are to benefit from the opportunities that exist to develop new environmental products and business ventures.

Strategic partnerships

One way of reducing or sharing any risks that may be associated with the development of either a new product or a new business venture is to enter into a strategic partnership. Such a partnership could take the form of a joint venture with an organisation that has already established a presence in the proposed market-place or which offers other advantages. This approach offers a number of advantages to the new entrant company: it can reduce the length of time taken to bring a product to market, it builds upon established market share and it reduces the entry cost into a market.

Although the majority of joint ventures will involve two or more businesses, or business organisations, other models of partnership may prove to be more suitable or mutually beneficial. A partnership with a community or a community group may offer a company the opportunity to share the costs of developing a new venture by agreeing with the community that it will purchase the new product or service. Other partnerships can be based upon the establishment of a working relationship between a business and an environmental conservation or promotional organisation. This model has already been illustrated in this chapter in the case of Easibind's partnership with the World Wide Fund for Nature; other examples include the Co-operative Bank's partnership with the Royal Society for the Protection of Birds, and British Telecommunications' sponsorship of the Environment City organisation. Local business organisations, such as a chamber of commerce or a local environmental business club or forum may also provide the basis for the development of a partnership. A final model of partnership is a joint venture with local or central government, a government agency or a utility organisation; such a partnership could prove to be suitable for the development of an advanced combined heat and power system or the establishment of a joint venture in the field of waste recycling.

Partnership models will vary according to the project proposed, but they all offer a degree of security to the partners on the basis of a shared risk or a guaranteed purchase arrangement. Local or regional environmental development partnerships, where the agreed objective for all partners is the economic and environmental development of a particular area, offer a more wide-ranging and comprehensive model; such partnerships are discussed at greater length in the following chapter.

Promotion and public relations

Having developed a new product or venture it is vital that a company should communicate the difference between its approach and performance, and that of its competitors. The need for good data and a clear understanding of the evolution of the market has been discussed earlier in this chapter. Effective promotion builds upon this information and is aimed at enhancing the image of a particular environmental product or business venture. In some instances a primary role of promotion will be to provide the public with basic information on the origins and impacts of a particular environmental problem. The stakeholder concept emphasises the need for the open disclosure of all relevant information and experience indicates that the most effective promotion is based upon the presentation of the maximum possible amount of information in the most direct and open manner. Welford and Gouldson (1993) point to the damage that can be done to the reputation of a company if its environmental information or claims are found to be excessive, meaningless, not explained or full of misleading jargon.

Promotion and public relations as a form of education and training is an appropriate model for an environmental product or venture. A company's educational message may be directed towards its customers and the general public, or it may wish to influence particular groups such as its workforce, its suppliers, any regulatory bodies with which it interacts, the community that acts as its host, its shareholders, the financial institutions and any other stakeholders that place a particular priority on the environment.

Above all any promotion or public relations exercise should follow a code of ethical behaviour. Any claims made for a product or service should be honest, and any information about a new business venture should be capable of withstanding a rigorous investigation. The burden of proof should be with the company rather than the customer, investor or partner. In the view of McCloskey, Smith and Graves (1993, p. 96) this implies that 'the interests of consumers would be given equal standing with those of managers'.

Conclusions

This chapter has demonstrated that a number of financial and other advantages are associated with the enhancement of environmental performance. Although some improvements in environmental behaviour will entail additional costs, many examples exist of efficiency gains and cost reductions. Areas of search for the reduction of costs include energy efficiency, waste management and pollution avoidance and control. The development by a company of a solution to its problem may also yield the basis for a new product or business venture.

New products have emerged in recent years as a result of higher regulatory standards, consumer pressure and the increased desire of companies to provide goods and services that are both profitable and environmentally sound. A process of evolution can be identified in terms of the adoption of enhanced environmental attitudes; most companies start by solving their own problems, they then offer new goods or services, and finally they may develop new business opportunities or enter into new ventures.

Irrespective of the position attained by an individual company in this process of evolution, three general issues require attention. The company will have to adopt a model of thinking and policy formulation that looks beyond the short term; it may have to enter into a strategic partnership in order to spread the costs of research and development; and it will need to ensure that it communicates the difference to its customers, stakeholders and society at large.

This chapter has also provided a basis for the discussion of the role of environmentally sustainable businesses in local and regional development that is presented in Chapter 9.

9

The role of environmentally sustainable business in local and regional development

In the Preface to this book it was argued that many of the existing treatments of the environment and business relationship pay insufficient attention to the importance of space and place. Even in a world where multinational businesses exercise considerable power and influence, many companies still value their association with a particular local or regional area. Location and local economic and environmental conditions are important factors in determining the way in which a business functions, and such conditions can also help or hinder the progress of a company as it strives to achieve a higher standard of environmental performance. Equally, the search by companies for improved environmental performance can contribute to the success or failure of a local or regional economy and to the quality of life in that area (Figure 9.1).

This relationship among business, the environment and place is an expression of the deep-rooted sense of attachment that people have to the places where they work, live and seek recreation. Traditional analysts of localities and regions, such as Patrick Geddes (1915), considered that an appreciation of the links between folk, work and place, as enshrined in Le Play's triad, was fundamental to understanding the origins and operation of local and regional economic systems in relation to the opportunities and limits imposed by the environment (Hall, 1974). People value places, and the often ill-defined notion of quality of life is, in reality, a spatial expression of that value.

In the modern era the clearest expression of the folk, work and place relationship can be seen in the many positive and negative ways in which economic enterprises interact with their host localities and regions (Hudson and Sadler, 1988). Whilst conservation groups, governments, companies and environmentally aware individuals all express general concern about global and national environmental issues, most individuals and local communities reserve their strongest protests against the undesired consequences of infrastructure developments and industrialisation for those schemes that are located in or adjacent to their backyards. The rise of the NIMBY (not in my back yard) phenomenon has coincided with an increased level of concern

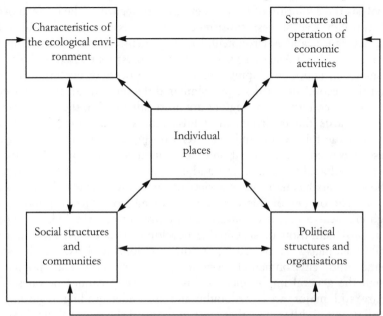

Figure 9.1   Business, environment and place

Source: adapted from Schaltegger and Sturm (1992)

for the environmental impacts of business; and public anxieties are unlikely to diminish as long as people feel threatened by actual or potential dangers that impinge upon their health and the environmental quality of their surroundings. This concern with place is reflected in the growth of ecocentrism; this view of the world is based on the 'belief that people's activities cannot be divorced from their relationship with the environment' (Gibbs, 1991, p. 225).

An additional point of importance should be noted at the outset: despite the efforts made in recent years to ensure that present and future environmental standards accord to a common norm of design and performance, little can be done to alter the inheritance of the past. The European Union, for example, has attempted to establish a 'level playing-field' with regard to the environmental quality required of new developments, but this equalisation of national and regional legal conditions will not, in itself, redress the very steep slope of the playing-field in terms of the wide variations that currently exist in the quality of the environment. As Shrivastava (1992a) observes, there is a huge contrast between the ability of citizens in the USA or Europe to influence the standard of environmental protection and industrial safety, and the relative powerlessness of citizens in developing countries. This factor is further illustrated by B&Q's (1993) analysis of international supply chains and the wider 'environmental footprint' left by the company's activities. In this analysis the evolution of business ethics with regard to the environment is traced through five stages: subsistence, ethical issues, health and safety, quality assurance, and environmental management. Whilst many companies in Europe and North America are now addressing issues related to the fifth of these stages, in many developing countries the process of evolution has only reached the second or third stages. Similar differences in attitude can occur within a single country; some regions are more advanced in their attitudes and policies towards the environment, whilst others tend to lag behind. This implies that the folk, work and place relationship is a matter of concern for business, irrespective of the location of an individual company or operation.

The mode of analysis and understanding that was advocated by Geddes and his fellow writers has its roots in a view of the world that is holistic and fundamental. The origins of this view can be traced from eastern philosophers, through classical concepts of nature, to the present day (Holliday, 1986). In the standard definition of sustainable development and environmental sustainability emphasis is placed upon the relationship between the socioeconomic and environmental conditions of an individual population. Although the general importance of this relationship cannot be questioned, there are still major areas of doubt and misunderstanding regarding the substantial spatial differences that exist in terms of the physical manifestation of this relationship. What may be accepted as normal or acceptable at one place may be unacceptable elsewhere.

The great variety of socioeconomic and environmental endowments that are inherited by individual places are the outcome of many long and complex processes of evolution. These processes have determined the form and condition of the present day natural and built environments and, as noted above, these processes reflect the broader socioeconomic, political and cultural traditions of a society.

Nowhere is this endowment from the past more apparent than in coalfield areas. Compare, for example, the influence of geography, or to be more precise geology, upon the areas either side of the north crop of the South Wales coalfield. To the north are the relatively unspoilt hills, moors and mountains of the central Wales massif whilst, to the south, the process of industrialisation during the last two centuries has left a legacy of despoiled environments and economic distress. An accident of geography left the area to the north without coal and without the profits that were gained from the mining of coal but, more importantly, it left them without the legacy of environmental degradation that will take many decades to erase. An even starker contrast can be found in Yorkshire. The Vale of York and the old North Riding where, until recently, the coal was considered to be too deep to be mined economically, represent an almost different world from the environmentally degraded coalfield area of South Yorkshire. These examples demonstrate the complexity and long history of the relationship among economic activity, environment and place.

One obvious reason for the occurrence of differences in the value that governments, companies and citizens attach to the environment is the presence of conflicting interests. In some countries, and in certain regions within a single nation, the reduction of a high level of unemployment may be given total priority, irrespective of the consequences for the environment. In other countries or regions the demands of powerful and vocal groups in society for better roads, for increased opportunities to express their power as consumers or for greater access to sensitive rural environments in the pursuit of leisure, may work against the overall best interests of the environment. Attempting to strike a balance between the various forces that have shaped, and continue to shape, the natural and built environments is no easy matter.

Business is obviously a key player in this search for a more balanced approach, but this balance is most likely to be achieved if business works alongside the other stakeholders who have an interest in the outcome of its decision-making processes. As Schmidheiny (1992, p. 27) has suggested 'it is now time that business becomes involved – with governments and other non-governmental organisations – in actively and thoughtfully charting the developmental and environmental paths of humankind'. Although much progress has been made at international level in creating a framework for the achievement of this objective, it is likely that the most effective partnerships for action will be established and function at a local or regional level.

This chapter examines the origins, evolution and objectives of local and regional development in order to establish the principles upon which an environmentally and economically balanced solution can be constructed and pursued. From this foundation, an agenda is developed that can be used to guide the evolution of the relationship between business and the environment at local and regional levels. This common agenda for business, as well as localities and regions, is illustrated by reference to the emergence of local business and environment organisations; the application of the concept of the sustainable city region; and the role played by the environment as a central feature in regional development strategies. The third section of the chapter looks forward to the integrated planning and management, or balanced development, of local and regional areas, and to the contribution that business is likely to make to this process. A final section of the chapter considers the benefits to business that can be obtained from the implementation of policies for an environmentally sustainable future through a balanced approach to local and regional development.

Local and regional development

Three dominant themes can be identified in the evolution of local and regional development and its relationship with economic and environmental matters:

1. The search for forms of economic activity and types of business organisation that demonstrate a high degree of consideration for the environmental

consequences of their operations and which attempt to minimise any
harmful effects.
2. The desirability of moving towards a pattern of spatial and social organisation that minimises the unnecessary or excessive use of resources, that
   maximises environmental benefits and which generates a higher overall
   standard of social welfare.
3. The benefit of meshing together these sectoral – both business and societal
   – and spatial elements in order to provide for the environmentally responsible and socially balanced planning and development of localities and
   regions.

These themes express the opportunity that exists for the integration of
company-based environmental management systems with the planning, development and management of local and regional areas. Welford and Gouldson
(1993, p. 189) refer to this process of balanced development as the creation of
a 'regional environmental management system', whilst Gibbs (1991) discusses
the importance of influencing investment decisions in order to guide the
restructuring of industry in ways that benefit the environment as well as the
economy. The attempt to create a mechanism for the simultaneous enhancement of the environmental and economic aspects of local and regional development has its antecedents in past attempts at spatial planning and
management.

A brief history of local and regional planning and development
Two separate, but parallel, strands of thinking and practice can be seen in the
history of environmental concern in local and regional development. The first
of these, in the USA, dates back to the 1920s, whilst the second, in Europe,
has its origins in the work of the nineteenth-century pioneers of the Garden
City movement and in the writings of Patrick Geddes. It does not really
matter whether the American or the European strand was the first or the
second to emerge, of far greater importance is the recognition that taken
together they represent the intermingling of the cultural, academic and professional traditions of North America and Europe. The American strand was
chiefly concerned with regions, and especially rural regions, whilst the
European tradition has its roots at a city or local level. The rediscovery of
these past attempts to achieve sustainable development is an important first
step towards the establishment of a more harmonious future between business
and the places where it is located.
   An early contribution to the debate as to how best to manage the distribution of environmental and economic resources across significant areas of territory, mainly at a regional scale, was articulated by a group of politicians,
conservationists, planners and business leaders who were later to become the
founders of the Regional Planning Association of America (Friedmann and
Weaver, 1979). This group developed and adapted a doctrine which was
aimed at creating, 'conditions that would establish a harmonious relationship

between human beings and nature, grounded in a bio-ethics that would show a deep respect for the limits of human intervention in natural processes and limit the cancerous growth of cities' (*ibid.*, p. 4).

These new ways of thinking ran counter to the dominant ethic of the nineteenth and early twentieth centuries, which placed great emphasis upon the achievement of economic growth at any price. This ethic regarded the environment as a storehouse of resources and a free dumping ground for unwanted residuals. It also placed considerable reliance upon advances in technology to overcome the resistance of natural processes to the forces of economic progress, and upon the capture of land and the other resources that were required in order to fuel further urbanisation and economic growth. Any damage done to the environment was considered to be unfortunate or was seen as an inevitable and unavoidable consequence of growth.

This ethic dominated societies on both sides of the Atlantic. In North America, the frontier mentality of exploit and move on was encouraged both by the rapid growth of population in the late nineteenth and early twentieth centuries, and by the desire of immigrants and government alike to develop the agricultural, mineral and other resources of a hitherto undeveloped continent. During the second half of the nineteenth century, 'the American landscape was transformed in ways that anticipated many of the environmental problems we face today' (Cronon, 1991, p. xv) and this process continued well into the twentieth century.

In Europe, the industrial revolution established the foundations for rapid economic growth, initially within the continent itself and later through the global expansion of European political and economic interests in the process of economic imperialism. This process of economic growth was not confined to capitalist economies, for in the 1920s nowhere was this search for growth more evident than in the then infant Soviet Union. In the Soviet Union planned industrialisation was seen as the chief weapon in the victory of technology over more gradual processes of change and evolution (Veblen, 1919). There were, however, a number of notable attempts to influence the headlong progress of economic growth. Perhaps the most important of these attempts in the UK was that of the Garden City movement. Ebenezer Howard in his *Garden Cities of To-morrow* placed emphasis upon the creation of an urban system in which industry would be decentralised from the inner parts of a city, and a new town would be built around the decentralised plant, in order to combine working and living in a healthy environment (Howard, 1902). Howard's notion of the 'Social City' (p. 126) was not aimed at creating a protected town or townscape; rather the intention was to create conditions in which 'the most valuable, and the most permanent of all vested interests – the vested interests of skill, labour, energy, talent, industry' (*ibid.* p. 138) might develop in a manner that respected the environment. Elsewhere in the UK, both before and after the first world war, other experiments in environmentally sustainable planning and practice took place, but these diminished in number and influence with the onset of the great depression of the late 1920s and 1930s and the relentless search for sources of economic revival and growth.

Other exceptions to the dominant ethic of growth at the expense of the environment emerged elsewhere in Europe. In 1920 the Siedlungsverband Ruhrkohlenbezirk (SVR) was established as an *ad hoc* planning body for the Ruhr. The creation of the SVR was a recognition that the acute economic, environmental and social problems of the region could not be met by the individual cities, and that action was necessary at a regional scale in order to promote the harmonious development of the economy and the environment (Alden and Morgan, 1974). French regional analysts such as Réclus and Le Play, although they were not in a situation to exert a direct influence upon local and regional planning, provided early insights into the causes and consequences of the dislocation of the economy from the environment. These analysts influenced Geddes and the other pioneers on both sides of the Atlantic and, more importantly, they provided the basis for the later development of integrated regional planning in France.

However, with the exception of the work of the SVR, the establishment of Garden Cities and new towns in the UK and elsewhere in Europe, and a limited number of early attempts at the comprehensive planning of regions using a model that sought to achieve the simultaneous development of the economy and the environment, the most significant and sustained challenge to the dominant ethic of the era occurred in North America. The ideas espoused by the Regional Planning Association of American (RPAA) coincided with the spirit of the times, and these 'dreamers with shovels' (Friedmann and Weaver, 1979, p. 5) were given the opportunity to apply their new doctrine in a direct and practical manner.

Fears that continued resource depletion would close future development options and, more importantly, that it would erode the possibility of achieving the economic and social revival of both urban and rural areas, led the RPAA to develop a new method of analysis and a new model for local and regional development. This model drew upon the new sciences of conservation, ecology and geotechnics, as well as the established tool of economic and social analysis. At the centre of the RPAA's philosophy were the ideas that cities could only survive in organic balance with the totality of their regional environment, and that the way to stop the destruction of this organic order was to use the natural building blocks of human settlement, or 'balanced regions' (MacKaye, 1928) as the basis for regional reconstruction.

Three fundamental tasks for balanced local and regional development have their origins in MacKaye's philosophy:

1. The conservation of natural resources.
2. The control of commodity flow.
3. The development of the environment.

These ideas can be seen to have a direct relationship with the business, environment and place (or place, work and folk) model that was outlined in the introduction to this chapter. In the view of MacKaye and Mumford (1929, p. 71) the quality of life in a successful area 'involves the development of cities and countrysides, industries and natural resources, as part of a regional whole'. This philosophy, and its method of expression through the integrated planning and implementation of the economic development and environmental management of river basin regions, was tested through the policies of Roosevelt's New Deal which established local and regional agencies such as the Tennessee Valley Authority (TVA).

Comprehensive river-basin regional development was the primary objective of the TVA. Drawing upon the themes and traditions of the RPAA and influenced, in part, by practice in Europe, especially the French practice of *l'aménagement du territoire* (in Sundquist's, 1975, p. 93, definition 'the search for a better distribution of people in relation to natural resources and economic activity'), the New Deal pioneers attempted to develop and utilise natural resources in a manner that was both sustainable and capable of supporting the 'economic and social well-being of the people' (Derthick, 1974, p. 20).

A helpful critique of these early attempts at sustainable regional planning was presented by Perloff and Wingo (1964) in their assessment of the relationship between natural resource endowment and economic growth. They argued that because the resource endowment is continuously redefined by changes in final and intermediate demand, production technology and economic organisation, factors other than those identified with the best environmental solution influence the pattern of resource development. In other words, resources and environment become the servant of the search for local and regional specialisation and economic growth. This move away from the environmental idealism of the 1920s to the modern paradigm of economic development was later reflected in attempts at comprehensive river-basin development in third-world countries during the 1950s and 1960s; a representation of what Friedmann and Weaver (1979, p. 78) describe as: 'resource development as a means of economic expansion'.

This brief excursion into the history of local and regional development serves two purposes. First, it positions the notion of sustainable development within its correct historical context. For example, many people regard sustainable development as a concept of the 1980s, but this is clearly not the case. Second, a historical focus illustrates the continuous tension that has existed in the theory and practice of local and regional planning between the notions of sustainability and of sustained economic growth. This second characteristic is of immense importance because, for almost five decades after the founding of the TVA, the environment has been perceived as a storehouse of resources to be plundered at will by those seeking to maximise local and regional economic growth. Until recently, many local and central government planners, industrialists and developers adopted a stance that placed economic growth above balanced development, and ignored the merits of a model of integrated comprehensive development that attempts to balance resource use with the social and economic missions of local and regional development. Friedmann and Weaver (*ibid.*) consider that 'territorial integration' (which places emphasis upon the operation and interaction of natural and socio-economic systems within a territory or locality) has been displaced by 'functional integration' (which emphasises the role of places and their resources in a wider economic order). It is only recently that territorial integration has sought to regain its rightful position and it is this re-establishment of a concern with the importance of place that provides the starting point for the introduction of the idea that environmentally sustainable businesses can play a central role in local and regional development.

Principles for environmentally sustainable local and regional development

Although views vary widely as to the definition and expression of sustainable development, four broad issues can be identified that need to be addressed in any attempt to develop localities and regions in an environmentally sustainable manner. These issues are as follows:

1. First, there are the standard elements of sustainable development related to environment, futurity, participation and equity.
2. Second, there are a number of issues that relate to the diversification and survival of a local or regional economy; resolving such issues is essential in order to allow the area to deal with any future adversity.
3. Third, there is the question of self-sufficiency; this is especially important in order to minimise environmentally and economically costly and wasteful resource inputs or transfers.
4. Fourthly, there is the question of territorial integration, both within an individual locality or region and between localities or regions.

Having defined these four broad issues it is possible to develop a number of principles that can be used to guide environmentally sustainable local and regional development. These specific principles have their origins in a number of concepts and principles, such as those for sustainable business development that were illustrated in Box 1.1, the principles adopted by the World Commission on Environment and Development (see Box 4.3), and the principles contained in the ICC's *Business Charter for Sustainable Development* (see Box 5.3). Addressing the issues outlined above, and building upon the work of Elkin, McLaren and Hillman (1991) environmentally sustainable local and regional development should

- comply with the primary principles of sustainable development: futurity (maintain a minimum environmental capital stock for future generations), environment (take into account the full and true environmental costs of an activity), participation (enable individuals to share in decision-making)

and equity (provide for social justice within current society and between generations);

- ensure that the local and regional economy is in good health in order that it can survive in the medium and long term; this should be based on policies that encourage diversification, full employment and a high level of local or regional control over capital and decision-making;
- encourage a higher degree of self-sufficiency, compatible with minimising resource use, and minimise costly and wasteful transfers of resources or the movement of waste; and
- allow a local area or region to develop a degree of territorial integration as a unified space, and ensure, at higher levels in the spatial hierarchy, that territorial rather than functional integration is regarded as the dominant force.

Although it will be necessary to identify detailed aims and objectives for each individual local or regional area, these general principles provide a broad indication of the structures and procedures necessary in order to achieve environmentally sustainable local and regional development. Even though the precise application of these principles will vary between areas, the new paradigm which they represent has more in common with the views that were expressed by the RPAA over half a century ago, than it has with the 'slash and burn' local and regional growth philosophy that has dominated much of the past forty years. The application of these principles in the practice of local and regional development is discussed in a later section of this chapter.

Environmentally sustainable business and local and regional development

Many attempts at local and regional development have sought to mobilise business investment in order to attract, stimulate and influence the spatial distribution and volume of economic growth. This implies that in order to implement sustainable development it is necessary to analyse and understand the dynamics of the relationship between business and the environment. The importance of understanding this relationship lies at the heart of any concern to ensure both the future prosperity and the environmental good health of localities and regions, and those who choose to ignore the relationship run the risk of working against the grain of the market.

As was noted in Chapter 2, Smith (1992) has stressed the need to consider the environmental dimension of the value chain and to consider those elements within the inbound–production–outbound parts of the chain that are likely to allow for the generation of green competitive advantage. Smith's expression of the value chain demonstrates the need to rethink many of the assumptions that currently dominate the practice of local and regional development and to redefine these assumptions in a more sustainable form. As the Town and Country Planning Association report *Planning for a Sustainable*

220   *Environmentally Sustainable Business*

Environment has noted, this implies that it is necessary to consider 'altering the way in which an economy is managed and relating this to the need for changed perceptions, lifestyles and livelihoods' (Clark, Burell and Roberts, 1993, p. 131).

In other analyses a similar message can be perceived. Coopers and Lybrand (1992) extend the message by noting that individuals – as residents and consumers – now place a high value on the achievement of more stringent environmental standards, and that this inevitably places pressure on business organisations to respond to such changes in consumer perceptions and preferences. The OECD (1990) shares this view and notes that the regeneration of city and regional economies is interlinked with the need to raise environmental standards in order to allow cities and regions to achieve success and maintain their status as successful places. Further evidence to support this view is provided in a study conducted by the University of Dortmund on the spatial impacts of the single European market (Ache, Bremm and Kunzmann, 1990). This study demonstrates the coincidence between environmental and economic factors that is important in determining the success of cities and regions. Amongst the factors that are identified by the Dortmund study as likely to determine the success of a city or region are

- the existence of an attractive, environmentally sound and well managed urban core with a wide range of facilities;
- the maintenance of a sound natural environment in the surrounding region and the existence of a built environment of high quality;
- the presence of a distinct and distinctive city and regional identity;
- the existence of effective links to the international transportation network;
- the presence of an international character in all sectors of activity, including manufacturing, services, cultural facilities and research and development; and
- the influence of a significant number of internationally minded actors in both the public and the private sectors.

Locational decisions and the views of localities

This accumulating evidence allows us to state with a degree of confidence, which was impossible to imagine even a decade ago, the value that many economic activities now place upon the environmental dimension. The increased value now placed on the environment by business is likely to prove to be a dominant force that will influence future locational and operational decisions. Equally, the greater emphasis now placed by local and regional development upon environmental quality will determine both the warmth of the welcome that is extended by localities and regions to new inward investments, and the willingness of localities to allow existing industries to remain if they are perceived to constitute a threat to the overall quality of the environment or to the environmental image of an area.

Although it is difficult to quantify the effects of increased environmental awareness upon the location of industry, some general trends can be observed. Quite clearly, from the evidence presented by the Dortmund study, large companies increasingly choose to avoid localities and regions that have a poor environmental performance or reputation. This has been recognised in both government-sponsored and academic research. At the inter-regional level broad investment shifts have occurred, exemplified by the relative shift of investment from the 'snowbelt' (or 'rustbelt') to the 'sunbelt' of the USA (Dicken, 1992) and, at a local and regional level, by the relative decline of manufacturing in the older urban areas and the growth of investment in the suburban and rural areas of the UK. There is evidence of a counter-tendency to both of these trends, but this is only apparent when derelict, contaminated and environmentally decaying areas and properties have been reclaimed, improved and regenerated. The 'rustbelt':'sunbelt' distinction between locations is often associated with the relative success of 'sunset' and 'sunrise' industries.

The reasons for the heightened awareness and response of industry to local and regional environmental conditions are many and complex, but they reflect the broad trends in corporate environmental awareness and preference that have been referred to elsewhere in this book. In addition, the response of companies indicates the difficulties of attracting qualified staff to work and live in environmentally degraded areas, the unwillingness of investors to purchase land or property in localities where returns are low or uncertain, and the desire of companies to avoid associating themselves with places that project a negative environmental image. Even traditionally attractive factors, such as the availability of cheap land or a plentiful supply of low-paid labour, are increasingly unlikely to prove sufficient to ensure the successful development of localities or regions. As the report of the Task Force on the Environment and the Internal Market (1989) has concluded, damage to the environment is not just a feature of the least favoured regions; it can also hinder or limit their development.

Examining this issue from the perspective of a local or regional area, it is clear that few areas wish to attract or retain industries that inflict serious or lasting damage upon a local or regional environment. The NIMBY syndrome has already been referred to and this manifestation of an area's unwillingness to accept new investment if it brings unacceptable environmental damage in its wake is increasingly reflected in local and community campaigns against existing bad neighbour industries. Horrendous environmental accidents, such as Seveso, Three-Mile Island and Bhopal, are well known, and they serve as a reminder to industry of its duty of care to its host location. Other more localised and less well-known accidents, such as the incident at Ellesmere Port that was referred to in Chapter 4, have generated fears and public protests in local communities in the UK and other advanced nations. Some localities and regions, wishing to rid themselves of bad neighbour activities, have recently enacted strict legislation that has, in effect, prohibited existing undesirable industries from continuing to function, and which deters potentially polluting industries from locating in the area. Chapman and Walker (1987, p. 256) consider California and Oregon to 'lie at the strict end of a subjective spectrum of environmental regulation', and equivalent differences in stance, at both national and regional scale, can be identified in Europe (Cannon, 1992).

Towards a common agenda

A number of common themes can be identified in the progress that has been made by business towards the adoption of enhanced attitudes towards the environment, and these are echoed in the rediscovery by local and regional planners of a mode of operation that seeks to achieve a more balanced form of spatial development. These common themes suggest that it is possible to develop a strategic link between business objectives and the stated desire of localities and regions to improve their environmental image and performance (Welford and Gouldson, 1993). Some of the most important themes in the emergence of the improved relationship between business and the environment can be summarised as follows:

- The adoption by companies of environmental assessment, auditing and management systems, and the development of corporate environmental policies.
- Growing environmental concern in accountancy and the employment by accounting practices of environmental specialists.
- The increased use made by the financial sector of environmental criteria in determining the availability and amount of funds to be provided for a project.
- Raised legal standards and the incorporation of environmental factors in the determination of insurance premiums.
- Improvements in packaging and product design that reflect the enhanced requirements of both businesses and consumers.
- The introduction of methods of marketing and public relations that emphasise the environmental values and preferences of consumers.
- Emphasis in the provision of training and skills development upon environmental issues.
- The rise of green consumerism and the increased provision of written and other material that provides guidance for consumers.
- Opportunities for the development of new business activities and for new ventures in the field of environmentally sound manufacturing.
- The emergence of major opportunities for manufacturing and service industries in relation to the control of pollution, including the design, manufacture and operation of pollution control equipment.
- The preparation of a number of important sector-specific studies of ways in which individual industries can adapt their operations in order to address particular environmental challenges, goals and opportunities.
- The recognition of the significance of locality as a determining factor in the development and adoption of environmentally sound solutions to business problems.

Many of the key themes that can be identified in the relationship between business and the environment (Roberts, 1992) have been translated into an agenda for action at the level of the individual company or a specific industrial sector. This experience of the adoption of environmental policies by companies and in individual sectors has recently been extended to the emergence of a broader concern for local environmental conditions. The key themes that have been identified in the relationship between business and the environment can be used to establish an agenda for a form of local and regional development that both meets the needs of business and respects the environment (Roberts, 1994). Taking each of the themes listed above, the implications for local and regional development are as follows:

- *Environmental auditing, assessment, management and policy.* Future local and regional development strategies should use parallel auditing and assessment methods in order to establish policies and management procedures that are designed to enhance the environment and to improve the attractiveness of an area as a location for economic activities.
- *Environment and accountancy.* The messages of green accounting, such as the need to take a long-term view and to utilise discount rates that incorporate the real gains that can be obtained by adopting enhanced environmental values, should become key elements in the design and implementation of plans for local and regional development.
- *Environmental funds.* Given the growing size and significance of this source of investment, it is important to develop local and regional policies that can be used to attract, encourage and support economic activities that can benefit from such funds, and which can contribute to the creation of a complex or network of green activities.
- *Law and insurance.* Strategies for local and regional development should respect current legal standards and anticipate more rigorous legislation in future. Any plans and programmes should seek to minimise hazards and risks, and should ensure that an environmental contingency plan is available in order to deal with any environmental accidents that might occur.
- *Packaging and product design.* New markets have emerged in relation to improved products, product design, methods of packaging and the reuse of materials. These represent opportunities for the development of local and regional niche and sectoral specialisations.
- *Marketing and public relations.* Environmentally sensitive marketing can assist both business and local and regional areas to establish their green credentials, and to ensure that the desired image is projected. This enhanced environmental image is an essential feature of a successful company or area.
- *Training and education.* Employee awareness, the provision of enhanced skills related to particular environmental issues and the preferences demonstrated by educated and mobile professionals for working and resi-

dential environments that are of high quality, are essential features of local and regional development.

- *Green consumerism.* The power of the citizen-consumer to influence issues such as quality of life, products, employment opportunities and investment possibilities, has grown in recent years. People live in places, and both consumer preferences and the support that can be provided by the local communities that are the hosts of businesses, should be incorporated into programmes for local and regional development.

- *Business opportunities.* New business opportunities, including environmental products, services and new ventures, can make a major contribution to the growth of a local or regional economy. Such activities can form the basis for a transition strategy, for new business start-ups or for the attraction of inward investment.

- *Pollution control.* This is a specific sector of economic activity that is currently experiencing rapid growth. Solving pollution problems at a local or regional level can both improve the condition of the immediate environment and can provide the basis for the future export of technology, services and expertise.

- *Sector studies.* Specialist sector studies can assist in the identification of environmental priorities and opportunities from local to international levels; such studies can form the basis for the development of specific policies at local and regional levels that are aimed at the generation of increased business opportunities for existing companies, the stimulation of new indigenous ventures and the attraction of inward investment.

- *Significance of locality.* Successful businesses and business managers are a strong and influential peer group, and they exert considerable influence upon other local and regional businesses. Peer group statements, and local examples which demonstrate the successful adoption of enhanced environmental behaviour, are important elements in a local and regional development programme that seeks to improve the environmental condition of an area. Local examples of successful environmental improvements can be used in a place marketing strategy.

The emergence of these common concerns, set within a framework provided by changed attitudes towards the environment and a new definition as to what constitutes an acceptable framework of development, can help to set a common agenda for business and for local and regional development. By internalising environmental issues within their decision-making structures, companies are now beginning to address the direct impacts and wider implications of their activities in a way that allows for any conflict between the ecological and competitive environments to be resolved. This internal resolution of the tension between economic pressures and environmental values is an important step in the right direction. However, unless this change is also reflected in the stance adopted by local and regional development, it is possible that the potential gains may be diluted or ignored. Such a situation would benefit neither firms nor those localities and regions that are seeking a new rationale for development.

Experiments in implementation

Much of the evidence presented in this book reflects a stance that places emphasis upon the importance of the role that is played by place in under-standing the business and environment relationship. This factor also empha-sises that strategies for the development of environmentally sustainable businesses need to be constructed on a foundation that reflects the uniqueness of the place in which a business is located. This should not be interpreted as suggesting that each individual locality or region can be considered as an economic or environmental island; rather it is stated in order to convey the need for a particular local blend of policy to reflect the environmental conditions and economic structure of an individual area. For example, it would be a pointless exercise to attempt to superimpose a model of economic and environment development that had originally been designed to provide a framework for the future balanced growth of Birmingham or Leeds upon the remote North West Highlands of Scotland or the moorland vastness of Mynydd Hiraethog. It is important that an appropriate response should be constructed on a basis that reflects the particular characteristics of an individ-ual place. Such a response should also recognise the potential that exists for the future economic and environmental development of that place.

Notwithstanding the need for a particular response to be provided that is matched to the conditions and requirements of an individual place, tremen-dous scope exists to demonstrate the many ways in which a business can improve its environmental performance, to publicise the methods available for the analysis of environmental problems, and to indicate the potential for the development of solutions. A number of local pilot projects, which seek to act as exemplars of the power of local networks to bring about change in the re-lationship between business and the environment, have been established by the Advisory Committee on Business and the Environment (ACBE). The ACBE Local Initiatives are intended as focused local schemes, each of which is tailored to the needs of local business and the conditions of the local environ-ment. Whilst the 11 initiatives concentrate upon meeting the needs of small and medium enterprises, they also draw upon the experience and expertise of the larger companies that are present in a local area. The local initiatives that are supported by ACBE are listed in Box 9.1.

Each of the local initiatives has its own individual style of operation, and they draw their support from a range of local and national companies and organisations. A common feature of the initiatives is the use of a partnership model of operation that brings together the public and private sectors in order to share expertise and experience. Because the local initiatives are situated in very different local and regional economies, each of which varies considerably in terms of size, economic structure and complexity, the methods of working and the services that are offered reflect different approaches to the resolution

Box 9.1   *Advisory Committee on Business and the Environment: Local Initiatives Network*

The ACBE Local Initiatives Network has been established to promulgate environmental messages to British business, especially small and medium-sized enterprises. Eleven pilot schemes have been supported in pursuit of the ACBE objectives. The selection criteria place emphasis on

- the need for local business leadership;
- the availability of private sector leadership;
- the involvement of the private sector in the operation of the initiative; and
- the need to demonstrate that the initiative can become self-funding within three years.

The 11 pilot projects are located in a variety of localities and regions that demonstrate different economic and environmental characteristics:

Amber Valley
Blackburn
Dudley
Hemel Hempstead
Leeds
Newcastle upon Tyne
Plymouth
Sheffield
Sutton
Wearside

A variety of different operational structures and approaches reflect the range of local opportunities. Some of the ACBE pilot projects operate within existing local partnerships, some work within existing schemes such as Business Link and others have been established as companies.

of the environmental problems that confront business. Although some of the services that are provided are designed to assist local companies to deal with specific environmental problems, the local initiatives are also proactive organisations. Typical services offered by the local initiatives include: the provision of briefings on the implications for business of existing and forthcoming environmental legislation, advice on energy efficiency, other utility audits; initial environmental reviews and more specialised advice on specific environmental problems; the presentation of solutions to particular environmental problems; and the provision of access to a range of environmental advisory and technical services.

Whilst it is too early to evaluate the success of the ACBE pilot project scheme, the importance of the model cannot be doubted. Building upon local initiatives, existing organisational arrangements and the influence that can be exerted by a local business peer group in order to influence the behaviour of companies, this locally rooted model demonstrates the synergies that can be harnessed in order to bring about change.

A second example of the local implementation and influence of business and the environment initiatives is provided by the Environment City movement. This organisation was established by the Royal Society for Nature Conservation with support from British Telecommunications, and has as its primary objective the implementation of local programmes for facilitating sustainability in urban areas. Each of the four Environment Cities that have been designated – Leicester, Middlesbrough, Leeds and Peterborough – reflect a variety of environmental, social and economic conditions, and each city has its own particular existing governmental and private sector structures. However, two common themes are central to each of the cities: the ethos of partnership and a holistic approach. In addition, each Environment City is organised around eight specialist working groups:

1. Energy.
2. Transport.
3. Waste and Pollution.
4. Food and Agriculture.
5. Economy and Work.
6. Built Environment.
7. Natural Environment.
8. Social Environment.

Each of these specialist groups operates a programme of activities centred around a common strategy that is aimed at defining what sustainability means in practice.

A number of these specialist working groups are of particular relevance to the development of environmentally sustainable businesses:

- Designing and developing schemes to save energy and to establish facilities, such as combined heat and power, that offer cost-effective and environmentally acceptable means of generating energy.
- Introducing more environmentally efficient modes of transport, and adapting conventional transport modes in order to reduce their environmental impact though measures such as car-sharing and easing the peak traffic loads experienced in many urban areas.
- Conducting research into more environmentally acceptable methods of construction and building conversion, and into the use and reuse of building materials that do not have adverse environmental impacts.
- Creating mechanisms for the minimisation of waste, including schemes for the collection and recycling of industrial materials.

All the Environment Cities are making progress towards the achievement of their objectives. The pace and impact of change varies from city to city and, within cities, from sector to sector. Given that urban areas are the places where a high proportion of the population live, and will continue to live, it is important that these experiments in the development and implementation of sustainable cities continue to be supported, and that their successes and failures are disseminated widely.

The Sustainable City Region

A further example of an attempt to promote environmentally sustainable local and regional development is provided by the Sustainable City Region project. This project has its origins in the work of the Town and Country Planning Association's Sustainable Development Study Group (Blowers, 1993b) and it represents an attempt to translate some of the broader principles of sustainable development into a form that will allow for their implementation at a local and regional level. The project has also promoted the need to consider simultaneously the environmental and social dimensions of sustainable development through the adoption of an integrated and balanced approach to spatial development.

The original report of the Study Group examined, amongst other themes, the objectives and characteristics of a sustainable economy, and suggested that sustainable economic development can be related to five major goals of sustainable development:

1. Conservation of resources.
2. Balanced development.
3. Environmental quality.
4. Reducing the waste of human resources.
5. Participation.

Three key aspects of sustainable economic development are identified by the study: the greening of business, the adoption of sustainable development in planning and economic development, and the creation of sustainable livelihoods (Clark, Burall and Roberts, 1993). Following a detailed analysis of these issues, the study group recommended a number of specific actions necessary to assist in the promotion of sustainable economic development. These include

- the promotion of life-cycle analysis and other tools necessary to design and develop green products;
- the requirement that companies should include an environmental statement in their annual reports;
- the development of local partnerships between industry and local authorities to promote recycling;
- the adoption by industry of environmental policies and strategies, and the promotion of environmental management systems;

- the use of planning powers to encourage changes in the location of business activities which match infrastructure and housing resources;
- the promotion of local environment and business organisations; and
- the need to investigate methods of home-based working and encourage the development of the infrastructure necessary to support such a mode of economic activity.

Together with a number of recommendations relevant to other sectors of activity – transport, energy, pollution, built environment and pollution – these proposals represent the fundamental elements necessary for the development of a Sustainable City Region. Drawing upon the specific characteristics and issues identified in the sectoral analyses, the study group has proposed an outline model for the further development of the Sustainable City Region concept. This model is based upon the identification of

- appropriate sets of strategic urban and rural policies; and
- the changes required in institutional and governmental structures in order to deliver such policies.

Urban and rural forms to achieve sustainability are at different stages in their development, but 'for maximum effect, these initiatives need to be co-ordinated' (Breheny and Rookwood, 1993, p. 151). The features of this process of integration have been investigated through the establishment and development of a demonstration project.

Greater Manchester has provided a test-bed for the application of some of the ideas contained in the original TCPA report. The scope of the Manchester 2020 project is set at the level of the city region, and it aims to 'create viable and practical scenarios for sustainable development in the planning and development of urban systems, for the short, medium and longer term' (Ravetz, 1994, p. 2). A city region, rather than an individual city or district, has been selected as an appropriate area for study because such areas more accurately reflect the bioregion within which an individual urban area is set. City regions also reflect the complex series of interactions among environmental, economic and social forces that act to generate urban change.

The business and environment dimension of the Manchester 2020 project places particular emphasis upon

- land use and transportation issues;
- energy demand;
- characteristics and trends in the local economy; and
- regional trends and influences.

In addition, the analysis of the business and environment relationship in the Greater Manchester area is dependent upon, and informed by, studies of other issues, including energy production, natural environment and resources, built environment, transport, waste and pollution, and the social and economic context. The intended output of the project will be based on three scenarios that anticipate a series of changes in the attitude adopted towards the environment. These scenarios are expected to develop in a number of phases:

- Stabilisation of current growth trends in environmental impacts – this equates to what is achievable under current conditions.
- Redirection and making the transition to a reduction in environmental impact trends.
- Sustainability of the urban system.

Some or all of these scenarios may occur at different places at a single point in time; certain parts of the city region are already further along the pathway towards sustainability than others and it is expected that the rate of progress will continue to vary in future. This variable spatial geometry in the progress of sustainability is likely to feature as a characteristic both within and between regions; it reflects the varied environmental inheritance of individual places, their capacity and opportunity to bring about change, and the strength of local determination to foster and implement an improvement in the environmental performance of human activities.

This and other experiments in implementation emphasise the need for the development of solutions to environmental problems to be constructed in response to the difficulties and opportunities that are encountered in a particular place. They also indicate the desirability of learning from experience and of transferring the messages of successful practice. However, no company, city or region can be considered in isolation.

Most forms of human activity have impacts across a wide range of environments, many of which may be distant from the final point of consumption of a product. Companies in advanced nations draw upon the resource base of developing countries through a complex international network of trading relationships; this ecological capital, which may be located thousands of miles from the region in which it is consumed, forms the 'shadow ecology of an economy' (MacNeill, Winsemius and Yakushiji, 1991, p. 58). Equally, a city draws water, energy and many other resources from distant points leaving an environmental or ecological footprint of its consumption pattern. Analysing the extent and implications of the environmental hinterland of a company or a city can assist in the promotion of a better understanding of the need for collective action to be taken in order to achieve a more sustainable environment.

Towards integrated environmental development

Having examined the history, content and outcomes of previous attempts at regional and local development, and having considered various aspects of the relationship between economic activity and the environment, this section now outlines some of the major issues that are likely to prove to be significant in the sustainable development of regions and localities.

The first point to note is that some past attempts at local and regional development have paid specific attention to environmental issues. The lessons from America, which were referred to in the second section of this chapter, provide one example, but others can be identified. Boudeville (1966) notes the importance of using natural resources in a harmonious manner in order to avoid excessive economic and environmental costs, and in order to allow for the *in situ* development of those localities and regions where resources are located.

Likewise, it has long been recognised that a poor environment detracts from the attractiveness of a locality or region, and that future success depends equally upon reclaiming the legacy of past environmental degradation (Secretary of State for Economic Affairs, 1969), and ensuring that, in future, policies are pursued which respect the environment.

The integration of environmental concerns with local and regional development aims to reduce the possibility of any future dislocation among environmental, economic and spatial processes. Past eras of development have been less effective than might have been expected due to the dislocation of the latter two issues; economic planning in the UK has been the responsibility of the Department of Trade and Industry, whilst the Department of the Environment has taken the lead in spatial matters. Any attempt at the integrated planning of localities and regions should recognise these previous failings. Bouwer (1993) observes that two types of integration are required: within environmental planning and management, and between environmental policy and spatial planning. A third category can be added if the need is accepted for integration between economic policy and the spatial and environmental aspects of local and regional development. This relationship among economic processes, the environment and space has been explored by Lipietz (1992) who argues that Fordist (mass-production) modes of production, spatial organisational and regulation create conditions in which the environmental consequences of production become the subject of neglect. In his view 'the natural tendency of firms is to deplete their resources or overwhelm them with waste' (*ibid*. p. 52). Lipietz also argues that place-based ecological problems are an extension of the link which exists between economic activity and place; the common roots of ecology and economy interact to create particular conditions in an individual locality.

If Lipietz is correct in his diagnosis and prognosis, then the roots of a strategy for the sustainable development of localities and regions can be found in the transition from a Fordist to post-Fordist mode of regulation, and in the emergence of the region, and especially the balanced region or bioregion, as the most suitable level of spatial organisation to tackle both ecological and economic problems. This view is supported by evidence from both developed and less developed nations. Cohen (1993) argues that individual urban areas are too small to cope with the transmunicipal and region-wide incidence of environmental problems, and that this implies the need to strengthen metropolitan and regional government. In order to intervene in an effective manner, an integrated policy should be constructed at what Stohr (1990) calls the 'meso level'; influenced by policy from above – such as international agreements regarding carbon emissions – and from below – for example, local schemes for waste reduction and recycling.

The spatial expression of policy also implies action at a regional level. City sprawl and the inherent environmental inefficiency of many current spatial forms suggest that individual areas working in isolation are unlikely to be able to generate satisfactory solutions. An integrated policy, which brings together local initiatives in order to allow for the development of localities and regions, requires, in the view of Elkin, McLaren and Hillman (1991), that

- the levels of pollution emitted and the demands made on resources be reduced;
- the transport required for the distribution of raw materials, goods and services be reduced;
- waste and pollution resulting from the consumption of products be reduced; and
- economic development which contributes to environmental sustainability be promoted.

These principles for sustainable economic and environmental development are similar in both origin and content to those advocated for urban areas by the OECD (1990). The OECD placed emphasis upon

- developing and monitoring long-term strategies which seek to enhance and maintain environmental quality;
- adopting a cross-sectoral approach which ensures that all organisations and agencies work towards common targets;
- facilitating co-operation within the public sector and among the public, private and voluntary sectors;
- enabling the producers of pollutants and waste to absorb the environmental and social costs of their operations;
- setting and enforcing minimum standards of environmental performance;
- increasing the use of renewable resources and recycling materials; and
- encouraging and building on local and regional initiatives.

Having set the broad principles and objectives for sustainable regional development, the next step is to outline a possible approach to the generation of a spatial expression of these objectives. It is difficult to isolate a single pathway towards a sustainable regional spatial structure because of the many differences which exist, in terms of resource endowment, natural form and built environment, both within and between regions. In addition, questions of equity need to be considered and it is important to acknowledge the variety of socioeconomic patterns that exists within regions. However, notwithstanding the need for local solutions, certain basic principles can be identified:

- The desirability of minimising the number and length of journeys – this suggests that work, home and leisure activities should be more spatially concentrated; there is little point in an environmentally aware company requiring its labour force to commute excessive distances.

- The need to reconsider the location of economic activities, such as industry, retailing and leisure, in order to ensure that such activities are accessible by public rather than private transport and, if environmentally acceptable, to locate them within or adjacent to residential communities.

- The need to reconsider the mix of economic activities and to segregate those activities that generate significant environmental problems in order that they might benefit from collective solutions to the problems of pollution and waste management.

- The desirability of developing forms of industrial and residential development that are in accord with the best practice of location, layout and construction in order to achieve maximum efficiency in the use of energy and materials.

- The generation of both hard and soft infrastructures that allow for the best use of natural resources (such as water), the collection and recycling of waste materials and the ability to substitute physical movement with other forms of interaction.

In developing an appropriate spatial strategy it is important to recognise that a balanced approach is required. Owens and Rickaby (1992) note that the identification of an environmentally sustainable solution is not the same as the adoption of a fuel-conserving strategy, and that this shift in values implies the need to reduce the physical separation of activities and to integrate land-use and transport planning. Of equal importance is the need to ensure that the desire to achieve environmental sustainability is balanced against social objectives; as Breheny (1993, p. 72) has observed: 'there is little point in creating an alienated community for the sake of energy conservation'.

This call for a balanced approach takes the environmentally aware local and regional planner or developer back to the 1930s and to the principles which were outlined in the second section of this chapter. Then, as now, there were no easy solutions, and the achievement of an environmentally sustainable approach to regional development and planning had to be set within the context provided by the full array of problems and opportunities visible in an individual region or locality.

Another vital element in the development of an environmentally sustainable approach to local and regional development is the principle of avoiding irreversible damage. In this case it is possible to identify recent advances in both theory and practice. Project managers, developers and planners can now call upon the tools of environmental auditing and assessment to assist them in their designs and deliberations. Strategic environmental assessment is now well established and has been incorporated into the procedures utilised by development agencies. At a lower spatial scale the Department of the Environment (1992b) now requires planning and development authorities to incorporate environmental considerations into the appraisal of policies as plans and schemes are prepared.

A further issue to be addressed is the role that enhanced strategic vision can play in the adoption of a more sustainable approach to local and regional development. A real danger exists that the 'quick fix' mentality which has dominated many areas of development during past decades will expect a rapid response to any environmental problems that are encountered and that it will require the problem to be solved within the time limits imposed by the electoral cycle. This is an unrealistic and dangerous assumption and it should be countered at the outset. Begg (1991) has argued that the adoption of sustainable attitudes implies the need to think beyond the usual time horizon of 10–15 years; indeed, it can be suggested that short-term palliatives are inherently dangerous because they are likely to generate complacency and the belief that an environmental problem can be solved for once and for all. A strategic vision approach is one which places emphasis upon

- the complex nature of a problem;
- the need for consistency of purpose;
- the importance of encouraging the widest possible participation;
- the creation of a system which is self-sustaining;
- the need to create consensus and then ensure that implementation adheres to agreed objectives; and
- the need to monitor, evaluate and disseminate the results achieved.

A strategic vision approach places particular emphasis upon co-operation and the development of confidence in the formulation and operation of the development process as a whole (Roberts, 1990). This approach is not restricted solely to a consideration of issues related to the design of policy; rather it is equally applicable to the implementation of local and regional programmes of development.

Although it is possible to identify and assess the challenges presented by the introduction of the notion of sustainable development, it is less easy to point to examples of the adoption of sustainable solutions to the development of localities and regions. Most evidence reflects action at a global, sectoral, or very local level. International agreements and actions often have profound implications for local and regional areas, whilst many sectoral and individual activities can be aggregated and merged to provide a regional or local response. However, such forms of action, whilst commendable in themselves, lack the integration among environment, economy and space which has been identified as the distinguishing feature of the balanced development of localities and regions.

Other clues as to the nature of future local and regional development practice can be gained from a study of the adaptation strategies of transnational companies as they seek to reorientate their structures and methods of production in order to comply with the principles of sustainable development. In those areas where such firms are well represented, it is likely that the prospects for future prosperity and quality of life will be enhanced. In addition, it is reasonable to assume that a vigorous and diversified base of small and medium environmentally responsible enterprises will develop. Conversely, those areas that are dominated by old, decaying and environmentally unsound economic activities are likely to experience a fall in demand for the traditional goods and services which they supply (Jacobs, 1991). An alternative view of the future prospects for environmentally degraded localities and regions is that they may face pressure to become the environmental 'sinks' or dumping grounds for other more environmentally advanced areas. One example of this new form of specialisation has been explored by the Task Force on the Environment and the Internal Market (Task Force, 1989). The report of the task force considered the case of waste tourism – a process whereby hazardous waste seeks out a location that is willing to receive it. Few areas aspire to become the garbage heap of the European economy, but some may find that this is their destiny unless they adopt sustainable attitudes and forms of development.

This prospect of a two-tier division of localities and regions, into environmentally aware and economically successful areas, and environmentally degraded and economically backward places, is now a reality and is becoming more so as time progresses. The implications of ignoring the economic and environmental opportunities, which are presented by an approach to local and regional development that is based upon the principles of sustainable development, may be likened to the consequences of failing to invest in skills and training. To fail to recognise the importance of the environmental market for goods and services in the generation and implementation of regional strategies is to ignore a large and growing market.

Examples now exist of how environmentally sustainable local and regional development might proceed. Most schemes are in their infancy, but they provide clues as to how both old industrial localities and less degraded areas can be revitalised using an environmental model. The recent *Report on Regional Planning Guidance for the West Midlands Region* (West Midlands Regional Forum, 1993) acknowledges the key role played by environmental sustainability, but it also notes the difficulties likely to be encountered in translating the concept into reality. Similar views have been expressed in other areas, including the interim *Green Plan* for South East England (South East Economic Development Strategy, 1990), which provides a comprehensive review of the various environmental challenges that face this region and outlines a work programme for the development of a strategic solution to all or some of them. Elsewhere in Europe similar messages can be identified, including some schemes that are at a more advanced stage. An important model for the sustainable planning of rural areas has been developed for the Avoca–Avonmore catchment region in Ireland (EMA, 1992).

More modest in scale, but important in terms of their adoption of environmental sustainability as the core concept in regeneration, are Project Genesis in Durham (Derwentside District Council, 1993) and The Earth Centre scheme for the Dearne Valley subregion of Yorkshire (The Earth Centre, 1992). Project Genesis is aimed at 'bringing together the many strands of the current environmental debate into a viable development strategy' (Derwentside District Council, 1993, p. 1), whilst The Earth Centre is planned as a national and international demonstration project to illustrate the many facets of sustainable living. The Earth Centre also aims to play a 'major role in the renaissance of the Dearne Valley' (The Earth Centre, 1992, p. 11) and, amongst other proposals under consideration, a green industrial park may be developed.

These examples illustrate the many ways in which sustainable development can be translated into the generation of strategies for the development of localities and regions. Their common characteristics include a recognition that the current paradigm of development no longer provides a satisfactory base from which to face the new challenges, and the realisation that changing course will take many years. An additional characteristic is the acceptance of the need to generate solutions that can be used both to tackle problems and to develop any opportunities that are presented. Top-down solutions are, on their own, unlikely to recognise the rich diversity of local and regional potential, whilst bottom-up solutions may fail to ensure the satisfactory use of resources. Local initiatives are vital in order to generate company-based and collective solutions that can then be integrated into more environmentally and economically efficient strategies at a regional level.

The contribution of business to the many processes that are associated with the sustainable development of local and regional economics can be identified in relation to

- the supply of environmentally sound goods and services;
- the promotion of enhanced standards of environmental performance within companies;
- the provision of help and assistance to other associated businesses and to the general business community; and
- the generation of new activities, either on an individual or a collective basis, that create new enterprises and employment.

The first three contributions have already been discussed at some length elsewhere in this book, and attention is now focused upon the final category of action.

Green growth poles

During the 1950s and 1960s the idea of establishing growth poles as a mechanism to enable the development of new economic activities was elaborated and applied in a number of countries. The theory that underpins the notion of a growth pole is that by concentrating investment in a single sector, or a cluster of linked sectors, of economic activity, then the propulsive effects created by this pole will spread throughout the sector or the area in which it is based. Glasson (1974) identifies a number of aspects of the theory that are relevant to the stimulation of growth:

- A leading industry (*industrie motrice*), a propulsive or growing industry or set of industries, is established in an area.
- The growth generated by this industry then induces the polarisation of other economic units into the pole of growth.
- This, in time, causes the propulsive effects to spread outwards.

Traditionally, an industry would be selected as an *industrie motrice* due to its proven qualities as a generator of backward and forward linkages, such as car assembly or steel making. These activities, in Glasson's view, would

- be new and dynamic with an advanced level of technology;
- have a high income elasticity of demand for its products which are usually sold to national markets;
- have strong interindustry linkages with other sectors;
- be relatively large;
- have a high ability to innovate; and
- belong to a fast-growing industrial sector.

Growth pole theory was applied through the designation and development of growth points, centres and areas in many different types of region and locality. Old industrial areas were the recipients of new industrial complexes, typically a car assembly plant; in rural areas growth centres were established based on, for example, new electronics industries; and in areas of higher growth, economic activities were concentrated in new towns. Some of these experiments succeeded in their mission, whilst others were less successful. Nevertheless, the creation of growth poles did stimulate growth, albeit sometimes not of an environmentally sustainable nature.

The rise in demand for environmental goods and services, and the opportunity to establish new economic activities, both large and small, could utilise the growth pole model as a method for the spatial and sectoral organisation of future economic development. It would, for example, be possible to establish a multimaterial waste reprocessing plant as the *industrie motrice* of a green growth pole. Backward linkages would include economic activities responsible for the collection and primary sorting of waste, whilst forward linkages could be established through the creation of enterprises that make use of recycled materials as a substitute for conventional raw materials. One major producer of packaging materials has already established an experimental plant with an annual processing capacity of 2,500 tonnes and is now planning to build a larger plant with four times this capability.

Parallel innovations could also be established at a local level, including more specialised facilities dealing with, for example, redundant computer systems or particular forms of toxic waste. A local, regional and national network of such plants offers the potential to create the growth poles of the future. The advantages of this approach are that green growth poles would be able to generate the necessary economies of scale that are currently absent in many reprocessing schemes and, by creating a network of plants, any problems related to the supply of materials and the distribution of products would be minimised.

By harmonising public and private investment in this manner the requirements of business could be integrated with the aims of local and regional development. Converting the problems associated with unwanted waste into a propulsive sector of activity offers both economic and environmental advantages. Similar schemes could be based upon the production of equipment for the prevention of pollution or, as has been discussed in earlier chapters, the dismantling of cars, white goods and other products that have a limited overall operational life, but which contain components that can be recycled or reused.

The benefits for business

The benefits for businesses of becoming involved with the promotion of environmentally sustainable local and regional development can be considered in relation to

- the advantages to be obtained through the establishment of a complex of like-minded economic activities;
- the creation of an infrastructure of environmental facilities and services in a locality or region; and
- the enhancement of the quality of life and attractiveness of an area.

Each of these issues is now considered in more detail.

By adopting a more sustainable approach towards the environment the process of local regional development will inevitably place particular emphasis upon the contribution that can be made by existing companies. Indeed, it is unlikely that a balanced development strategy will be successful if it fails to command the active support of industries that are already located in an area. Whilst inward investments may help to support the objectives of a strategy, it is increasingly likely that such investments will only be attracted to a locality if it can offer a high quality of life and an established base of economic activities that are already working towards the goals of environmental sustainability.

Given the coincidence that exists between the objectives of sustainable local and regional development and those of an environmentally sustainable business, there is considerable potential for mutual benefit. By encouraging and supporting the implementation of higher environmental standards in existing companies, and through the provision of advice, financial assistance and environmentally sound infrastructure, local and regional development organisations can help to stimulate business confidence and improve economic performance. Companies will gain immediate benefits from this support and may, in time, also experience an increase in demand for their products and services from other companies in the area.

New business opportunities will emerge from this virtuous cycle of improvement. Some of these may be associated with an increase in demand for existing products and services, whilst others may result from new initiatives such as the creation of recycling industries. The green growth pole effect that was discussed in the preceding section could accelerate the process of development.

Above all, companies will benefit from their participation in a collaborative partnership for positive change. The public sector partners in this venture – local authorities, regional development organisations and government departments – are also frequently the regulators of environmental standards and, by working in partnership with these bodies, companies will gain from the greater understanding and trust that is generated.

A second major benefit from which companies will gain competitive advantage relates to the establishment of a framework of environmental policies and services. Some of these have already been mentioned, but other important policies include the provision of environmental advisory services, the creation of environmental business forums and associations, the establishment of green purchasing networks and the enhancement of public transport. Gibbs (1991) has suggested that these policies may be extended, subject to the terms of competitive tendering, to include the development of local authority purchasing strategies that encourage green local firms, and the provision of packages of financial assistance that are aimed at the encouragement of environmental production.

The provision of environmental infrastructure could be extended through the establishment of environmentally sound and economically efficient methods for the generation of combined heat and power, the creation of research and development facilities aimed at the support of innovation and the introduction of new products, and the provision of cost-effective means for the safe disposal of waste. The latter example also represents a new business opportunity.

A third benefit for business may emerge from the overall improvement of the environment of a locality or region. A number of authors have pointed to the benefits that may be obtained by businesses through the adoption of balanced local and regional development (Bowen and Mayhew, 1991). Chief amongst such benefits are the enhanced ability of companies located in environmentally sound areas to attract and retain qualified staff, and the positive image that is projected by localities and regions that have adopted a balanced approach to development. A region or locality that has placed emphasis upon the rehabilitation of derelict and polluted areas, the encouragement of environmentally sound production, and the enhancement of quality of life is more likely to be successful than other areas. Such an area will also be a place in which indigenous business prospers.

Projecting the difference that results from a balanced approach to local and regional development offers companies the opportunity to report their own environmental progress. The best advertisements for a successful place are the success stories of individual companies, and free advertising provided through the medium of a good environmental practice handbook or guide is of far greater value to a company than any amount of self-promotion.

The modern expression of the folk, work and place relationship is to be found in the balanced development of localities and regions, organised and supported through a partnership between the public and private sectors, and working towards the creation and realisation of mutual benefits.

Conclusions

In this chapter attention has been focused upon the relationship between environmentally sound business and the balanced development of local and regional areas. Achieving balanced development requires a return to the basic principles that are expressed by the relationship among folk, work and place. People value places, and the interface between business and the environment is subject to stringent scrutiny when it impinges upon the quality of life of an individual locality or region.

The process of generating a balanced approach to development can be assisted by returning to the lessons first elucidated by Geddes, Howard and the Regional Planning Association of America. They emphasised the need for economic activities to work in harmony with the environment, and demonstrated the mutual benefits that can be obtained if business and the community work hand in hand.

Balanced development implies the need to change present ways of working and the desirability of adopting new practices in both industry and the public sector. But it also implies the creation of new business opportunities that will benefit both companies and the areas in which they are located. It is argued that net gains will result from the adoption of environmentally sound attitudes and practices.

Initial results from a number of experimental schemes and projects indicate the benefits that are likely to accrue from the adoption of balanced development. Local projects, such as those promoted by the ACBE initiative, also point to the desirability of ensuring that balanced development is locally rooted. Individual solutions that are tailored to the problems and opportunities evident in a particular locality are more likely to be successful than the imposition of a standard package of measures that has been developed elsewhere. By basing a balanced development strategy upon the characteristics of a locality or region, an appropriate and lasting framework can be established.

A sustained and integrated approach that involves the public and private sectors in positive partnership is a necessary precondition for successful implementation. An integrated approach implies that the strategy should be directed towards the achievement of long-term and lasting measures. This can best be undertaken through the generation of a strategic vision for the locality or region.

By contributing to balanced local and regional development companies will benefit from improvements to the local environment, through the generation of additional trade and by the creation of a positive image of the locality in which they are situated. It may also be possible to establish a complex of activities that can generate new business opportunities through the operation of a green growth pole.

10

Environmental challenges and the business response

In the Preface to this book it was argued that insufficient attention has been paid to the spatial dimension of the relationship between business and the environment. The intention of the book has been to correct this imbalance and, therefore, as well as providing broad coverage of the main elements of the business and environment debate, emphasis has been placed upon demonstrating the merits and advantages of thinking globally but acting locally.

However, it would be foolish to believe that all the actions that are necessary in order to bring about a change in business attitudes can be taken at a local level, or in isolation from the national and international dynamics of economic and ecological transformation. The internationalisation of economic activities, together with the widespread occurrence and consequences of environmental damage, implies the need for action to be taken at all spatial levels from the global to the local. This final chapter reviews the lessons that can be gleaned from previous experience, and it looks forward to ways in which business can adapt its structures and operations in order better to meet the rapidly emerging environmental challenge.

There is now little doubt about the scale and severity of the environmental problems that confront business. Chapter 2 outlined some of the major difficulties that are encountered and suggested that many of these difficulties may take decades or even centuries to resolve. But it is easy to become overawed by the scale of the problem and to ignore the possibilities of implementing a succession of small, and in themselves insufficient, actions that cumulatively can bring about the resolution of problems. There are positive signs that an incremental strategy of this nature can achieve effective and lasting results.

The need for a wholesale change in the prevailing value or belief system, expressed through the promotion of more responsible and realistic economic attitudes, higher standards of environmental regulation and more sophisticated methods of environmental assessment and analysis, lies at the heart of the adoption of enhanced business behaviour towards the environment. Chapter 7 outlined ways of making progress towards the development of a corporate environmental strategy, whilst Chapters 8 and 9 demonstrated the benefits, for both business and local and regional development, that may be attained through the adoption of enhanced environmental attitudes and behaviour.

The term value or belief system is used in order to express the fundamental nature of the change that is necessary. Studies of the ecological modernisation of business, conducted in Europe and elsewhere, point to the need for a transformation in business structures to be built upon a transformation in the ideologies of both the public policy and business communities (Weale, 1993). To expect business to change its attitudes and operations in the absence of public policy inducement and regulation is naive and unrealistic; whilst to expect governments to be able to implement change in the absence of support from business is to indulge in a degree of fantasy that has little foundation in terms of the realities of late twentieth-century economic control and management.

The pace of progress towards the achievement of the goals of sustainable development in general, and environmentally sustainable business development in particular, varies from country to country and between industrial sectors. This is to be expected, because the different economic and environmental inheritances of industries and of places has resulted in businesses starting from many different positions. An analysis of the various stages in the evolution of business ethics – this was presented in Chapter 9 (B&Q, 1993) – suggests that it is equally likely that businesses located in different areas of a country, or industries within a single sector, may make progress at varying speed and from different starting points. A variable spatial geometry of progress towards the goals of sustainable development has been the hallmark of previous decades, and it is likely that this pattern of variable spatial and sectoral progress will be perpetuated in future.

This implies that progress, if it is to be effective and at a sufficiently rapid pace to prevent further environmental damage, will have to be accelerated wherever and whenever possible through the promotion of experiential learning and the transfer of good practice. As has been demonstrated in the case studies of business improvement that have been presented throughout this book, good practice can be identified at all scale levels of company, from multinationals to small enterprises, and in all sectors of the economy. The establishment of mechanisms for the transmission of the messages of good practice is still in its infancy, but positive signs are now emerging that provide a degree of encouragement. National and international networks have been established in some sectors of industries, although their influence outside Europe and North America is somewhat restricted, and local and regional environmental business organisations are beginning to make inroads into the backlog of inherited environmental problems.

Building on good practice

One of the major messages of this book is that it is important to identify and transmit the lessons that can be gained from good practice. Whilst such lessons and messages may be based upon the experience of a major company in the development of recycling procedures for redundant products, it may be possible to develop local equivalents of these multinational ventures, or to point to low-technology and low-cost schemes aimed at the reduction of energy consumption. Irrespective of the size of the company from which an example of good practice is drawn, it is important to root the transplanted practice in the economic and environmental conditions that prevail at a local level. Transplanting experience is likely to fail if it is not tailored to local circumstances and needs.

This implies that good practice should be transferred in a manner appropriate to the needs of the intended recipient, and that care should be taken to ensure its effective transmission. As in all exercises in marketing, a good idea or product will not sell itself; good environmental practice has to be targeted and sold to a selected section of the market. Likewise, it is important to establish priorities in a clearly defined order. Returning to the basic principles for environmentally sustainable business development that were outlined in Chapter 1, five priorities for future action can be established:

1. Prevent further damage to the environment.
2. Promote the incorporation of environmental costs within a product or service.
3. Produce more with less through minimising waste and recycling.
4. Practice strategic thinking and publicise achievements.
5. Partnership solutions are normally the most effective.

Building upon the progress that has already been made, the first priority is to prevent any further deterioration in environmental quality. However, whilst it is easy to state this as a global priority, it is less easy for the developed world to persuade newly industrialising nations to forsake what they perceive of as the material benefits that result from economic growth. At local and regional level the same dilemma can be observed; less prosperous areas still strive to attract and establish new economic activities although, at least in developed nations, this desire for increased economic activity is tempered by a greater environmental awareness than in the past.

Multinational companies have an immense responsibility, at both global and local levels, in the promotion of environmentally sustainable policies for future business development. In one continent alone, Europe, the national distinctions between east and west, advanced and newly reindustrialising, are stark. In western Europe there is now a general move towards environmental progress, whilst much is yet to be done in the ex-Soviet nations of the east. At local and regional level, whilst it is true to suggest that multinational companies can play an important leadership role, it is unlikely that real progress can be made without the active participation of the majority of small and medium enterprises in partnerships for environmental stewardship. Such partnerships should also involve the public sector, voluntary conservation and environmental organisations, and local communities. As has been demonstrated in earlier chapters of this book, progress towards the establishment of such partnerships is now beginning to gather pace. A further discussion of the role of partnerships is presented below.

Preventing further environmental damage through the avoidance of pollution, reducing the consumption of non-renewable resources and preventing the misuse of other environmental factors such as land, implies the adoption of the tools of analysis and assessment that were discussed in Chapter 5. Environmental assessment and auditing, initial environmental reviews and life-cycle analysis are now beginning to be accepted as part of normal business practice, at least in larger companies. The latter technique, life-cycle analysis, has much to offer in terms of its ability to present a complete picture of the overall impact of a business operation and it is important to promote its general adoption. However, irrespective of the progress made to date, the development and very existence of such procedures demonstrates a growing awareness that prevention is better than cure.

Some of the examples that have been presented in this book indicate that it may take some time before the eventual realisation of the extent and seriousness of an environmental problem is fully acknowledged. However, as in the case of the use of CFCs in aerosols, it is also apparent that procedures and methods now exist that can provide evidence and information, and that, once acknowledged, further environmental damage can be avoided. At a more proactive level, environmental damage can be avoided altogether by rejecting unsuitable projects and products, and by searching for ways of satisfying specific social goals and aspirations without creating environmental problems. The current debate in the UK on the future of public and private transport provides an interesting and crucial test of the degree of progress that has been made towards the adoption of the precautionary principle and the political acceptability of placing environmental values towards the top of the agenda.

A second priority, having prevented the further deterioration of the environment, is to reclaim and repair the damage of the past. A basic requirement here is to ensure that the costs of environmental damage are incorporated within the costs of production or the provision of services. This issue was discussed at length in Chapter 3 and, as was demonstrated by reference to attempts to incorporate environmental values in the accounting procedures of governments and companies, the most difficult elements of any such exercise are the determination of costs, the assignment of responsibilities and the need to adjust current accountancy procedures in order fully to reflect the value of environmental resources. Ponting (1991, p. 406) has analysed this issue and notes that 'a pricing system continues to operate that takes no account of the fact that these [resources] are irreplaceable assets in which future generations have a vital interest'. Determining and assigning responsibility for meeting the current environmental costs that are associated with the production of goods or services, whilst difficult in itself, is a relatively easy task compared to the assignment of historic costs. Nevertheless, a substantial legacy of environmental damage awaits repair and restoration, and the costs associated with clearing this backlog of neglect frequently prove to be considerable. Some of these costs are currently met through the public purse, such as the reclamation of derelict land, whilst certain other costs are included within the current capital and revenue programmes of private sector and voluntary organisations. If the full costs associated with clearing the backlog of environmental damage have to be met by the public sector, this implies either a considerable increase in taxation, or an extension of the time that will be required to reclaim and repair environmental damage. As was the case in the first priority, it is likely that the implementation of environmental programmes will be more effective and efficient if promoted through a partnership mode of organisation.

For the individual company the restoration and repair of past environmental damage may mean investing in new plant and equipment, changing operational procedures or reclaiming areas of land and premises that have been the subject of pollution and toxic deposition in the past. These examples demonstrate the extensive nature of historic environmental problems and they also point to the need for action at all levels from the individual small enterprise to the large multinational company. Taking responsibility for past environmental damage is often also a legal obligation, and it is certainly a matter of central concern in the determination of the financial or insurance status of a company. An increasing number of loans, takeovers and insurance renewals have either stalled, or been abandoned, following the discovery or disclosure of historic environmental problems. Prevention is better than cure, but if an environmental problem exists then it should be treated. Ignorance is not bliss if inaction forces a company into receivership.

The third priority is to ensure that the consumption of non-renewable resources is minimised or eliminated, and that the use of renewable resources is geared to the rate of replenishment of such resources. This implies the need for the development of waste minimisation policies and the encouragement of reuse, repair, recycling and reconditioning. Although much progress has been made in recent years, especially in relation to resource substitution and the development of recycling schemes, there are still many instances and examples of profligate behaviour and an unwillingness to change course.

In part this perpetuation of environmentally irresponsible behaviour results from the absence of policies, laws and regimes of enforcement that require business organisations fully to incorporate within their core business the historic and current environmental costs that are associated with their operations. It also reflects the unrealistic pricing structures used to value many resources, even in cases where non-renewable resources are extremely scarce, or in circumstances where the continued exploitation of such a resource may lead to permanent environmental damage. The undervaluation of many non-renewable resources and the seeming inability of governments and business organisations to protect threatened habitats, species and landscapes does little to encourage greater economy in the use of non-renewable resources. A parallel to the undervaluation of non-renewable resources can be seen in the continued unwillingness of some public and private bodies to invest in the development of renewable resources; but such investment is urgently required in order that the call upon non-renewables can be reduced.

Whilst local and regional action to manage non-renewable resources may be constrained by national or international policies and pricing, a higher degree of capability exists in relation to the development and adoption of renewables. Although there are economic and environmental limits to the substitution of non-renewable by renewable resources, certain important limitations to the adoption of renewable resources are imposed by political aspirations and policies. This is true of a wide range of issues, from support for public transport through the design and implementation of renewable energy technologies, to the extent to which policy recognises the need to seek renewable alternatives to a scarce resource such as oil or natural gas.

Reuse, repair, recycling and reconditioning, the 4 Rs, are more likely to be achieved if national and international policies are designed with local and regional implementation in mind. Even projects that are designed as national facilities have to be sited at a specific location. The choice of location may reflect both the pre-existing level of development of recycling activities present in the area, and the likelihood that a local or regional market exists, especially for some of the heavier or bulkier items that emerge from the recycling process. By adopting and promoting the 4 Rs, companies can both benefit their balance sheet and enhance their image.

The fourth priority is concerned with the full adoption and integration of environmental concerns in business. Once a policy issue is embedded within the corporate strategy of a company, it is likely to remain as a central consideration in all aspects of company policy for some considerable time. Greater regulation, peer group and supply chain pressures, and a growing awareness that green business is good business, have combined to make the environment a central business issue. The inclusion of environmental factors and out-turns in many annual reports is the clearest demonstration that the environment is now taken seriously by business. As has been noted in earlier chapters, certain countries, such as Norway, have gone further and now require the inclusion of environmental results in the annual reports of companies.

Whilst the development of environmental strategies at the level of the individual companies may prove to be sufficient to guarantee the improvement of the environmental performance of larger or more specialist concerns, many small and medium enterprises lack the resources, expertise and confidence that are necessary in order to embark upon a process of strategic planning for environmental improvement. Indeed, in many such companies it is unlikely that any formal process of strategic planning exists. An alternative mode of strategic planning is one that is based upon local and regional characteristics, needs and opportunities. To a certain extent this form of inter-company collaboration is already encouraged through formal mechanisms such as the Chemical Industries Association's Responsible Care Network, and through informal arrangements including personal contact networks and membership of local environment and business organisations. An area-based strategy might, for example, assist in the development and promotion of a joint waste disposal or recycling scheme.

Ensuring publicity for the achievements that flow from enhanced environmental performance of a company is an important element in further extending the environmental content of business. Achievements, even if they are modest, are important factors in boosting confidence, demonstrating technical capability and indicating the potential for further cost savings. An area-based strategy also requires a mechanism to publicise its achievements.

The final priority is concerned with the promotion of partnership. Many of the actual and potential improvements in environmental performance that have been discussed in this book result from the adoption of a partnership mode of operation. In some cases partnerships are intracompany – two or more departments within an organisation may decide to work together to tackle a common problem – whilst others are based upon a common desire, expressed by a number of companies or by companies working with each other in a group of local organisations, to bring about a substantial and lasting improvement in the condition of the environment.

In the future environmentally sustainable business development is most likely to be successful if the chosen pathway of development reflects five priorities:

1. Changes in the nature and expression of value systems.
2. Pressures for change from above and below.
3. The search for greater knowledge and learning.
4. The desirability of constructing a response at local or regional level, whilst maintaining awareness of global issues.
5. The characteristics of the individual company.

Whatever its precise form and method of operation, a partnership implies the adoption of a shared agenda for change, and the pooling of financial and other resources in the pursuit of common goals. By working through partnership the synergies that are all too often confined within the boundaries of a company can be released and can create the driving force that is necessary in order to promote further change.

These five priorities, built upon the experience of good practice, represent the future agenda for business. They indicate what can be achieved if a sustainable development agenda is pursued with determination and a willingness to share with others in the evaluation of common problems and successes.

Facing the future

As has been demonstrated in the previous section, a change in value systems is essential to making further progress in improving the environmental performance of business. As has been suggested throughout this book, it is no longer the case that a company has to choose between economic efficiency and environmental quality; both are possible, and the achievement of one of these goals is likely to improve the prospect of achieving the other. This is true for all types of business organisation: large or small, local or multinational, manufacturing or service. Indeed, the achievement of environmental quality is rapidly becoming the benchmark of a successful company.

But the change in value systems that lies at the heart of sustainable business development requires support both from above and from below. From above – at national and international levels – it is important to move away from what Simonis (1993) refers to as 'tonnage ideology'. In many advanced economies the traditional indictors used to measure success are measures of output, such as coal or steel tonnage, miles travelled and units of electricity generated. These are inappropriate measures for monitoring the achievement of sustainable development, and they should be replaced with new benchmarks that reflect sustainable values, such as a reduction in energy and materials consumption. Moving from a 'tonnage ideology' to a more sustainable economy requires businesses, governments and environmental organisations to agree and operationalise realistic goals and targets that reflect the necessary change in values. An alternative index of sustainable welfare that can be used to measure sustainable development has been constructed by the New Economics Foundation (1993).

Of equal importance in the achievement of change is influence from below – originating in individual companies and from local and regional levels – for this is where the real battleground for change is to be found. There is little hope of achieving positive results in the absence of the active co-operation of local stakeholders and communities, and these groups share a common agenda with those companies that are orientated towards the improvement of the overall condition of the environment. They are, of course, also directly involved in the preservation and generation of jobs and in the improvement of social welfare. It is important to recognise that both of these aims, economic and environmental, can be achieved; it is not a case, as Simonis (1993) argues, of having to choose between jobs and trees. The key question, asked by Gardiner and Portney (1994, p. 19), is 'how can we get environmental protection and economic progress at the same time?'

By building strategies that draw equally upon pressures and preferences from above and below, the desired change in value systems can be attained. Ecological modernisation has already achieved some notable successes; it is, for example, claimed that over 300,000 Germans now work in companies that serve the market for environmental products (Ossenbrugge, 1991).

Further successes can be built upon the realisation that respecting the environment can be a creator rather than a destroyer of jobs.

Accelerating the progress of environmentally sustainable business development also depends upon the extent to which the attitudes of business managers and leaders can be adjusted in order to meet the new challenges. This implies the need for simultaneous adjustments to be made in business practice and in business education. Changes in the attitudes and approach of management formed the subject of Chapter 7. This discussion demonstrated the need for a corporate commitment to be made to the enhancement of environmental values, and for strategy to encompass all aspects of a business and the full range of operations from the shopfloor to the boardroom. The need for change in the attitude of management towards the environment is now beginning to bring about the adoption of enhanced environmental practices. As Hill, Marshall and Priddey (1994, p. 12) observe 'good environmental management is in many ways simply good management'.

Whilst employees will gain many valuable insights from their experience of designing and implementing environmental policies, and from undertaking job-related training, it is also important to ensure that managers and other workers are equipped with initial education and training that is appropriate to the task in hand. Although some managers will have benefited from environmental modules as part of their academic or professional education, the majority have received little formal guidance on such matters. Roome (1993, p.3) notes that 'management and business educators have been rather slower to respond to the environmental agenda than the leading business organisations', and this deficiency must be addressed. The initial stimulus for this book was provided by the authors' involvement in the development of an Anglo-German programme of management education, and the requirements of that programme placed ecomanagement at the centre. It is vital that future MBA and other management programmes, including continuing professional development, should incorporate material that allows managers to identify the challenges that confront them, and provides the technical knowledge and understanding that is necessary to face such challenges with confidence. This knowledge and understanding, set within the context that is provided by the conditions encountered in an individual company, should then be transmitted through training to all members of the workforce. Self-directed action on the part of an individual worker is no substitute for a training programme that is calibrated in order to reflect the environmental characteristics and priorities of a company.

A penultimate element of considerable importance in meeting environmental challenges in the future is the need to realise that changing course takes time and that the nature and characteristics of the environmental challenge will evolve throughout the period of transition. In one sense it is impossible to solve an environmental problem; having polluted a river or destroyed a habitat no amount of compensatory action can restore the environment to its previous state. The last two centuries have been dominated by the growth ethic and any adjustments to business practice that seek to reflect environmental priorities face a long and often uphill struggle. But this statement should not be mistaken for a counsel of despair; it simply reflects the realities of long-term business planning and need for persistence and consistency in the pursuit of the goal of sustainable development.

Above all it should be recognised that managing the environment is essentially a local and regional affair. Even the largest multinational company produces its goods and services at a specific location, and the characteristics of the environment and the economy vary from place to place. The vast majority of people work in small and medium companies, most of which are locally or regionally based. An economic action that is possible, or even welcome, at one place may be unacceptable or impossible to achieve elsewhere. Furthermore, despite the desirability of transferring good practice between companies and between places, this process of transfer should respect the uniqueness of an individual place and should seek to identify a mode of business operation that respects the interests of all stakeholders, both at present and in the future. This emphasis upon the local and regional scale of action is also in accord with the principle of subsidiarity; this principle is a central element in the environmental and other policies of the European Union (Agyeman and Evans, 1994).

This emphasis on local and regional solutions does not deny the wider global obligations of business towards the environment, nor does it absolve companies and governments of their responsibilities for ensuring that the pre-conditions for environmentally sustainable development are specified and achieved. What it does do is to assign all or part of the cause of a particular environmental problem to the actions of an individual company located in one place at a specific moment in time. To fall into the trap of assigning all causality to 'a somehow unlocatable level of the global' (Massey, 1994, p. 117) is to ignore the reality of the direct link that exists between cause and effect. For a business this is an important realisation, because by embedding its choices and modes of operation in the conditions of a place, it can reasonably expect to be able to call upon the support of other local actors in the pursuit of its environmental goals and policies. The spatial dimension of the link between cause and effect in the field of environmental policy is frequently only considered to be of importance when an environmental incident occurs, or when a company seeks to assess its plans for a new or expanded operation. However, the local field of concern can, and often does, provide the most direct testing ground for a company's claim to have adopted an environmentally sustainable mode of development.

Despite advocating the case for the adoption of the local and regional level as the most appropriate spatial scale for the elaboration and better manage-ment of the relationship between business and the environment, it is acknowledged that it is essential to maintain a close watch upon the inter-regional, national and global impacts of business operations. As has been noted elsewhere in this book, irrespective of their size or location, businesses cast a shadow over other areas of the globe's surface. These ecological 'footprints', or 'shadow ecologies', are the spatial manifestation of the supply chain links that have been discussed earlier in this chapter. A company that conducts its business in an exemplary manner at a specific location, but which continues to utilise scarce and finite resources, is likely to have a negative overall environmental impact, despite its local performance and image. The spatial dislocation of production from the source of raw materials, and the isolation of a final user from the initial point of entry of a resource into the supply chain, means that a company may not be aware of the origins of the materials that it uses. Whilst this state of affairs is understandable in some cases, it is no longer an acceptable way of doing business. Life-cycle analysis can assist in the identification of the occurrence and severity of both internal and external environmental impacts.

Having argued the case in favour of adopting a local and regional context for the future development of the relationship between business and the environment, the responsibility for ensuring that positive action results rests with the individual business. No amount of exhortation from government, business organisations, local communities, trade unions or individual members of the workforce can persuade an antediluvian management to adopt enhanced environmental values if it does not wish to do so. What may persuade such a company of its responsibilities are factors such as falling sales, increased insurance premiums and bank charges, frequent prosecutions and a poor public image. However, most companies when questioned are open to the suggestion that enhanced environmental values are an essential part of future business life. The real problem for many businesses, and especially small enterprises, is identifying what needs to be done, how to do it and where to obtain support and advice. Although home-grown solutions that meet the requirements of an individual enterprise are normally preferable to imposed models of environmental management, much can be gained from lessons of good practice gained from elsewhere, and from participating in sectoral and local networks and initiatives.

The changes that have already taken place in the stance adopted by business towards the environment have resulted from a greater degree of pro-activity on environmental matters than was evident in the past. This greater proactivity reflects responsible leadership by informed managements, the increasing adoption of a holistic approach to environmental problems and opportunities, a willingness to disclose and discuss common problems with others, and a realisation that working within a local context will assist in the identification and implementation of the most appropriate solution.

Much has been achieved, but much remains to be done. Changing course is difficult, and may take a considerable period of time, but ignoring the need for change is no longer an option for a company that wishes to remain in business. There is no escape from the environmental responsibilities that are associated with economic activity and there is a need to anchor such responsibilities at the point of production. As Gro Harlem Brundtland suggests in her introduction to *Our Common Future*, 'the environment is where we all live and development is what we all do in attempting to improve our lot within that abode. The two are inseparable' (WCED, 1987, p. xi).

References

Ache, P., Bremm, H.J. and Kunzmann, K. (1990) *The Single European Market: Possible Impacts on Spatial Structures of the Federal Republic of Germany*, IRPUD, University of Dortmund, Dortmund.

Adams, D. and Carradine, M. (1990) *Last Chance to See*, Heinemann, London.

Advisory Committee on Business and the Environment (1993a) *The Environment: A Business Guide*, Department of Trade and Industry, London.

Advisory Committee on Business and the Environment (1993b) *The Business Case for the Environment*, Department of Trade and Industry, London.

Agyeman, J. and Evans, B. (1994) The new environmental agenda, in J. Agyeman and B. Evans (eds) *Local Environmental Policies and Strategies*, Longman, London.

Alden, J. and Morgan, R. (1974) *Regional Planning: A Comprehensive View*, Leonard Hill, Leighton Buzzard.

Ansoff, I. (1987) *Corporate Strategy*, Penguin Books, Harmondsworth.

Autocar and Motor (1991) Who's the greenest of them all?, 12 June.

Ball, S. and Bell, S. (1994) *Environmental Law* (2nd edn), Blackstone Press, London.

B & Q (1993) *How Green is my Hammer?*, B & Q plc, Eastleigh.

Barrett, S. (1992) Strategy and the environment, *Columbia Journal of World Business*, Vol. 27, pts. 3/4, pp. 202–8.

Beaumont, J.R., Pedersen, L.M. and Whitaker, B.D. (1993) *Managing the Environment*, Butterworth-Heinemann, Oxford.

Bebbington, J. and Gray, R. (1993) Corporate accountability and the physical environment: social responsibility and accounting beyond profit, *Business Strategy and the Environment*, Vol. 2, pts. 2, pp. 1–11.

Begg, H. (1991) The challenge of sustainable development, *The Planner*, Vol. 77, no. 22, pp. 7–8.

Bennett, E. (1992) European industry and the environment: the developing role of the EC and a strategy for industry, *European Environment*, Vol. 2, pt. 6, pp. 2–4.

Bennett, R.J. and Chorley, R.J. (1980) *Environmental Systems*, Methuen, London.

Bennett, S.J., Freierman, R. and George, S. (1993) *Corporate Realities and Environmental Truths*, John Wiley, New York.

Berry, D. and Steiker, G. (1974) The concept of justice in regional planning: justice as fairness, *Journal of the American Institute of Planners*, Vol. 40, no. 6, pp. 414–21.

Bigham, D.A. (1973) *The Law and Administration Relating to Protection of the Environment*, Oyez Publications, London.

Blair, I. (1992) Greener products, in M. Charter (ed.) *Greener Marketing*, Greenleaf Publishing, Sheffield.

Blowers, A. (1993a) Pollution and waste – a sustainable burden? In A. Blowers (ed.) *Planning for a Sustainable Environment*, Earthscan, London.

Blowers, A. (ed.) (1993b) *Planning for a Sustainable Environment*, Earthscan, London.

Blunden, J. (1985) *Mineral Resources and their Management*, Longman, Harlow.

Blunden, J. (1991) The environmental impact of mining and mineral processing, in J. Blunden and A. Reddish (eds) *Energy, Resources and the Environment*, Hodder & Stoughton, London.

Body Shop International (1992) *The Green Book*, Body Shop International, Littlehampton.

Boudeville, J.R. (1966) *Problems of Regional Economic Planning*, Edinburgh University Press, Edinburgh.

Booth and Co. (1993) *Public Registers of Land Which May be Contaminated*, Booth and Co., Leeds.

Boulding, K.E. (1966) The economics of the coming spaceship earth, in H. Jarrett (ed.) *Environmental Quality in a Growing Economy*, Johns Hopkins University Press, Baltimore, Md.

Bouwer, K. (1993) *Integration of Regional Economic Management and Physical Planning in The Netherlands*, Institute of British Geographers, London.

Bowen, A. and Mayhew, K. (1991) *Reducing Regional Inequalities*, Kogan Page, London.

Breheny, M. (1993) Planning the Sustainable City Region, *Town and Country Planning*, Vol. 62, no. 4, pp. 71–5.

Breheny, M. and Rookwood, R. (1993) Planning the Sustainable City Region, in A. Blowers (ed.) *Planning for a Sustainable Environment*, Earthscan, London.

British Aggregate Construction Materials Industries (1992) *Environmental Code*, British Aggregate Construction Materials Industries, London.

British Standards Institution (1991) *Specification for Environmental Management Systems*, British Standards Institution, Milton Keynes.

Burke, T. and Hill, J. (1990) *Ethics, Environment and the Company*, Institute of Business Ethics, London.

Business in the Environment (1992) *A Measure of Commitment*, Business in the Community, London.

Button, J. (1988) *A Dictionary of Green Ideas*, Routledge, London.

CAG Consultants (1993) *A Guide to the Eco-Management and Audit Scheme for UK Local Government*, HMSO, London.

Cairncross, F. (1991) *Costing the Earth*, Business Books, London.

Cannon, T. (1992) *Corporate Responsibility*, Pitman Publishing, London.

Carruthers, J. (1993) Down to earth and cleaning up: Reckitt and Colman's environmental policy, in M. McIntosh, J. Raistrick, A. Shaw and J. Mortimer (eds) *Good Business?*, School for Advanced Urban Studies, University of Bristol, Bristol.

Catlow, J. and Thirwall, C.G. (1976) *Environmental Impact Assessment*, Department of the Environment, London.

Centre for the Exploitation of Science and Technology (1990) *Industry and the Environment: A Strategic Overview*, CEST, London.

Centre for the Exploitation of Science and Technology (1993) *The UK Environmental Foresight Project*, HMSO, London.

Chapman, K. and Walker, D. (1987) *Industrial Location*, Basil Blackwell, Oxford.

Chapman, M. (1991) Building consensus on environmental policy: a new approach, *Policy Studies*, Vol. 12, no. 4, pp. 20–9.

Charter, M. (1992) Greener marketing strategy, in M. Charter (ed.) *Greener Marketing*, Greenleaf Publishing, Sheffield.

Chemical Industries Association (1992) *Responsible Care*, Chemical Industries Association, London.

Chemical Industries Association (1993) *Indicators of Performance*, Chemical Industries Association, London.

Chem Systems (1990) *The Chemical Industry and the Environment*, Chem Systems, London.

Clark, B.D., Chapman, K., Bisset, R. and Wathern, P. (1976) *Assessment of Major Industrial Applications: A Manual*, Department of the Environment, London.

Clark, M., Burall, P. and Roberts P. (1993) A sustainable economy, in A. Blowers (ed.) *Planning for a Sustainable Economy*, Earthscan, London.

Clutterbuck, D., Dearlove, D. and Snow, D. (1992) *Actions Speak Louder*, Kogan Page, London.

Cohen, M. (1993) Megacities and the environment, *Finance and Development*, Vol. 30, no. 2, pp. 44–7.

Collis, C. and Roberts, P. (1992) Foreign direct investment in the West Midlands: an analysis and evaluation, *Local Economy*, Vol. 7, no. 2, pp. 114–30.

Commission of the European Communities (1985) Council directive of 27 June 1985 on the assessment of the effects of certain public and private projects on the environment, *Official Journal L175*, pp. 40–8.

Commission of the European Communities (1986) *The Europeans and their Environment in 1986*, Commission of the European Communities, Brussels.

Commission of the European Communities (1992a) *Towards Sustainability: A European Community Programme of Policy and Action in Relation to the Environment and Sustainable Development*, Commission of the European Communities, Brussels.

Commission of the European Communities (1992b) *Report on the State of the Environment*, Commission of the European Communities, Brussels.

Commission of the European Communities (1992c) *European Community Environment Legislation* (7 vols), Commission of the European Communities, Brussels.

Confederation of British Industry (1973) *The Responsibilities of the British Public Company*, Confederation of British Industry, London.

Confederation of British Industry (1990) *Narrowing the Gap: Environmental Auditing*, Confederation of British Industry, London.

Confederation of British Industry (1992) *Environmental Education and Training*, Confederation of British Industry, London.

Coopers and Lybrand (1990a) *Environmental Issues: An Executive Briefing*, Coopers and Lybrand, London.

Coopers and Lybrand (1990b) *Environment and the Finance Function: A Survey of Finance Directors*, Coopers and Lybrand, London.

Coopers and Lybrand (1992) *Protecting and Enhancing the Physical Environment: the New Challenge*, Coopers and Lybrand, London.

Cope, D. and James, P. (1990) The enterprise and the environment – measuring performance, *UK CEED Bulletin*, no. 30, pp. 6–9.

Cottrell, A. (1978) *Environmental Economics*, Edward Arnold, London.

Cranfield School of Management (1990) *How Green are Small Companies?* Cranfield Institute of Technology, Cranfield.

Cronon, W. (1991) *Nature's Metropolis*, W.W. Norton, New York.

Cutter, S.L. (1993) *Living with Risk*, Edward Arnold, London.

Daly, H.E. and Cobb, J.W. (1989) *For the Common Good*, Beacon Press, Boston, Mass.

Davis, J. (1991) *Greening Business*, Basil Blackwell, Oxford.

Department of Employment (1993) *1991 Census of Employment, GB and Regions*, Department of Employment, Runcorn.

Department of the Environment (1988) *Town and Country Planning (Assessment of Environmental Effects) Regulations*, Department of the Environment, London.

Department of the Environment (1989) *Environmental Assessment: A Guide to the Procedures*, HMSO, London.

Department of the Environment (1990) *This Common Inheritance*, HMSO, London.

Department of the Environment (1991) *Policy Appraisal and the Environment*, HMSO, London.

Department of the Environment (1992a) *The UK Environment*, HMSO, London.

Department of the Environment (1992b) *Planning Policy Guidance Note 12: Development Plans and Regional Planning Guidance*, HMSO, London.

Department of the Environment (1994) *Sustainable Development: The UK Strategy*, HMSO, London.

Department of Trade and Industry (1992a) *Environment: Foam Blowing*, Department of Trade and Industry, London.

Department of Trade and Industry (1992b) *Environment: Chlorinated Solvents*, Department of Trade and Industry, London.

Derthick, M. (1974) *Between State and Nation: Regional Organization in the United States*, Brookings Institution, Washington, DC.

Derwentside District Council (1993) *Project Genesis Information Sheet*, Derwentside District Council, Consett.

Dicken, P. (1992) *Global Shift*, Paul Chapman Publishing, London.

The Earth Centre (1992) *The Earth Centre: The Earth's Future*, The Earth Centre, Denaby Main, South Yorks.

EC Committee of the American Chamber of Commerce (1994) *EC Environment Guide*, EC Committee of the American Chamber of Commerce, Brussels.

ECOTEC Research and Consulting (1989) *Industry Costs of Pollution Control: A Report Prepared for the Department of the Environment*, ECOTEC, Birmingham.

Ekins, P., Hillman, M. and Hutchison, R. (1992) *Wealth Beyond Measure*, Gaia Books, London.

Elkin, T., McLaren, D. and Hillman, M. (1991) *Reviving the City*, Friends of the Earth, London.

Elkington, J. and Burke, T. (1989) *The Green Capitalists*, Victor Gollancz, London.

Elkington, J., Knight, P. and Hailes, J. (1991) *The Green Business Guide*, Victor Gollancz, London.

English Tourist Board (1991a) *Tourism and the Environment*, English Tourist Board, London.

English Tourist Board (1991b) *The Green Light: A Guide to Sustainable Tourism*, English Tourist Board, London.

Environmental Management and Auditing Services (1992) *Avoca-Avonmore Catchment Conversion Plan*, Environmental Management and Auditing Services, Dublin.

Essery, G. (1993) Managing environmental improvement within a major chemical complex, in D. Smith (ed.) *Business and the Environment*, Paul Chapman Publishing, London.

Eversheds, Hepworth and Chadwick (1992) *Environmental Compliance*, Eversheds, Hepworth and Chadwick, Leeds.

Farman, J. (1990) Halocarbons and stratospheric ozone – a warning from Antarctica, in D.J.R. Angell, J.D. Comer and M.L.N. Wilkinson (eds) *Sustaining Earth*, Macmillan, Basingstoke.

Faulkner, J.H. (1992) Forward, *Business Strategy and the Environment*, Vol. 1, pt. 1, pp. i–iii.

Fields, P.R. (1992) Deep shaft effluent treatment technology, in T. Alabaster, D.J. Blair and B. Simpson (eds) *Environmental Progress: Spotlight on the North East*, Bewick Publications, Sunderland.

Fleming, D. (1993) *The Fifth EC Environmental Action Programme*, European Research Press, Bradford.

Friedmann, J. and Weaver, C. (1979) *Territory and Function*, Edward Arnold, London.

Gabel, H.L. (1992) A primer on the economics of the environment, in D. Koechlin and K. Muller (eds) *Green Business Opportunities*, Pitman Publishing, London.

Garbutt, J. (1992) *Environmental Law*, Chancery Law Publishing, London.

Gardiner, D. and Portney, P.R. (1994) Does environmental policy conflict with economic growth? *Resources*, no. 115, pp. 19–23.

Geddes, P. (1915) *Cities in Evolution*, Williams & Norgate, London.

Generalitat de Catalunya (1992) *Nuria Valley*, Generalitat de Catalunya, Barcelona.

Gibbs, D.C. (1991) Greening the local economy, *Local Economy*, Vol. 6, no. 3, pp. 224–39.

Gilbert, M.J. (1993) *Achieving Environmental Management Standards*, Pitman Publishing, London.

Gladstone, B.W., Morris, D.S. and Haigh, R.H. (1992) Quality implications of the greening of energy supply, *ASQC Quality Congress Transactions – Nashville*, American Society for Quality Control, Milwaukee, Wis.

Gladwin, T.N. (1993) The meaning of greening: a plea for organisational theory, in K. Fischer and J. Schot (eds) *Environmental Strategies for Industry*, Island Press, Washington, DC.

Glasson, J. (1974) *Regional Planning*, Hutchinson, London.

Glasson, J. (1994) EIA – only the tip of the iceberg? *Town and Country Planning*, Vol. 63, no. 2, pp. 42–5.

Godet, M. (1993) *From Anticipation to Action*, UNESCO, Paris.

Goldsmith, E., Allen, R., Allaby, M., Davoll, J. and Lawrence, S. (1972) A blueprint for survival, *The Ecologist*, Vol. 2, no. 1.

Goudie, A. (1990) *The Human Impact on the Natural Environment*, (3rd edn), Basil Blackwell, Oxford.

Gouldson, A. (1993) Fine tuning the dinosaur? Environmental product innovation and strategic threat in the automotive industry: a case study of the Volkswagen Audi Group, *Business Strategy and the Environment*, Vol. 2, pt. 3, pp. 12–21.

Gray, R., Bebbington, J. and Walters, D. (1993) *Accounting for the Environment*, Paul Chapman Publishing, London.

Greeno, J.L. and Robinson, S.N. (1992) Rethinking corporate environmental management, *Columbia Journal of World Business*, Vol. 27, pts. 3/4, pp. 222–32.

Hall, P. (1974) *Urban and Regional Planning*, Penguin Books, Harmondsworth.

Hardin, G. (1968) The tragedy of the commons, *Science*, Vol. 162, pp. 1243–8.

Hill, J. (1992) *Towards Good Environmental Practice*, Institute of Business Ethics, London.

Hill, J., Marshall, I. and Priddey, C. (1994) *Benefiting Business and the Environment*, Institute of Business Ethics, London.

Holliday, J. (1986) *Land at the Centre*, Shepheard-Walwyn, London.

Hoskins, W.G. (1955) *The Making of the English Landscape*, Hodder & Stoughton, London.

Houghton, J.T., Jenkins, G.J. and Ephraums, J.J. (eds) (1990) *Climate Change: The Intergovernmental Panel on Climate Change Scientific Assessment*, Cambridge University Press, Cambridge.

House of Lords Select Committee on the European Communities (1981) *Environmental Assessment of Projects*, HMSO, London.

House of Lords Select Committee on the European Communities (1993) *Industry and the Environment*, HMSO, London.

Howard, E. (1902) *Garden Cities of To-morrow* (3rd edn), Swan Sonnenschein, London.

Huddle, N., Reich, M. and Stiskin, N. (1975) *Island of Dreams*, Autumn Press, New York.

Hudson, R. and Sadler, D. (1988) Contesting works closures in western Europe's old industrial regions: defending places or betraying class? In A.J. Scott and M. Storper (eds) *Production, Work, Territory*, Unwin Hyman, London.

Hughes, D. (1992) *Environmental Law* (2nd edn), Butterworth, London.

Independent Commission on International Development Issues (1980) *North–South: A Programme for Survival*, Pan Books, London.

International Chamber of Commerce (1991) *Business Charter for Sustainable Development*, International Chamber of Commerce, Paris.

International Institute for Sustainable Development (1992) *Business Strategy for Sustainable Development*, International Institute for Sustainable Development, Winnipeg, Manitoba.

Jacobs, M. (1991) *The Green Economy*, Pluto Press, London.

James, P. (1992) The corporate response, in M. Charter (ed.) *Greener Marketing*, Greenleaf Publishing, Sheffield.

Joly, C. (1992) Green funds, or just greedy, in D. Koechlin and K. Muller (eds) *Green Business Opportunities*, Pitman Publishing, London.

Kempton, W. (1991) Lay perspectives on global climate change, *Global Environmental Change: Human and Policy Dimensions*, Vol. 1, no. 3, pp. 183–208.

Kneese, A.V. (1977) *Economics and the Environment*, Penguin Books, Harmondsworth.

Kneese, A., Ayres, R.U. and D'Arge, R. (1970) *Economics and the Environment: a Materials Balance Approach*, Resources for the Future, Washington, D.C.

KPMG Management Consulting (1992) *Coping with a Changing Market*, KPMG Management Consulting, London.

Lee, N. and Wood, C. (1978) EIA – a European Perspective, *Built Environment*, Vol. 4, no. 2, pp. 101–10.

Leeds Environmental Business Forum (1993) *Good Environmental Business Practice Handbook*, Leeds Environmental Business Forum, Leeds.

Leeds Environmental Business Forum (1994) *The Leeds Waste Manual*, Leeds Environmental Business Forum, Leeds.

Lipietz, A. (1992) *Towards a New Economic Order*, Polity Press, Cambridge.

Lockyer, K., Muhlemann, A. and Oakland, J. (1991) *Production and Operations Management*, Pitman Publishing, London.

Lowe, R.J. and Olivier, D. (1993) Global warning and architecture (Royal Institute of Chartered Surveyors Continuing Professional Development Seminar), Leeds Metropolitan University, Leeds.

MacKaye, B. (1928) *The New Exploration: A Philosophy of Regional Planning*, Harcourt Brace, New York.

MacKaye, B. and Mumford, L. (1929) Regional planning, *Encyclopaedia Britannica* (14th Edn), Vol. 19, pp. 71–2.

MacNeill, J., Winsemius, P. and Yakushiji, T. (1991) *Beyond Interdependence*, Oxford University Press, New York.

Marshall, T. and Roberts, P. (1992) Focus on business and the environment, *Planning Practice and Research*, Vol. 7, no. 2, pp. 25–8.

Massey, D. (1994) *Space, Place and Gender*, Polity Press, Cambridge.

McCloskey, J., Smith, D. and Graves, B. (1993) Exploring the green sell: marketing implications of the environmental movement, in D. Smith (ed.) *Business and the Environment*, Paul Chapman Publishing, London.

McGrew, A. (1993) The political dynamics of the new environmentalism, in D. Smith (ed.), *Business and the Environment*, Paul Chapman Publishing, London.

McIntosh, M., Raistrick, J., Shaw, A. and Mortimer, J. (eds) (1993) *Good Business?* School for Advanced Urban Studies, University of Bristol, Bristol.

Meadows, D.H., Meadows, D.L. and Randers, J. (1992) *Beyond the Limits*, Earthscan, London.

Meadows, D.H., Meadows, D.L., Randers, J. and Behrens, W.W. (1972) *The Limits to Growth*, Universe Books, New York.

Millichap, D. (1994) Public develops an interest in the global environment, *Planning*, no. 1051, pp. 20–1.

Mintzberg, H. (1994) The fall and rise of strategic planning, *Harvard Business Review*, January–February, pp. 107–14.

Morphet, J. (1993) *Towards Sustainability: A Guide for Local Authorities*, Local Government Management Board, Luton.

Moss, C. (1992) Evaluating green performance, in M. Charter (ed.) *Greener Marketing*, Greenleaf Publications, Sheffield.

Muller, K. and Koechlin, D. (1992) Environmentally conscious management, in D. Koechlin and K. Muller (eds) *Green Business Opportunities*, Pitman Publishing, London.

Murphy, T. (1981) EIA and developing countries, *Planning Outlook*, Vol. 24, no. 3, pp. 109–12.

New Economics Foundation (1993) *An Index of Sustainable Economic Welfare for the UK 1950–1990*, New Economics Foundation, London.

Newman, O. and Foster, A. (1993) *European Environmental Statistics Handbook*, Gale Research International Ltd, Andover.

Nordhaus, W.D. and Tobin, J. (1972) Is growth obsolete? *Economic Growth, Fiftieth Anniversary Colloquium*, Vol. 5, National Bureau of Economic Research, New York.

Norton, G.A. (1984) *Resource Economics*, Edward Arnold, London.

Organisation for Economic Co-operation and Development (1972) *Guiding Principles Concerning International Economic Aspects of Environmental Policies*, OECD, Paris.

Organisation for Economic Co-operation and Development (1990) *Environmental Policies for Cities in the 1990s*, OECD, Paris.

Organisation for Economic Co-operation and Development (1991a) *The State of the Environment*, OECD, Paris.

Organisation for Economic Co-operation and Development (1991b) *Environmental Policy: How to Apply Economic Instruments*, OECD, Paris.

Organisation for Economic Co-operation and Development (1992) *Long-Term Prospects for the World Economy*, OECD, Paris.

O'Riordan, T. and Turner, R.K. (1983) Economics and ecology: towards a new paradigm? In T. O'Riordan and R.K. Turner (eds) *An Annotated Reader in Environmental Planning and Management*, Pergamon, Oxford.

O'Riordan, T., Wood, C. and Shadrake, A. (1992) *Landscapes for Tomorrow*, Yorkshire Dales National Park, Grassington.

Ossenbrugge, J. (1991) Impacts of environmental protection on regional restructuring in northern Germany, in T. Wild and P. Jones (eds) *De-industrialisation and New Industrialisation in Britain and Germany*, Anglo-German Foundation, London.

Otter, J. (1992) Some aspects of environmental management within a chemical corporation, in D. Koechlin and K. Muller (eds) *Green Business Opportunities*, Pitman Publishing, London.

Owen, D. (1992) The implications of current trends in green awareness for the accounting function: an introductory analysis, in D. Owen (ed.) *Green Reporting*, Chapman & Hall, London

Owen, D. (1993) The emerging green agenda: a role for accounting? In D. Smith (ed.) *Business and the Environment*, Paul Chapman Publishing, London.

Owens, S.E. and Rickaby, P.A. (1992) Settlements and energy revisited, *Built Environment*, Vol. 18, no. 4, pp. 247–52.

Papp, D.S. (1977) Marxism-Leninism and natural resources, *Resources Policy*, Vol. 3, no. 2, pp. 134–48.

Pearce, D.W. (1976) *Environmental Economics*, Longman, London.

Pearce, D. (1977) Are environmental problems a challenge to economic science? *Ethics in Science and Medicine*, Vol. 2, pp. 79–88.

Pearce, D. (1991) Toward the sustainable economy: environment and economics, *Royal Bank of Scotland Review*, no. 172, pp. 3–14.

Pearce, D. (ed.) (1993) *Blueprint 3: Measuring Sustainable Development*, Earthscan, London.

Pearce, D., Markandya, A. and Barbier, E.B. (1989) *Blueprint for a Green Economy*, Earthscan, London.

Pearce, D.W. and Turner, R.K. (1990) *Economics of Natural Resources and the Environment*, Harvester Wheatsheaf, Hemel Hempstead.

Peattie, K. (1992) *Green Marketing*, Pitman Publishing, London.

Perloff, H. and Wingo, L. (1964) Regional resource endowment and regional economic growth, in J. Friedmann and W. Alonso (eds) *Regional Development and Planning*, MIT Press, Cambridge, Mass.

Ponting, C. (1991) *A Green History of the World*, Penguin Books, Harmondsworth.

Ravetz, J. (ed.) (1994) *Manchester 2020: A Sustainable City Regional Demonstration Project*, Town and Country Planning Association, London.

Rees, J. (1985) *Natural Resources: Allocation, Economics and Policy*, Methuen, London.

Roberts, C. (1992) Environmental disclosures in corporate annual reports in western Europe, in D. Owen (ed.) *Green Reporting*, Chapman & Hall, London.

Roberts, P. (1990) *Strategic Vision and the Management of the UK Land Resource*, Strategic Planning Society, London.

Roberts, P. (1992) Business and the environment: an initial review of the recent literature, *Business Strategy and the Environment*, Vol. 1, pt. 2, pp. 41–50.

Roberts, P. (1994) Sustainable regional planning, *Regional Studies*, Vol. 28, no. 8, pp. 781–7.

Roberts, P. and Shaw, T. (1981) EIA: links to practice, in M. Breakell and J. Glasson (eds) *Environmental Impact Assessment*, Oxford Polytechnic, Oxford.

Roberts, P.W. and Shaw, T. (1982) *Mineral Resources in Regional and Strategic Planning*, Gower, Aldershot.

Roberts, P.W., Shaw, T. and Adkins, M.G. (1980) *Environmental Impact Assessment: A Practice Guide*, Department of Urban and Regional Planning, Lanchester Polytechnic, Coventry.

Rookwood, R. (1993) Making it happen, in A. Blowers (ed.) *Planning for a Sustainable Environment*, Earthscan, London.

Roome, N. (1992) Developing sustainable management strategies, *Business Strategy and the Environment*, Vol. 1, pt. 1, pp. 11–24.

Roome, N. (1993) *Management and Business: Pre-Seminar Report*, Manchester Business School, Manchester.

Royal Bank of Scotland (1993) *Corporate Environmental Policy Statement*, Royal Bank of Scotland, Edinburgh.

Royston, M. (1979) *Pollution Prevention Pays*, Pergamon, Oxford.

Sadgrove, K. (1992) *The Green Manager's Handbook*, Gower, Aldershot.

Sainsbury's (1992) *Energy Efficiency*, J. Sainsbury plc, London.

Schaltegger, S. and Sturm, A. (1992) Eco-controlling: an integrated economic–ecological management tool, in D. Koechlin and K. Muller (eds) *Green Business Opportunities*, Pitman Publishing, London.

Schmidheiny, S. (1992) The business of sustainable development, *Finance and Development*, Vol. 29, no. 4, pp. 24–7.

Schofield, J.A. (1987) *Cost-Benefit Analysis in Urban and Regional Planning*, Allen & Unwin, London.

Searle, G. (1975) Copper in Snowdonia National Park, in P.J. Smith (ed.) *The Politics of Physical Resources*, Penguin Books, Harmondsworth.

Secretary of State for Economic Affairs (1969) *The Intermediate Areas (Hunt Report)*, HMSO, London.

Sells, B. (1994) What asbestos taught me about managing risk, *Harvard Business Review*, March–April, pp. 76–90.

Sharratt, T. (1994) Explosion averted in gas leak blaze, *Guardian*, 3 February, p. 3.

Shrivastava, P. (1992a) *Bhopal: Anatomy of a Crisis*, Paul Chapman Publishing, London.

Shrivastava, P. (1992b) Corporate self-greenewal: strategic responses to environmentalism, *Business Strategy and the Environment*, Vol. 1, pt. 3, pp. 9–21.

Simmons, P. and Wynne, B. (1993) Responsible care: trust, credibility and environmental management, in K. Fischer and J. Schot (eds) *Environmental Strategies for Industry*, Island Press, Washington, DC.

Simonis, U. (1993) Industrial restructuring: does it have to be jobs vs. trees? *Work in Progress of the United Nations University*, Vol. 14, no. 2, p. 6.

Smith, D. (1992) Strategic management and the business environment: what lies beyond the rhetoric of greening? *Business Strategy and the Environment*, Vol. 1, pt. 1, pp. 1–9.

South East Economic Development Strategy (1990) *Green Plan: Interim Report*, South East Economic Development Strategy, Stevenage.

Stead, W.E. and Stead, J.G. (1992) *Management for a Small Planet*, Sage Publications, London.

Steer, A. and Lutz, E. (1993) Measuring environmentally sustainable development, *Finance and Development*, Vol. 30, no. 4, pp. 20–3.

Stohr, W.B. (1990) *Global Challenge and Local Response*, Mansell, London.

Sundquist, J.L. (1975) *Dispersing Population: What America can Learn from Europe*, Brookings Institution, Washington, DC.

Tanega, J. (1994) *Eco-Management and Auditing: A Practical Guide to the EC Regulation*, IFS International, Kempston, Beds.

Task Force on the Environment and the Internal Market (1989) *Report on the Environment and the Internal Market*, Commission of the European Communities, Brussels.

Taylor, A. (1992) *Choosing our Future*, Routledge, London.

Therivel, R., Wilson, E., Thompson, S., Heaney, D. and Pritchard, D. (1992) *Strategic Environmental Assessment*, Earthscan, London.

Tietenberg, T. (1992) *Environmental and National Resource Economics*, Harper Collins, New York.

United States Government (1969) *National Environmental Policy Act*, United States Government Printing Office, Washington, DC.

Vaughan, D. and Mickle, C. (1993) *Environmental Profiles of European Business*, Earthscan, London.

Veblen, T. (1919) *The Place of Science in Modern Civilization and Other Essays*, Viking Press, New York.

Wahlstrom, B. and Lundqvist, B. (1993) Risk reduction and chemicals control, in T. Jackson (ed.) *Clean Production Strategies*, Lewis Publishers, Boca Raton, Fla.

Wathern, P. (ed.) (1988) *Environmental Impact Assessment: Theory and Practice*, Unwin Hyman, London.

Watson, R.T., Meira Filho, L.G., Sanhueza, E. and Janetos, A. (1992) Greenhouse gases: sources and sinks, in J.T. Houghton, B.A. Callander and S.K. Varney (eds) *Climate Change 1992: The Supplementary Report to the IPCC Scientific Assessment*, Cambridge University Press, Cambridge.

Weale, A. (1993) Ecological modernisation and the integration of European environmental policy, in J.D. Liefferink, P.D. Lowe and A.P.J. Mol (eds) *European Integration and Environmental Policy*, Belhaven, London.

Wehrmeyer, W. (1992) Strategic issues, in M. Charter (ed.) *Greener Marketing*, Greenleaf Publishing, Sheffield.

Welford, R. (1992a) Linking quality and the environment: a strategy for the implementation of environmental management systems, *Business Strategy and the Environment*, Vol. 1, pt. 1, pp. 25–34.

Welford, R. (1992b) *A Guide to Environmental Auditing*, European Research Press, Bradford.

Welford, R. (1993) Breaking the link between quality and the environment: auditing for sustainability and life cycle assessment, *Business Strategy and the Environment*, Vol. 2, pt. 4, pp. 25–33.

Welford, R. and Gouldson, A. (1993) *Environmental Management and Business Strategy*, Pitman Publishing, London.

West Midlands Regional Forum (1993) *Report on Regional Planning Guidance for the West Midlands Region*, West Midlands Regional Forum, Stafford.

Wheeler, D. (1994) Why ecological policy must include human and animal welfare, *Business Strategy and the Environment*, Vol. 3, pt. 1, pp. 36–8.

Wimpenny, J.T. (1991) *Values for the Environment*, HMSO, London.

Winter, G. (1987) *Business and the Environment*, McGraw-Hill, Hamburg.

Wood, C. and Jones, C. (1991) *Monitoring Environmental Assessment and Planning*, HMSO, London.

Worcester, R.M. and Corrado, M. (1991) *Attitudes to the Environment: A North/South Analysis*, MORI Social Research Institute, London.

World Commission on Environment and Development (1987) *Our Common Future*, Oxford University Press, Oxford.

World Health Organisation (1992) *Our Planet, Our Health*, World Health Organisation, Geneva.

Zola, É. (1970) *Germinal*, Dent, London.

Index

treatment 55, 89

water pollution 10, 21, 24, 31, 79, 82, 84, 85, 87, 112, 116, 145

welfare 50, 51, 55, 58

West Midlands 24, 192, 225, 235

Wildlife Trusts Partnership 71

World Bank 21

World Commission on Environment and Development 14, 15, 26, 36 *et seq.*

World Industry Conference on Environmental Management 4, 70

Yorkshire and Humberside 18, 70, 71, 90, 113, 128, 166, 183 *et seq.*

zero growth 54

Zetland County Council Act 73